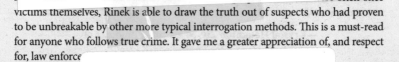
victims themselves, Rinek is able to draw the truth out of suspects who had proven to be unbreakable by other more typical interrogation methods. This is a must-read for anyone who follows true crime. It gave me a greater appreciation of, and respect for, law enforce

"This book is not only a rare glimpse into the remarkable and dedicated work of the FBI; it is also a ringside seat into the heart and soul of a federal agent doing the most demanding work. Jeffrey Rinek's personal story punctuates the pages and takes the reader on the journey for justice for America's most vulnerable victims. Rinek the federal agent? I'd say federal angel."

—**Diane Dimond**, journalist, former Court TV reporter,
and author of *Be Careful Who You Love: Inside the Michael Jackson Case*

IN THE NAME
OF THE
CHILDREN

AN FBI AGENT'S
RELENTLESS PURSUIT
OF AMERICA'S
WORST PREDATORS

JEFFREY L. RINEK
and MARILEE STRONG

Quercus

First published by Benbella Books, Inc., Dallas, TX, in 2018

This paperback edition published in 2019 by

Quercus Editions Ltd
Carmelite House
50 Victoria Embankment
London EC4Y 0DZ

An Hachette UK company

A CIP catalogue record for this book is available
from the British Library

PB ISBN 978 1 52940 188 2
EBOOK ISBN 978 1 52940 187 5

This is a true story. The events in this book all took place, and conversations are based on court
transcripts, FBI recordings, public statements, and Jeffrey L. Rinek's recollections and perceptions.
Some names and other identifying details have been fictionalized to protect the privacy of those
individuals. Any resemblance between a fictionalized name and a real person is strictly coincidental.

10 9 8 7 6 5 4 3 2 1

Front cover design © Pete Garceau
Full cover design © Sarah Avinger

Printed and bound in Great Britain by Clays Ltd, Elcograf S.p.A.

This book is dedicated to my wife, Lori, and my sons, Joseph and Jordan. A father always hopes that his children will be better than he is and accomplish more. You both have made me so very proud. Lori, you make life worth living, and along with our sons, anything I have done well in my life is because of you. You are my best friend, my love, my better half.

Steve and Gail Nee, I love you and I am so proud of the family you have made and for you to have included me in yours.

—Jeffrey L. Rinek

"Whoever fights monsters should see to it that in the process he does not become a monster. And if you gaze long enough into an abyss, the abyss will gaze back into you."

—FRIEDRICH NIETZSCHE

Prologue

THE RADIO ROOM notified us that the pizza and the polygrapher had arrived at the same time. John asked Stayner which he wanted first. Stayner could have asked for the pizza and stalled for time, or he could have said he changed his mind about everything and got up and walked out the door. But what he said next sent a shiver down my spine.

"Let's skip the polygraph," Stayner said. "I'd like to speak to Jeff alone."

I went out to advise my longtime partner and our acting FBI supervisor that day, Ken "Hitman" Hittmeier, that Stayner had asked to speak with me privately. This wasn't the first time someone had asked to speak to me alone right before a polygraph was to be administered, and Hitman kind of rolled his eyes at me like, "Here we go again." I had become known in the FBI as someone who was particularly good at obtaining confessions, and Hitman and I felt that what Stayner was saying sounded like the beginning of a confession. But we were told Stayner was just a witness, so I was thinking the thing he wanted to confess might concern something different from why we were here, maybe about his uncle's murder. Hitman told me to go find out what that was, so I went back into the interview room.

Stayner was slumped over with his head down, sobbing, when I reentered the room. I asked him what he wanted to talk to me about and he said, "Jeff, I'm a bad person and I've done some really bad things." He said he struggled all the time with terrible, obsessive thoughts—thoughts about molesting and even killing prepubescent girls.

"Hold on," I said. I told him what I believed, that doing bad things doesn't necessarily mean someone is a bad person, nor does having bad thoughts. "So let's talk about what's going on with you," I offered, "and we'll figure this out together."

"I can give you closure," he said.

Prologue

"On what?" I asked.

"This," he responded. "And more."

"Are you talking about the three tourists?" I asked with trepidation, and he slowly nodded. But before he would say any more he wanted something from me, something that rocked me back on my heels. This was not an attempt to plea bargain. He did not ask for any kind of deal or to even have the death penalty taken off the table but requested something extraordinary, something out of left field, and something I could not possibly deliver. We were on that fragile, delicate precipice together—the threshold of a confession—and one false move could send it crashing down. I had no idea how to get around the obstacle Cary Stayner was now placing in front of me.

I went back to consult with Hitman again, for moral support and to strategize where to go from here. Hitman assured me that I could get through this, that everything I experienced in my life and career had prepared me for that moment.

Introduction

I'M HAUNTED BY THEIR NAMES, forever coursing through my mind like a mantra of pain. For those I was fortunate to meet while they were still alive, who managed to survive the ordeal that caused our paths to cross, it is their voices that shake me to my core—the sheer incongruity between the sweet tones of youth and the words they spoke to me that no child should ever have to utter. In most cases, it breaks my heart to say, I only came to know them after their death. Their faces swirl endlessly through my mind: a nausea-inducing kaleidoscope of school pictures and family snapshots freeze-framing a moment in happier times and the indignities inflicted upon them that I witnessed at their murder scenes.

The memories of all I've done and all I couldn't do to rescue them or find their killers ravage my sleep, burden my conscience, flood my body with sudden waves of terror and grief. I spent twenty-eight years as an FBI agent, mostly working cases of missing and murdered children, and I can't let go of those I couldn't find and couldn't help. I mourn for those whose lives were taken or irrevocably damaged. I agonize for those I fear I've hurt when my actions, however well intentioned, had unforeseen and dire consequences. I am especially sorry for the pain I've caused my own family, who could not help but get caught up in the fallout of the horrors I could not escape.

Retirement has not erased the pain of all this accumulated grief. Neither has medication, or therapy, or the brotherhood and sisterhood of FBI agents and other law enforcement officers with whom I shared so many grim tasks. The choking weight of tragedy compounded upon tragedy, a sense of impotence and futility in the face of so much darkness, led me at one point to attempt to take my own life—feeling that I belonged with the kids I couldn't save.

Introduction

Other than my testimony at trial and occasional comments to the press, I've never talked about most of the investigations I worked to anyone outside of my family. It was my wife, Lori, who urged me to write everything down, an account of an improbable life and a record to leave our sons.

As I thought about what my wife asked of me, I realized that she and our sons were victims, too. My marriage to Lori is a true partnership. I shared with her everything I experienced and I didn't hide the painful facts of my work. I couldn't have even if I tried—the effects were patently obvious—and I couldn't have survived if I kept everything I saw and experienced wholly inside me. The cases I investigated affected me physically and emotionally and bled over into my relationship with Lori and our boys, who were forced to grow up in the shadow of other children's suffering. I can honestly say that without my family's love and selfless support I would not be alive today. I hope they think that what I did as an FBI agent was worth it. I sometimes need to convince myself of that when I realize how it impacted their lives. So I tell these stories now to honor the victims, living and dead, to whom I tried to deliver justice, and to honor my family as well.

I did my job to the best of my abilities and I embraced it with a passion I didn't even know was in me. I loved the work, and at times I hated it. I always did what I thought was right, yet there is much that I regret. I've learned that nothing in life is as black and white as we would like to believe, not even murder. The victims and killers I dealt with were by turns heroically brave and horrifically broken, vessels of innocence and volcanoes of rage. And, to a greater or lesser degree, I empathized with them all.

To handle the horrors we must deal with on a daily basis, many in law enforcement become hardened and compartmentalize their emotions, which has its own deleterious effects. I was not able to do that, nor could I stand at a clinical distance and rely on some technique or one-size-fits-all theory of criminality and remain untouched by the horrors I saw. All the simplistic strategies you see depicted on TV and in crime novels—playing good cop/bad cop, using lies and trickery or force and intimidation—have limited success in my opinion. You cannot get a sex offender to confess by looking upon him as nothing more than a monster. You cannot gain the trust and cooperation you need from families of missing and murdered children by judging those who, through neglect or inattention or because of their own demons, placed their kids in harm's way.

The only approach that worked for me, and by which I was able to obtain confessions in even the most unlikely situations, was to open my heart and soul not just to the victims but also to their killers. When I managed to get perpetrators in the interrogation room, I had to bond with them on a deep emotional level, to risk and expose a part of myself in order to get them to reciprocate my investment. I had to try as best I could to understand how they had come to this place in their lives, and then leverage whatever vestige of good I could find inside of them. I had to convince them that despite all the terrible things they had done and could never undo, there was still a way to help those they had hurt. I had to make them believe that by confessing their crimes, leading us to their victims' bodies, and helping the victims' loved ones find some semblance of closure, their lives could still have meaning and value.

Looking back, I'm proud of what I was able to accomplish and what I continue to strive to do since my retirement from the FBI to help find missing children and bring their kidnappers and killers to justice. It has been more than a professional calling to me; it is a mission to which I have dedicated my life. However, the cost—not just for me but also for all of those who fight in the trenches every day trying to protect the lives of children—is almost unbearably high. You cannot emerge from this type of work unscathed. You cannot be exposed to such horror and tragedy without having it affect your life in terrible ways.

I have learned that PTSD and vicarious or secondary trauma are real phenomena and affect not just those in combat but also those waging the war at home: from first responders of all types to therapists, social workers, emergency room doctors, and many people in law enforcement. For some of us, the things we hear and see on a daily basis are so overwhelming we can't adequately process them. They accumulate in the body and eventually overload our emotional response system. This can result in an array of symptoms: anxiety, insomnia, nightmares, flashbacks, and intrusive thoughts and memories that replay constantly in the mind and can be triggered by sounds or smells or certain types of situations. PTSD can have a profound effect on the mind and body. It can lead to depression, suicide, immune disorders, and depletion of the hormones our body needs to cope with stress.

This book is written quite literally in the name of the children to whom I tried to bring justice: kids abducted and murdered by strangers, others abused and killed by their parents, and children exploited by pimps and predators who had discovered a wonderful new tool—the Internet—to advertise their wares, share their predilections, and find and groom potential victims. Their killers tried to erase them, their abusers to silence their voices, their exploiters to reduce them from a flesh-and-blood human being to an object that existed purely to serve and satisfy others. I want these children to be remembered. I want the loss of each and every one of their lives to be mourned as the tragedy it is. I want society to reckon with what happened to these kids, how we failed to protect them, and what we need to do to prevent other kids from becoming victims. Perhaps one of the hardest truths we need to confront is how many victimizers were once victims. We need to break the code of silence that still shrouds childhood abuse, face the full ramifications, and intervene to break this awful, perpetual cycle.

CHAPTER ONE

Jeffrey

I'VE ALWAYS HAD an unusually intimate relationship with death. My father worked as an undertaker, and when I was born in 1952 we actually lived in the funeral home in downtown Philadelphia where he was employed. I was always interested in those my father attended to and wondered what had brought their lives to an end. Some had died the way we all hope to die: peacefully, at the end of a long and fruitful life. Others died suddenly, violently, miserably at the hands of another. I came to realize that every death told a story, and I became obsessed with trying to figure out what each person's story was.

As a child, I would occasionally sneak into the embalming room, more curious than repulsed by the ministrations that went on in there. Eventually, my father invited me to spend time with him inside this sanctum sanctorum. Once it was because he wanted to teach me a valuable lesson by showing me what the lungs of someone who died from lung cancer looked like. Dad was a heavy smoker himself, but he didn't want me taking up the habit. His scared-straight tactics worked; I never had any desire to smoke. Maybe there was a little bit of cop in him, too.

My father, Sidney Rinek, was highly respected in our community. He loved his job and was supremely dedicated to it. He understood that families called upon him in the darkest hours of their lives and he felt that it was his responsibility to help them get through a perilous passage as best they could. At the time, as fascinated as I was by my dad's work, I also resented the demands it placed on him and the time it stole from our family. He was never able to come to any of my school activities; that was left to my mom. Dad worked all day and late into the night, and when he was with us he was usually on the phone making plans with another family about yet another funeral. As a kid, I was unable to appreciate the acute sense of duty and moral obligation my father felt to perfect strangers, and it created a distance between us. Yet as an adult, be it ironic or simply inevitable, I would choose a calling with the same overriding sense of duty and obligation, and my own wife and kids would pay the price of its voracious demands.

When I turned sixteen my parents expected me to start working, and my dad got me on at the funeral home. My job was to attend to the needs of grieving family members during funeral services, get them water and tissues, and stand by their side stoically and respectfully. I also had to transport the hearse between the funeral home's two Philadelphia locations. Attending services allowed me to hear stories about the deceased that before I had only imagined. But I didn't last long in the profession, not yet mature enough for the seriousness of the task. I laughed out loud once in the middle of a service when an elderly mourner coughed and his dentures came flying out of his mouth. I'm also embarrassed to confess that when the hearse was empty I sometimes took the funeral home nameplates out of the windows and drag raced it up Broad Street, its 472-cubic-inch engine the closest I had yet come to the muscle cars I dreamed of owning. One day, with the engine visibly steaming when I got back to our funeral home, my father asked if I had done anything unusual with the hearse.

"Nothing I don't normally do," I answered honestly, if cryptically. My dad's face bore a mixture of skepticism and a look of what was probably acute disappointment, but he questioned me no further.

Finally, in my gravest breach of decorum, I football-tackled a mourner to the ground. The latter transgression was at the funeral of a woman who had married twice. My father had told me that the woman's second husband, to whom she was still married at the time of her death, would be attending but that a former husband was not welcome and posted me at the door to keep an eye out for him. When a man roughly matching the description of the ex-husband came running up to the door just as the service began, I knocked him down and pinned him to the ground until my red-faced dad pulled me away, screaming that I had the wrong guy. It never occurred to my father, nor should it have, that instead of using polite yet firm persuasion I would resort to physical force on a mourner. With much awkwardness, my dad had no choice but to fire me.

By that point I had learned enough to know that I did not want to follow his footsteps into a career as an undertaker. But the respect and dignity my father afforded both the dead and the grieving left a big impression on me. I would later come to see my work investigating homicides as a way of honoring my father and carrying forward the values he instilled in me by his example.

The job I longed for, the profession I dreamed of since I was a little kid, was to be an FBI agent. Typical boyhood icons like Batman and Superman meant nothing to me. FBI agents had been my superheroes ever since I happened to stumble across the book *The FBI Story* by Don Whitehead and saw the film version with Jimmy Stewart playing a fictionalized agent named "Chip" Hardesty, a zealous and *Zelig*-like special agent who was depicted as having a hand in taking down nearly every major bad guy in FBI history: from murderous Ku Klux Klansmen to treacherous spies to the colorfully monikered gangsters "Pretty Boy" Floyd, "Machine Gun" Kelly, and "Baby Face" Nelson.

One time when I was about ten, a mobster's service was held at my dad's funeral home. I remember the deceased was missing one of his lower legs, although I believe that the loss of that body part long preceded his death. So many of the man's friends and associates turned out for the funeral that the police were dispatched to help with traffic. While the service was going on, I noticed that FBI agents were actually outside writing down the license plate numbers of cars parked on the streets nearby, just like I'd seen them do in the movies. It was amazing to see real agents on the job and I tried to take in everything I could about them, from the way they talked to each other to how they carried themselves.

When I was a teenager, the popular TV series *The FBI* came along with Efrem Zimbalist Jr. playing the iconic Inspector Lewis Erskine, and after watching his weekly exploits I became even more obsessed with the idea of a career with "the Bureau." Some episodes of the show ended with Zimbalist appealing for the public's help in finding real-life criminals featured on the FBI's "Most Wanted List," including, in the most famous instance, the assassin of Martin Luther King Jr., James Earl Ray, who when that episode aired was still at large. At a time of great political and social chaos in the country, the incorruptible Inspector

Erskine seemed so reassuringly foursquare and heroic that many Americans sent fan letters addressed to the fictional character to the real FBI headquarters, believing Erskine actually ran the Bureau. Bringing kidnappers and murderers to justice—while tooling around in a sharp Mustang like Erskine did—was the kind of guy I wanted to be. Jeffrey Rinek didn't have the ring to it that "Chip" Hardesty did, but to be able to have the words Special Agent in front of my name and the ability to do anything remotely as important with my life as he was depicted as doing was the greatest thing I could possibly imagine.

Yet the chance of me ever becoming an FBI agent seemed highly unlikely due to two immutable facts of my life. The first seemingly insurmountable impediment to me having any career in law enforcement was the fact that I was born with a mild case of cerebral palsy and as a result suffered from birth defects that caused physical deformities. I initially appeared to be a normal baby but soon it became apparent that my left leg and foot were not developing in the usual way. As I grew, my foot pointed further and further inward toward the other leg. To call me pigeon-toed would have been a gross understatement: I had a clubfoot. I had great trouble learning to walk to the point that I was a danger to myself. My very first memory, in fact, is of me getting stuck between the door and the doorframe of my parents' chain-locked bedroom door. Seeking a little nighttime comfort, I was unable to negotiate the simple task of passing my left foot across the sill to reach the warmth of my parents' arms.

At age nine my spine started to curve as well. It seemed as if my entire body was being brutally tugged and twisted by some unremitting force. Even today I continue to suffer from shoulder and knee problems that are probably the result of my skeleton being innately off-kilter. My childhood is a blur of the innumerable doctors my parents took me to in search of a solution, which seemed impossibly elusive, and the hell that was school for a deformed kid. I couldn't run and play like the other kids and was never allowed to participate in P.E. but always excused, which enhanced my "different" status. Any day we had to go out into the yard or field for some school activity was not a good day for me. I had no friends at school. I was made fun of, beat up for appearing weak, ostracized for being "defective." As long as I live I'll never forget the trapped, humiliating feeling of being pinned to the ground by some kid sitting on my chest, my legs kicking uselessly, unable to get enough footing to escape my tormentor's grip.

In the summer my parents sent me to a day camp called Happy Acres. That was a little better because there were some activities that did not require a lot of movement, like tetherball and fishing. I could never just buy shoes in a store like regular people but had to get corrective shoes specially made for my left foot. For years I wore all sorts of torturous devices on and between my legs to try to make my left leg and foot turn in a normal direction, but nothing worked. I grew up lonely, embarrassed, ashamed, and, increasingly, angry. I vented my feelings onto my brother, David, and consequently do not consider myself to have been a good brother. My sister, Rebecca, was born eight years after me, which prevented her from being exposed to my anger and anguish.

One of the myriad doctors my parents took me to see was a man named Anthony DePalma, whose son Brian De Palma would become a famous film director. Dr. DePalma was a lauded orthopedic surgeon, the author of textbooks that became standards in the field. I first saw him when I was five and he suggested a radical surgical procedure to completely reconstruct my left leg, which included straightening my clubfoot. But because the surgery was experimental and unproven my parents were scared off and the visits from doctor to doctor continued for several more years.

After my spine began to contort as well and my future looked increasingly compromised, my folks took me back to Dr. DePalma. He believed that due to the cerebral palsy my muscles were weak and constantly in spasm and thus were contorting my leg. This had led in progressive fashion to the curvature of my spine, known medically as scoliosis. The experimental procedure that he hoped would give me a shot at walking normally involved breaking and resetting my leg bone while cutting away muscle and releasing tendons that would, in turn, release pressure on my spine and stop the progression of the scoliosis. At last, my parents agreed and I underwent the procedure.

I woke up in a hospital room with my mom and my aunt Ethel. My left leg was encased in plaster from my knee to the top of my toes. A heavy metal bar was implanted in the cast at my heel, forcing my foot to remain face-forward at a ninety-degree angle to my leg. It was too early to tell what the outcome would be, but just seeing my foot pointing for the first time in the correct direction filled me with excitement at the thought that I would finally be "normal." The torture was not over yet, however. For two weeks I had to lie in my hospital bed in the same position, unable to move. The hospital staff did try to get me up once to see if I could stand, but I could not lift the weight of the cast and metal bar. I began to despair, but Aunt Ethel, who worked near the hospital, snuck hamburgers in to me to raise my spirits. For months, even after I got out of the hospital, I was on crutches.

Eventually, the cast came off and I began to walk—albeit with specially made shoes because my left leg would always be shorter and smaller than my right. While my physical challenges were eased thanks to Dr. DePalma, emotional scars as deep and gnarled as the ones that marked my leg remained. For a long while I seethed with anger and resentment toward those who had bullied me. Where once I had been afraid, I now wanted to get even. Walking on crutches so long had built up my arm strength and given me the power to fight back. I fought a lot and got into various kinds of trouble. At one point in elementary school the vice principal became so fed up with me that he pulled me out of class and threw me up against the wall; the thud of my body into the hallway lockers was loud enough for everyone in class to hear.

I still struggle today with anger to some degree, but over time feelings that had once been so self-directed and self-destructive became the gifts and signposts that would help me along the particular career path I chose. Free-floating, useless anger transformed into a passion for seeking justice. I no longer wanted to "get back" at my own victimizers but to bring to account those who would victimize others—especially predators who chose children, those least able to protect themselves, as their targets. The vulnerability I felt as a kid produced a deep sense of empathy for child victims and the desire to protect them from exploitation and abuse. At the same time, the loneliness and ostracism I had experienced as a kid gave me a measure of insight, and at times great empathy, into those torn and twisted souls who take out their pain on the flesh of others.

Jeffrey

College was the first place where I fully began to escape the stigma of my childhood deformity. I didn't travel far to Albright College in Reading, Pennsylvania, a small liberal arts college less than an hour and a half from Philadelphia, yet to me it was worlds away. But when I graduated I realized that I did not want to follow the culturally acceptable path and go to law school. I went to work in the credit department of Sears, where I had worked as a salesman part time during school. I even went through the application process to become a store manager but realized that wasn't for me either. I became very depressed. It felt like I was playing that game you see during intermission at sporting events where people run around a set of chairs and when the buzzer rings everybody scrambles for a seat—and I kept ending up without a chair to sit on. About a year after school ended I moved back home with my parents and began working at a local department store in security. That began to turn my mind back to law enforcement.

I still dreamed of becoming an FBI agent, but there was a second reason I doubted that my dream would ever become a reality: I'm Jewish, and the FBI was notorious for being the WASPiest, or at least the most Christian, of all law enforcement organizations. While religion might seem like a minor or even irrelevant fact in considering fitness to serve as an FBI agent, the notion of who best fit the mold was set by the man who played the largest role in shaping the organization: J. Edgar Hoover.

The Bureau of Investigation, or BOI, the forerunner of the FBI, was first established not long after the turn of the previous century under President Teddy Roosevelt. In his previous stint as superintendent of the New York City police commission, Roosevelt had implemented a series of bold reforms to professionalize and root out rampant corruption in that city's notoriously corrupt and patronage-riddled police force. As president, he and his attorney general, fellow Progressive Charles Bonaparte, shared the belief that government intervention was necessary to ensure a fair and just society, and they brought together a small cadre of federal investigators under the jurisdiction of the U.S. Department of Justice specifically tasked with fighting crime and corruption. The notion of any kind of national police body was initially controversial, as the prevailing constitutional view at the time was that law enforcement, like most government functions, should be left to the purview of states and municipalities. But with Prohibition and the Great Depression, a massive uptick in crime and criminal syndicates led to an expansion of laws for which the federal government was given jurisdiction.

Hoover took over as director in 1924 and in 1935 changed the name to the Federal Bureau of Investigation. He further sought to enhance the image of "special agents" as the most professional and highly skilled in all law enforcement. He wanted agents who were highly educated, preferring those with degrees in law and accounting while also recruiting experts in the developing field of forensics and other scientific specialties. Over the years of his long reign, he established a national laboratory and an academy through which new agents would receive formal, centralized training in the latest crime detection techniques, which evolved from fingerprint analysis thanks to the first national fingerprint database to later advances in forensic testing and DNA analysis and the bold new field of criminal psychological profiling. And with zeal equal to that of Roosevelt and the Progressives, Hoover wanted his agents to be incorruptible, scandal free, above reproach—in stark contrast to local beat cops and federal Prohibition agents who were all too often on the take of those they were supposed to police.

However, Hoover had a much more circumscribed view of who fit the bill to be part of this elite force than did the Progressives who preceded him. Though he was not a Catholic himself, Hoover believed the principles espoused by Catholicism best embodied his particular view of a well-ordered and morally pure society. Under Hoover's nearly half century at the helm of the FBI, the agency mostly hired graduates of Catholic universities and especially prized those with a Jesuit education. In fact, there were so many Jesuit-educated agents that some referred to the Bureau by the same nickname applied to the Jesuit order: God's Marines. Mormons were also highly recruited due to their faith's emphasis on strong family values and abstinence from alcohol and drugs. Concomitantly, there existed a streak of anti-Semitism in the institution that lasted well into my tenure, rearing its head in surprisingly ugly ways at the precise moment when I achieved what would be considered my greatest success in the Bureau.

Jeffrey

My community wasn't exactly gung-ho in support of my dream either. Both sides of my family were from Eastern Europe—Germany and Lithuania on my mother's side, Prussia and Romania on my father's—where police, and government authorities in general, were something to be feared and avoided at all costs. The section of Philadelphia I spent most of my childhood in, and where nearly all my extended family lived, was predominately Jewish. Next door to us lived the Goodmans, Uncle Jimmy and Aunt Lee. Across the street were the Inselmans, Uncle Marvin and Aunt Margie. Two or three doors down lived another uncle, Paul Friedman, with whom we celebrated a huge Fourth of July block party every year, with the national holiday also happening to be his birthday.

My whole life revolved around that neighborhood. In fact, I had never been outside of Pennsylvania for an extended period of time until I went to work for the FBI. All my friends and relatives were Jewish, and Jewish parents of my generation, who fled war and oppression and anti-Semitism for the Promised Land of America, wanted their kids to become doctors or lawyers, professions that not only offered a route to prosperity but also commanded status and respect. For people with memories of pogroms and Secret Police, locking people up for a living did not seem like a particularly noble profession. In fact, to have a cop in the family was a source of embarrassment to a lot of Jewish families. A low-level police officer, without any status or rank, was actually referred to in some Jewish circles as a "double failure."

Disgusted with the twenty pounds I had gained in my post-college depression, I had began to run and quickly became an obsessive runner—as if forever trying to prove to myself that I could really do it. As someone who could once barely walk, running made me feel as close to normal as I would ever be, and I was driven—and would be for the rest of my life—with presenting myself as normal. I still couldn't sprint very fast because of my legs being different lengths, but I began to run longer distances and I dropped the weight and began to feel more powerful. I also began to feel more hopeful. Running gave me a feeling of accomplishment, which represented the first big personal change in my life.

In the Name of the Children

It was 1975 and I decided to take my life by the horns. I applied to state police forces, Secret Service, DEA, and every law enforcement agency I could think of except for the FBI, still believing the FBI was out of reach. Then one day, after a good run, I thought, what the hell, and sent in an application to the Bureau.

I couldn't believe it when I got a call back from the FBI and they asked me to come in for an interview. As I sat in the reception room of the Federal Building in downtown Philadelphia waiting for my interview, I scrutinized the agents walking in and out just as I did during that mob funeral when I was a kid. I looked for the telltale bulge under the jacket where they wore their firearm and wondered about the cases they were working on behind that closed door. Eventually someone came out, brought me into an interview room, and told me that I did not have the qualifications to be an agent, not having a degree in law or accounting (mine was in history).

My heart sank, but then he told me there was another route. He said I could go to work at the FBI as a clerk and that if I worked hard for three years and earned the opportunity I would be able to apply to become an agent. The pay for a clerk position was minimal—$5,200 a year—but there could have been no pay for all I cared. I jumped at the chance and after getting my appointment letter I moved into a small apartment in Alexandria, Virginia, where I would commute by bus into Washington, D.C., to my position as a clerk at the J. Edgar Hoover Building, the FBI headquarters just four blocks from the White House.

On my first day I found myself among a crowd of eager, newly hired clerks. The FBI building was bigger than life and it was amazing to actually be there. We were told that by the end of the week we would be assigned to a particular division within the Bureau, such as the Identification Division, which was fingerprint comparison, or the Records Division, where case files were kept. While those at least sounded interesting, the assignment I received was more humbling. An agent approached me and asked if I would be interested in working in the Exhibits Section of the Administration Division. I responded that I wanted to do whatever would improve my chances of getting into the new agent class.

The job I received was making clerk badges in a workshop in the sub-basement of the nearly three-million-square-foot Hoover Building.

Jeffrey

This involved layering an acrylic mixture until it became hardened like a credit card. We had to keep remaking badges because people would use them to scrape ice off of their cars in the winter. Not only was the job pretty dismal, but also I soon learned that the chance of graduating from clerk to agent was more tenuous than I had anticipated. At that time in the mid-1970s, the FBI was desperate for clerks to perform the more routine tasks in its various divisions, and dangling the hope of becoming a full-fledged agent was little more than a recruitment tool to fill clerk positions. As I got to know other clerks, I realized how talented and incredibly dedicated they were. So many young dreamers like myself came in through that door believing that if we just worked hard and long enough we would get our shot. But the odds were against us. At the time I was there, I believe there were 1,500 clerks trying to do what I was hoping to do, and the average number of candidates admitted to a new agent class was between twenty and thirty. In fact, I learned, having been a clerk was actually stigmatizing in terms of upward mobility.

I tried to stay out of trouble and do as good a job as I could in hopes of advancing my needle in the haystack of would-be agents. I moved up one level higher and began doing silk screening, which was used to make signs of all sorts. One day I was hammering a screen-printing frame when a unit chief, whose office was nearby, complained about my hammering. This was a man who had long seemed to dislike me, who would never speak to me, but I didn't know why. A few weeks later we had another run-in in the stockroom, which culminated with him screaming that I was a "fucking Jew." At last I, and everyone within earshot around me, knew what the issue was. It was out in the open. I was called into the section chief's office and asked to apologize. For what, I wondered—being Jewish? I refused, saying that if I had to apologize I would resign.

About six months into my employment, the Bureau issued a proclamation that it would no longer accept three years of clerkship as a qualification for admission to the new agent class. My dream had gone from sure shot to long shot to no shot, and I was devastated. I had finally found it in myself to believe that I could be an FBI agent and I was on my way to getting there—and now some heartless bureaucrat behind a desk was taking it away.

In the Name of the Children

While I was trying to figure out what I was going to do I saw a memo that laid out requirements for a Special Agent Accountant applicant. Applicants needed special training in some area, such as law, accounting, foreign languages, or computer science, and accounting seemed the most doable route for me. While still working full time at my clerk's job, I spent every weeknight and Saturday for the next fifty-two weeks in school, first at community college and then at George Mason University and the University of Virginia to complete the course work required for an accountant agent.

For the first time in my life I had fully committed to something, and neither the tedium of my day job nor the arduousness of my course schedule would dissuade me. I simply went to work, went to class, and made sure I got a run in each day. As a result of my run-in with the anti-Semitic unit chief, I was notified that I was going to be transferred, and because I was taking accounting classes I was sent to work as an analyst in the budget unit. The move was intended as a way of defusing the situation but ended up putting me on the path to becoming an agent. The administrative division that included the budget unit is arguably the most powerful division of the FBI, because it controls how resources are allocated. I was thrust into the belly of the beast, and although the work was still pretty mind-numbing, I was exposed to more actual FBI agents than I had been in the exhibits section. Part of the job involved attending to the needs of the higher-ups, including those in the Director's Office on the seventh floor, which we called "Seventh Heaven." Going up to the seventh floor to perform some gofer task was like an out-of-body experience. You were so close to power yet so far from having any power of your own.

But I didn't have time to think about myself or obsess over any of my perceived shortcomings, which was a good thing. I found comfort in my routine. I recognized a couple of other clerks in some of my accounting classes and we enjoyed the camaraderie of pursuing a shared dream.

I became good friends with two of them, Tim Tracy and Randy Ewy, who were taking accounting classes like I was to try to get into agent's class. We finished our course work about the same time and were waiting to take the next test to be qualified as accountant applicants. Unlike my history and general education courses, I did really well in the accounting classes. But I was still precariously short of the score needed for the Special Agent appointment. I was extremely fortunate that my unit chief at that time in the budget unit was Dale Anderson, a man of extraordinary patience and magnanimity, who painstakingly taught me what I needed to know to get by. Dale truly embodied the FBI motto— Fidelity, Bravery, and Integrity—and my friend Tim and I wanted to emulate him when we became agents.

Ultimately, my greatest talent as an agent would lie not in excavating evidence through forensic accounting or analyzing spreadsheets and databases but in the human interaction of interviewing suspects, victims, and witnesses. Accounting was simply my way through the door. I passed the test for accountant applicants, equivalent in scope and difficulty to the qualifying exam to become a CPA; a series of written exams to be considered for entry into the FBI training academy; and an interview with a panel of three FBI agents. I even passed the requisite physical, the thing that I feared the most. I had been working out every day, running along the National Mall with Tim and weightlifting with another clerk friend who was a major power lifter. I was the strongest I had ever been but worried that the scar bearing witness to my childhood deformity would out me as unworthy. Fortunately, no questions were raised about my leg, and I was admitted to the next agent class, scheduled to begin on June 26, 1978, along with Tim. Randy was assigned to a different class that started a few weeks later.

After being administered the oath at the Hoover Building, Tim and I reported to the FBI Academy in Quantico, Virginia, where the final hurdle began: sixteen weeks of classroom and hands-on training in federal law, forensic science, investigative techniques, intelligence gathering, firearms usage, and arrest tactics. Quantico was a wonderment to behold and I could hardly believe that I was there to become a Special Agent. We had to pass numerous tests on all these areas as well as a physical fitness test that included a two-mile run in which we had only two chances to make the cutoff time. I was proud that after all our running, Tim and I were able to ace that particular exam.

There were forty would-be agents in my class, including ten women, the largest number of women to date in an agent class. The sprawling campus outside D.C. is like the Disneyworld of law enforcement, a web of buildings linked by air-conditioned tunnels that meant you could visit all of them without ever leaving the comfort of climate control. We stayed in high-rise dormitories that appeared (I was never totally sure) to be wings of the Academy. About the only time we had to endure the humid Virginia summer was to run and climb the ropes hanging outside the gym door, ropes that Jodie Foster can be seen climbing in *The Silence of the Lambs*, as well as for firearms and other outdoor training activities.

Today, in my opinion, the campus has more of a Universal Studios vibe with the addition of Hogan's Alley, a movie set–like street of mock homes and businesses where tactical training scenarios are acted out, such as bank robberies and terrorist attacks. Hogan's Alley is so realistic that a nearby Marine academy sometimes borrows it for urban combat training. We in the pre–Hogan's Alley generation had to make do with a little more imagination in our training. I remember one scenario that involved using a pizza delivery ruse to gain access to where the "bad guys" were holed up in an open-walled apartment built on a stage. Even in these play-acting scenarios adrenaline would get pumping and emotions could get very real. The agents-in-training in this particular simulation were supposed to knock and wait for the suspects to open the door, enter with the pizzas, then drop the ruse and make the arrest. Instead, when the instructor acting as the suspect opened the door all hell broke loose. The "arrest team" rushed the door, the pizzas boxes went flying as if they had been shot from a missile, and the students pounced on the instructor so aggressively that the participants almost came to blows.

The simulation gone awry seemed kind of comical at the time, but looking back it was a good lesson. One of the most challenging aspects of working in law enforcement is learning to control your emotions, something the job tests you on every day in the real world. Fear, anger, and heart-pumping adrenaline make a dangerous mix, a corrosive chemical cocktail that clouds judgment and overwhelms reasoning. An inability to tamp down these feelings and their resulting biological responses and make strategic, measured decisions can have deadly consequences, as we have seen with frightening rapidity in recent years in some of the officer-involved shootings that have created a chasm of mistrust between police and those we are sworn to serve and protect. Equally challenging is learning to live with the cavalcade of horror we in law enforcement are forced to experience as part of the work—the grief and tragedy we witness and the helplessness and frustration we feel when we are unable to solve a case or bring justice, and it eats away at our souls.

The training we received at the Academy was first-rate, but with it lasting just sixteen weeks (it's twenty weeks nowadays) it is a little like trying to become a doctor after attending medical school for four months. For example, the only thing I learned in the Academy about interviewing suspects came from a single two-hour course. I've subsequently become aware of a huge controversy surrounding an interrogation technique used by a large number of police and military agencies around the world known as the Reid Technique—a technique some believe is at risk for inducing false confessions. But I was never taught or employed any particular interrogation technique. For me, interviewing suspects as well as victims and witnesses, gaining their trust and cooperation, was a very intuitive and internally driven process, honed over many years on the job and informed by steps I took outside the FBI to learn more about the particular type of suspects—sex offenders—that I would spend most of my career pursuing.

Perhaps the most important thing I learned while in the Academy, and in subsequent specialized trainings at Quantico over the years, was about the breadth and depth of resources the FBI has at its disposal. These were the tools I could bring to the table when partnering on cases with local police and sheriff's departments, which did not have access to facilities and expertise on the caliber of the FBI forensic lab, or rapid response teams the FBI could deploy at a moment's notice to mount searches or canvass crime scenes and gather and preserve evidence, or specialists like behavioral profilers who look for patterns and "signatures" that can help direct an investigation and narrow the list of potential suspects.

Before we graduated from the Academy we were asked to rank field offices to which we would like to be assigned. My dream had been so focused on becoming an FBI agent that I had never even thought about where I might want to live. I don't remember what I put down, but I was assigned to Chicago. I drove out in my Camaro—yes, I'd managed to obtain my first muscle car—with my gun, my badge, and my two cats to the Windy City, the first time in my life I had ever been west of Pittsburgh.

I was initially assigned to the fugitive squad under a training agent named Mike Ryan, whom many called Captain America because the inveterate smoker always seemed to be emerging from a cloud of smoke. Rounding up bad guys wanted on warrants was a pretty exciting task for a newly minted agent, but after six months I was reassigned to the accounting squad, my port of entry now coming back to haunt me. I can't even remember the cases I worked on as an accountant agent. I had already gotten my taste through the fugitive squad of what seemed to me like real meat-and-potatoes crime fighting, and forensic accounting did not compare.

It was pretty obvious that I was unhappy and began being loaned out to other squads on what were known as "specials," temporary assignments that for me almost invariably involved working in a wire room monitoring phone-tapped conversations—what in police parlance we refer to as "wearing the muffs." The most interesting wire room case I worked involved the massive casino profit-skimming operation that was the real-life inspiration for Martin Scorsese's 1995 movie *Casino*. The Chicago "Outfit" had set up the skimming scheme at several casinos they controlled in Las Vegas. The part of the case I was involved with included embezzlement of funds from the Teamsters pension fund, extortion, the attempted bribery of a U.S. senator, and the murder of several informants. Both of our targets ended up getting killed by other mobsters during our investigation. The conversations we listened to were so colorful, with salacious innuendo about all kinds of celebrities beholden to the mafia, that it was not surprising to see these larger-than-life characters later depicted on the big screen by the likes of Robert De Niro, Alan King, and Joe Pesci.

Just over a year after I started work as an FBI agent, my father was diagnosed with lung cancer and was told he had maybe two more years to live. It was a sad irony that the smoking habit he had scared me away from would claim him as a victim. Because my dad had always been so consumed by his job, I never felt that close to him, but now felt that I needed to be there to help him in his time of need. The FBI granted me a temporary hardship transfer to the Philadelphia office, but that was for just one month. While there I requested a longer-term transfer to Philadelphia. I had no idea at the time that some agents had abused the hardship excuse to get a more preferred assignment. I was livid when I was called in to the Assistant Special Agent in Charge's office and grilled with what seemed like enormously insensitive questions. "What are your *FBI reasons* for being assigned to Philadelphia?" I was asked, followed by, "Can you prove your father is dying?" The man who held my fate in his hands then told me, "If I could lie and get myself transferred to Tampa, I would. So how do I know you are not lying?"

He eventually threw me a bone: if an agent volunteered to serve in the New York office for five years, then after that stint was completed he or she could request a transfer and would be guaranteed placement at an office within five hundred miles of the requested location. At the same time, he said, he was certain I would not be assigned to Philadelphia. I wondered how he could be assured of that and why he seemed so dead set against helping me help my father. I also wondered why the FBI felt the need to offer a special incentive to get people to work at what should be one of its most prestigious offices. I enjoyed living in Chicago, but I needed to be closer to Philadelphia and if the New York assignment was the best I could do, so be it. Philly was just 97 miles from New York City, a two-and-a-half to three-hour drive each way. I would make it work. In April 1980, I made the move to New York and for the next two years, every Friday night, I made the long drive down to Philadelphia to help take care of my father.

Those first two years in New York—the last two years of my father's life—were the best years of my relationship with him. Despite the hellish bouts of chemo and the radiation, the highs of hopeful days and despairing lows each time the disease came roaring back, I came to see the man my father was and appreciate the charisma and character he had in spades. I came to understand the love and respect people held for him and recognize that I felt the same way about him. At times I convinced myself that maybe the cancer could be overcome, but the next X-ray or chemo order always shattered those hopes. Eventually truth prevails.

One summer day, a month shy of my dad's fifty-fifth birthday, I was awakened by a phone call from the hospital telling me I needed to get there right away. I drove as fast as I could to Albert Einstein Medical Center, racing the last few blocks up Broad Street just as I did as a young hellion in the funeral home's hearse. As I entered my dad's room, I saw my entire family there looking as shocked as I was at finding Dad tied to the bed, struggling wild-eyed against the restraints. The staff explained that Dad's lungs were giving out and that only the oxygen being delivered through a mask attached to his face was keeping him alive. When I looked into my dad's beseeching eyes, I realized that he wasn't pulling at the restraints out of pain or fear; he was trying to pull off the oxygen mask. I released his arms and took off the mask. We all sat on the bed and held him as his breathing became shallower and slower until he stopped breathing altogether. I can feel the sensation of his frail body cradled in our arms even as I recount this story now. It was the first time I experienced death in such a personal manner. I don't know how much time passed, but I stayed with him until the people from the funeral home came to pick him up. That night I drove home with the top down on my convertible, wanting to believe that my dad was all around me in the sky. In the end, I had only *really* known my father for two years, but that, for me, felt like a lifetime's worth of love.

About a thousand people turned out for Dad's funeral, so many that just like for the mobster's service back when I was a kid the police had to provide traffic control. I was touched by how many friends from the Bureau came down to attend my dad's memorial. It was the first time as an agent I felt that sense of camaraderie that exists in law enforcement, the brotherhood that would sustain me through many dark times to come. The loss of my father left a deep void in my life. I was twenty-nine years old, and no longer needing to devote all my free time and energy to the care of my father exposed the dissatisfaction I felt with both my career and my personal life.

It hadn't taken me long to see that, at least for someone like me, being at the nerve center of the FBI was not an ideal posting. With a thousand agents under its roof and layers and layers of management, the New

York office was so big and bureaucratic that it had an Assistant Director in Charge (ADIC) rather than the mere Special Agent in Charge (SAC) you find in most field offices. If your goal was to move up the ranks of Bureau management, New York was the place to make connections and get noticed. But I had no such ambitions and little respect for those who did because they were sentencing their families to a life of frequent moves and thus making their family subordinate to their career.

When I arrived I was assigned to the white-collar crime squad investigating government program fraud. As someone who had longed to be a crusading crime fighter in the mold of Inspector Erskine and Chip Hardesty, busting people who lied on FHA mortgage applications and other fairly petty offenses was not what I had in mind. I just wanted to work cases on the street, cases that really mattered, where life or death hang in the balance. For a long time, it seemed like that was never going to happen.

The logistics of getting into and out of Lower Manhattan every day where the FBI office was located to somewhere an agent could actually afford to live was another reason the New York posting was not, as many higher-ups claimed, "the best work in the Bureau." I had originally moved to Long Island, where I lived with my closest friends, Steve Nee and his wife, Gail, whom I considered family. I eventually moved to Plainsboro, New Jersey, to make the weekend commute to Philadelphia a little easier. After my dad died and I no longer had to make the weekend treks to Philadelphia, I still had to contend each workday with the nightmare that was the crawl up the New Jersey Turnpike and then the agonizing squeeze into Manhattan through the Holland Tunnel, where a gazillion lanes merged into just two—a trip that took me at least two and a half hours each way.

The Bureau tried to make it easier by assigning cars, known as Bucars, so that agents could carpool. On my very first week in the New York office, I witnessed a fistfight between agents over a Bucar, which was assigned as one car to six agents. Trying to coordinate the schedules of four to six agents for every trip was a logistical nightmare and much emotional energy was spent each day figuring out that day's ride home and the next day's ride in. Regular carpool-mates became like pseudo families, with both the bonding and the aggravation families confined in such close quarters experience. Driving habits became legend in the carpools, as we jockeyed for every advantage in making the trip a little quicker. While my passengers slept, or tried to, I developed the habit of miming that I was screaming at other drivers while I cut in and out of traffic, then registering silent satisfaction if I could see the other drivers' faces redden in anger. It was a game driven by aggravation and boredom.

The fraternity of agents and the humor that develops through shared endurance helped us get through. I sat at a desk with four agents sharing one phone. There were no personal cell phones at that time, so everyone knew everyone else's business. No one had cubicles except for the supervisor, who had shoulder-high walls separating him from the rest of his squad. I was a practical joker, always trying to come up with ways to lighten the day, like hiring a singer in a gorilla suit to come in and serenade our secretary on Valentine's Day. We considered ourselves good agents if we knew how to get anywhere in the city by subway, such as to all the establishments called Ray's that claimed to have the best pizza in New York, with desk jockeys easily identifiable by their inability to do so.

I admired the bachelors in the office who didn't have a wife or kids waiting for them at home and, thus, for whom the commute was a little more tolerable. But I feared that a bachelor was all I might ever be. While I had girlfriends from time to time, there was always an emotional distance between me and these women. That sense of otherness was still a part of me. I could never really believe that someone would accept me for who I really was. With more free time in my life now that I no longer had to take care of my father, the loneliness I felt loomed large.

Friday nights were always the worst. My apartment complex had a clubhouse and Friday nights were social nights. I was tired of brief relationships but also longing for one that would be truly meaningful. One Friday night I took a female friend with me to the clubhouse just to make the situation less awkward and my friend pointed out another woman across the room. I can't really describe it, but there was just something special about her. I made my approach and we ended up talking the night away.

Jeffrey

Over the course of the evening, I learned that her name was Lori and that her life was in a lot of upheaval. Her mother had passed away two years before, her father had recently passed away, and her marriage had just broken up. While I felt very attracted to Lori, the information she revealed provided a natural brake to any thoughts of jumping into a romance. She would only give me her work number, and we went on a movie date. We had to negotiate a raging snowstorm that night, which may give an indication of how much I wanted to see her. The reality of her life hit me again as I dropped her off at her house, which had clearly been intended to be the starter home for her and her husband. She was not ready for a new relationship, so we both agreed just to be friends and keep each other company. We did not want anything more complicated, which came as a relief to me because I didn't have to worry so much about how she perceived me. Lori was a research biologist at a major pharmaceutical firm in New Jersey. She was smarter than me and had a better-paying job, which was intimidating. But we had a lot in common and really enjoyed hanging out together.

Things went along this way for a while. Lori's divorce went through and we were still palling around as friends, but I had begun to notice a different feeling, a sense of "concern" for Lori, which in guy terms meant that I had developed deep feelings for her and didn't want her dating anyone else. She was feeling the same way, but neither of us wanted to take the risk of losing the deep friendship that had developed between us. She probably thinks I don't remember such things, but I clearly recall the moment everything changed, when I dropped her off one night and we shared our first romantic kiss. The big declaration came not long after, but it took a funny, if telling, incident to bring it out.

When Lori was feeling down after her marriage broke up, her brother gave her a puppy for companionship that she named Mocha. She would bring that dog over to my apartment, where it loved to chase my cats. One day it chased the cats onto my bed and then Mocha stopped to urinate on my pillow. My temper reached its flash point and I punched the wall in anger. An hour later as a doctor at the ER was manipulating my broken knuckle back into place, I told Lori, in between screams of pain, that I loved her. When the drugs he gave me wore off, I realized that it was true: I did love her. I say the incident was telling because that moment was also the beginning of our "family"—the menagerie of dogs, cats, and birds, and, eventually, our children that would populate every home we ever shared.

About six months into our post-friendship relationship we decided to move in together. We were actually looking at townhouses in Plainsboro when we decided to take a very different route, purchasing a 150-year-old farmhouse on an acre of land on the outskirts of Plainsboro that a friend of mine from high school owned. As we worked to mold that house into a home that was uniquely ours, I realized that our relationship had passed the kinds of tests that make for a good marriage. We had been friends before becoming lovers, had helped each other through the grief of losing a parent and, in Lori's case, a first marriage, and had survived the stress of endless home improvements.

Although I'd like to think that just being an FBI agent means I'm an adventurous person, she was the adventurous one and made me look tame by comparison. She brought daring and excitement into my life. By the time we had been together five years, we had gotten our open-water scuba diving certification together and Lori had taught me how to ski. Lori had always wanted to learn how to fly a plane and gave me the wonderful gift of flying lessons for my birthday one year. She pursued the training as well and we both obtained our flying licenses. We piloted our way around the East Coast, and if you think your spouse is a back-seat driver, try flying with them. Flight training enabled me to become a copilot in the Bureau's aviation program.

Another gift Lori gave me was a John Deere lawn and garden tractor, seeing as I had an acre of grass to mow at our farmhouse. I've perhaps never been the most romantic guy, as the following may attest. When the tractor was delivered, I put the engagement ring I had gotten for her on the tractor's key ring and told her she had to take it for its test drive. She cried, we hugged, and after we got rid of the neighbor kid who broke into our emotional moment to ask if his dad could borrow our new machine, she said yes.

From that point on, I no longer looked upon the bachelor agents as the guys who had it all together. I was marrying my best friend and I could not imagine anything being better. On September 15, 1984, two days after my thirty-second birthday, Lori and I said our vows on the back deck of our home. The town mayor officiated and our friends came from far and wide. It was an overcast autumn day, but when the DJ cranked up a Beach Boys song at the reception in our backyard, the sun popped out as if right on cue. I cried that night, realizing how blessed I was to have so many wonderful people in my life.

Despite all the TLC we put into our converted farmhouse, I was looking forward to the day we could get out of the rat race and move somewhere more amenable to raising children. It is important for me to say that while I was always wanting to move to a less congested area, Lori was truly a "Jersey girl" and was not sure whether moving was what she wanted. She went along with it because of her adventurous spirit, and because she loved me. But once again, the Bureau changed policy, reneging on the promise made to me and many other agents of a guaranteed transfer after "voluntarily" putting in five years at the New York office. A slew of young agents, feeling they had been lied to, simply quit the Bureau. In fact, so many agents who came in around the time I did were leaving or looking to leave that one day someone hung a sardonic sign up in the office that said, "New York FBI: your pathway to private industry."

By the time I was finally allowed to transfer to a placement of my choosing, I had served eleven years in New York. Over my time there the work got better. I got assigned to meatier white-collar investigations, but it was often hard to gauge the value of my own contribution when working in a large bureau or on a sprawling task force. Running down amorphous leads or producing bits of intelligence might yield a single thread that when woven together with hundreds or thousands of other threads might someday produce a discernable picture. On a daily basis, however, it was often hard to know whether I was being useful at all. I still wasn't sure where my particular talents lay. I wanted for so long to be an FBI agent, but was it where I actually belonged? Was there somewhere within the organization where I could truly make a difference?

In the late 1980s, the FBI Agents Association, a union-like group that advocates on behalf of agents with management, finally succeeded in getting the FBI to honor its transfer promises to the New York "volunteers." Those affected began to receive calls asking us to confirm our "office of preference." In preparation for this decision, Lori and I took numerous trips to different cities to evaluate them as good places to raise a family. By that time, we'd already had our first child, a son we named Joseph but always called Joe, so picking a good, livable place for our family was the paramount factor in our decision.

We planned to visit one last place, Sacramento, where California's state capital is located, but hadn't yet had time when my call came through in 1990. We had already crossed some of the cities we had visited off our list, wanting to avoid the traffic congestion and density that made the New York metropolitan area so logistically challenging. While Sacramento is one of the largest cities in California, with about a million and a half residents at that time, it was in no way dense by the standards of big East Coast cities. And it is linked in every direction by major highways and interstates, which made it possible to commute fairly easily from more rural areas in the surrounding valley and foothills.

Neither Lori nor I had ever been to Sacramento. The closest either of us had ever been was Lake Tahoe, the beautiful mountain lake where Lori had spent her first honeymoon, which seemed inappropriate to factor into our decision. We chose Sacramento anyway, sight unseen. Right after making our decision, we found out Lori was pregnant again. As excited as we were to get on to the next phase of our lives, we asked the Bureau to give us an extension on the transfer so Lori could give birth without the stress of the move. On October 28, 1990, our second son, Jordan, was born.

A week later, we went to see the pediatrician for a routine well-baby visit. Jordan checked out fine, but we were concerned about Joe, because his weight had doubled in a period of just two weeks and he had blown up like a balloon. The doctor took a urine sample and asked us to wait. Fifteen minutes later he returned and we could see the concerned look on his face. He measured his words carefully and it seemed like time slowed down to a crawl as he spoke. The amount of protein in Joe's urine sample was far too high, which meant that his kidneys were not working properly. He sent us to a specialist at Rutgers, who confirmed that Joe was suffering from pediatric nephrotic syndrome, a potentially serious condition that is diagnosed in just two in one hundred thousand children a year.

In a healthy person, the kidneys filter the blood, sending needed minerals back into the bloodstream and flushing waste and excess fluid out of the body as urine. Tiny blood vessels in the kidneys normally prevent large molecules, such as protein, which is essential for regulating fluids in the body among other important functions, from leaking out into urine. In Joe, these capillaries were failing to do their job. The loss of protein was causing fluid to back up into the tissues and cavities of his body. This swelling, or edema, is often one of the first signs of the syndrome. While nephrotic syndrome may result from other conditions that can damage the blood vessels in the kidneys—such as some autoimmune diseases, diabetes, and cancer—in most patients there is no known cause. We were told to keep Joe at home and give him the corticosteroid prednisone, a drug his doctors claimed was successful in treating 98 percent of children. If it didn't work, things could get dire. Joe's kidneys could be permanently damaged. He might need dialysis or even a transplant. Even when treatment works, the condition often recurs, with periods of relapse and remission that can extend into the child's early teen years.

Both Lori and I stayed home with Joe and gave him the medicine as instructed. Prednisone is not an easy drug to tolerate. It suppresses the immune system, which alone was worrisome because it made Joe susceptible to other illnesses and infections. At the high doses being administered to Joe, it also comes with a range of nasty side effects, from headaches, nausea, and insomnia to disturbing mood swings and 'roid-like rages. As parents it was incredibly hard to watch our child suffer and know that the medicine we were giving him was causing even more suffering.

We were told that we would know that the medication was working when he started to urinate out the swelling that had been building up. The edema continued to increase, however. In a span of just two weeks this fluid buildup caused his weight to balloon from twenty-nine to fifty-eight pounds. About a month after starting the drug regimen Joe started doing better, but a few weeks later he again began retaining fluid. Doctors kept ratcheting up the amount and frequency of prednisone our son was receiving, which got to a level that was the highest non-lethal dose a child his size could tolerate. Eventually, the specialists at Rutgers sent us to a different set of specialists at Children's Hospital in Philadelphia. We were living in limbo defined by the progression each day of Joe's disease.

After wanting out of New York for so long we first had to ask to delay the transfer for almost a year due to Jordan's birth and then extend it for several more months due to Joe's health. The FBI had been gracious, but then I was told that I needed to go now or not at all. Though Joe was still sick, the doctors felt he was stable enough to make the cross-country trip.

Leaving New York ended up being harder than I expected. I had forged so many strong relationships at the office. And then there were the neighbors who lived down the road from us who had provided childcare for Joe while Lori and I worked. I used to drive down to their house in the John Deere tractor to pick up Joe, and he always wanted to take the controls and drive home. He only ever hit one thing, a sapling that he knocked down on a ride with his mother; he asked Lori to transplant it across the street so his dad wouldn't know.

Lori and I cherish those who cherish ours, so when it came time to say good-bye to that couple it was very hard, but we believed we were doing the right thing for our family. With heavy yet hopeful hearts, and much trepidation due to Joe's precarious health, we packed up the car and headed west. Traveling with our menagerie of three dogs and six cats made accommodations on the road challenging. So like wanted criminals, we looked for rooms whose doors opened right onto the parking lot. We would back up the car as close as possible to the door of the room. Lori would go inside and raise her arms up like Moses parting the Red Sea when she determined the coast was clear. Then we would all pile out and stampede into the room.

To cheer Joe up we promised we would stop in Moline, Illinois, for a tour of the John Deere factory. But by the time we reached Pittsburgh, Joe started to go downhill. When he said he did not want to stop at the factory we knew that things were really bad. We called his doctors in Philadelphia and they told us to proceed directly to Nebraska's University of Omaha Medical Center. When the doctors there saw him they immediately hospitalized him. The increasing doses of prednisone he had been receiving had reached such a high level that the drug alone was endangering his life. Yet he was still massively edemic, so much so that the nurses were having a difficult time finding veins to set him up on an IV. Joe was pumped with diuretics to reduce the swelling from all the fluid accumulated in his body.

I called the Sacramento FBI office to tell them about our situation. My soon-to-be-boss in Sacramento apparently got in touch with his counterpart in Omaha and within a few hours I got a call from the SAC at the Omaha office offering his home to us as a place to stay while Joe was in the hospital. As I write this, the emotion wells up in me all over again at the generosity of this offer, extended from someone I had never even met. Many people outside law enforcement find it hard to believe that such warmth and kindness exists behind the cold façade of organizations like the FBI. Yet it was something I would see over and over again throughout my career, directed not just to those within the fraternity but also to victims, witnesses, survivors, and even suspects whose lot in life made their crimes nearly inevitable. The staff at the hospital went out of its way as well, arranging boarding for our pets and lodging for Lori, six-month-old Jordan, and me—which we accepted, not wanting to inconvenience the Omaha SAC. The benevolence extended to us was like nothing we had ever experienced and we were overwhelmed with a feeling of gratitude we were not sure we could ever repay.

It took a week before the doctors in Omaha thought Joe was well enough to resume our journey. However, his health was still quite precarious, and the Omaha doctors had arranged with physicians at the University of California at Davis Medical Center, near Sacramento, to see Joe as soon as we could get there. Again we had to travel like thieves in the night. When we hit the Nevada desert, we had a new problem. Our dogs have never "done their business" anywhere but on grass and for long stretches through the Mojave Desert there was nothing but dirt and sand. The best and most accessible lawns we found happened to be at the casinos that dot Nevada. So we guiltily took three dogs onto the casino lawns, and then scampered away as soon as they finished.

Before our move, Lori and I had purchased a home outside Sacramento, the home we still live in today. A realtor had found almost a hundred houses for us to see on our house-hunting trip, fifty in places off Interstate 80 and another fifty off Route 50. We settled on a house on ten acres perched on a hill thirty-five miles northeast of Sacramento that looked off into the distance onto the snow-capped Sierra Nevada Mountains that surround Lake Tahoe—a view that looked like a window onto paradise after a decade of choking commutes and hermetically sealed skyscrapers. It was in a tiny rural area called Rescue, reportedly named for the rescued fortunes its gold mines produced, now long since depleted of the valuable ore. The town moniker would later seem intensely meaningful to my family and me, as I would spend the rest of my professional life trying to find, save, protect, and bring justice to vulnerable children who had fallen into the hands of predators. When we first arrived, however, the name Rescue was almost mocking. Would we be able to save the life of our own son?

The prednisone was no longer working and Joe's new medical team at UC Davis, which included the head of the pediatric nephrology department, wanted to try an even scarier course of treatment. Chlorambucil is a chemotherapy agent, used in fighting cancers of the blood and lymphatic systems. It has also shown success in pushing children with nephrotic syndrome who have not responded to steroid treatment into remission and reducing their risk of relapse, sometimes permanently. However, like all chemotherapy drugs, chlorambucil is toxic, can cause cancer in its own right, and suppresses the immune system. Children undergoing a course of chlorambucil are specifically warned to avoid exposure to childhood illnesses for which they have not yet been vaccinated. To authorize the treatment, we were given papers to sign that contained all kinds of disclaimers, including stating that Joe might not survive. I insisted on being the only signatory. Lori and I did everything as partners, but if Joe didn't make it or something else bad happened to him, I did not want Lori to feel culpable.

It was Lori who was the absolute rock of our family during Joe's illness, as she has been for me throughout our marriage. I had to start work when we got to California, so she had to put her career aspirations on hold to provide full-time care for our very sick and volatile child. With Joe taking up to 100 milligrams of prednisone a day at the height of his disease, our sweet little five-year-old boy was in extreme discomfort and suffering from painful edema, which caused him to be aggressive and angry, mad at everyone and everything. He threw terrible temper tantrums and collapsed in crying jags. His physical appearance also had altered, his features so distorted he was barely recognizable. He was grossly large and bloated due to the swelling, and had developed the ruddy, rounded "moon face" characteristic of heavy corticosteroid use. When a stranger in the supermarket commented on his strange looks, Joe snapped at her: "That's the prednisone." During chemo, Lori had to take Joe to the hospital several times a week to have his white blood cell count checked, a scene that was always stressful because there were few phlebotomists capable of drawing blood from Joe's massively edemic body.

I thought I was being the best father and husband I could be only to be rocked out of my denial. One day in the Sacramento office, an agent who had lost his fifteen-month-old son in a drowning accident passed by my desk. I offered my condolences. He was aware of what I was going through and he said that he felt worse for me, because his situation was finite but mine was ongoing, that I didn't know from day to day what would happen. We closed the door to the room we were in and cried together for about two hours. Three days later the office chaplain came by my desk and invited me to lunch. I wasn't even aware at that time that the FBI had a chaplaincy program. But here was this kindly man asking me how I was doing. By the end of our lunch together he had made me see how I kept finding things that needed to be done in our garage each night when I got home. He said that was called avoidance and that I was avoiding my family because I felt so helpless in the face of my son's disease. I felt terrible when I finally realized what I had been doing to Lori and how difficult this was for her. I worked very hard after that not to avoid those who meant everything in the world to me.

Seven weeks into treatment with the new drug, an unthinking mother with a sick child exposed our son to chickenpox. The chemotherapy had to be stopped. Joe was given high doses of gamma globulin in hopes of warding off infection. Amazingly, Joe did not come down with chicken-pox. Even more amazingly, seven weeks of chemo seemed to have done the trick. Joe went into remission and the disease did not recur.

In the Name of the Children

I felt an enormous sense of debt and gratitude to all the doctors and nurses who fought so hard to save our son's life and to the FBI and all the great people who worked there who had shown me so much patience and compassion. I wanted to repay that debt the best way I could think of, which was to dedicate the rest of my life to helping other children and families in dire circumstances.

For a long time, I was forced to stand by helplessly and watch while my child suffered. With Joe in remission, I was now blessed with two healthy children, a wife I dearly loved, and the job I had always wanted. I was at last in a place I wanted to live and with the opportunity to do the kind of work where I thought I could make a difference. I made a vow to do everything in my power as a law enforcement officer to protect and defend vulnerable children, to bring the same level of passion and commitment to my work as an FBI agent as those medical professionals brought to theirs as they so valiantly fought for my son.

CHAPTER TWO

Frankie

THE FBI HAS A FIELD OFFICE in every federal court district throughout the country. The Sacramento office covers a huge swath of California, thirty-four counties in total: from the Northern California border to as far south as Bakersfield, from the easternmost parts of the San Francisco Bay Area to the Nevada border. While most of this area is rural and seemingly sedate, it has been home to some of the most notorious crimes in American history. These include all but one of the confirmed killings attributed to the "Zodiac," a terrifying hooded figure who ambushed young couples parked in lovers' lanes and taunted police and the media in cryptograms and threat-filled communiqués; the kidnapping of an entire school bus full of children in the Central Valley town of Chowchilla; the murder of twenty-five itinerant workers by a fellow farm worker, Juan Corona; the bank robbery and killing involving then-fugitive Patty Hearst; the horrific series of rape-murders perpetrated by serial killing partners Leonard Lake and Charles Ng, who may have killed up to twenty-five people and raped and tortured their female victims in a homemade dungeon; and the horrific attempted killing by mutilation perpetrated by Lawrence Singleton. In the latter case, after raping a fifteen-year-old hitchhiker named Mary Vincent, Singleton hacked off the girl's forearms, and then threw her off a thirty-foot cliff and left her for dead. But Mary refused to die, and her determination to live is one of the most inspirational survival stories in the annals of crime. Miraculously, the badly bleeding girl managed to climb back up the cliff, flag down a passing driver, and survive to put her would-be killer behind bars.

When I first arrived in Sacramento, I was assigned to the foreign counterintelligence squad, but after a year my boss could see that I was restless and better suited for something different. So I was transferred to the violent crimes squad, which is where I wanted to be. Also known as the reactive squad, we mainly investigated bank robberies, kidnappings, extortion, and other violent crimes for which there is federal jurisdiction. Almost by accident I was thrust into what would turn out to be one of the biggest investigations in FBI history, a baptism by fire into the world of violent crime investigations and an experience that taught me the dangers both of clinging too fiercely to any particular lead or theory and of swimming against the tide in an agency as hierarchical as the FBI.

As it happened, an agent was leaving our squad and asked me if I would take over a case for him that was in a status the FBI called "pending inactive." That meant the investigation was still technically open but for some reason was not currently being worked. When I agreed I had no idea what the case was and certainly no inkling of what it would become. When I looked over the file, I saw it went by the unique type of shorthand the FBI uses to designate major cases. The case was called UNABOM.

In a major FBI investigation, when the identity of the perpetrator is still unknown, an acronym-like descriptor is assigned to the case based on salient facts. The first crimes that would eventually be attributed to Ted Kaczynski dated back to a mail bomb sent to a Northwestern University engineering professor in 1978 and the discovery a year later of a smoking but unexploded bomb in the cargo hold of an American Airlines jet en route from Chicago to D.C. Thus the case became known as UNABOM, for university and airline bomber, and the suspect as the Unabomber.

For the next several years, parcel bombs were mailed to various academics around the country and to executives at United Airlines and Boeing. The first fatality occurred in 1985, when a shrapnel-covered bomb left at a computer rental store in Sacramento killed the store's owner, which is when the Sacramento office got involved in the case. Then, after an inexplicable six-year break, the Unabomber resumed his campaign of terror, sending package bombs to a Yale University computer science professor and a UC San Francisco geneticist on the same weekend in 1993. On both of those packages the return address was listed as the California State University in Sacramento, and the dormant investigation I'd been handed suddenly became very active. All told, sixteen separate bombings over a period of seventeen years, resulting in three deaths and the maiming of twenty-three others, would be tied to Kaczynski.

When you have a case that becomes really big like this, everybody wants to be a part of it. All these managers and agents started transferring in, hoping that having this case on their resumes would better their chances of promotion. As case agent—lead investigator in FBI-speak—I was supposed to be in charge of the investigation out of Sacramento. But then they brought someone in to supervise me, and someone in to supervise that person, and that inspector, who was based in San Francisco, decided the investigation should be headquartered in San Francisco. They wanted me to move with it, but I refused. My son was still sick and we had just finally settled in a place we wanted to live. I wasn't politic in my refusal, voicing my distaste for the naked ambition of so many putting careerism over family and the case itself. I continued to work on the case from Sacramento, but what I said had begun to seal my doom on that investigation.

The inspector overseeing the case believed the answer to the mystery was already somewhere in our files and for a long time instead of being able to go out and pursue new leads we were confined to the office reviewing what we had already done. We were working six days a week, twelve hours a day, pursuing what, to me, were dead ends. The wasted time angered me, knowing it was depriving me of time with my son when I didn't know how much time I would end up having with him.

I was working one particular lead that initially looked promising. I won't use the suspect's name, which was never made public, but he was a strange guy like Kaczynski who didn't fit in anywhere and couldn't get along with anyone. I believe it was his ex-wife who brought him to our attention. He had been violent toward her, but we weren't finding any evidence linking him to any of the bombings. We had submitted samples of his handwriting to see if it matched writing on any of the parcels and had just received word that no match was found when I was told I needed to go to a big meeting of the task force at the FBI headquarters in Washington, D.C. At the D.C. gathering, I hadn't expected to speak but suddenly heard the supervisor from San Francisco say, "When Jeff gets up he'll tell you . . ." A lot of people were hot on the suspect we had been investigating in Sacramento, but I got up in front of the directors of the FBI and ATF and told them that while some things looked promising about him, I didn't think he was the guy and that it was dangerous to put too much stock into that particular lead.

My own role in the Unabomber case is but a footnote in its long and fraught history. Within six months of refusing to move to San Francisco, I was removed as case agent but brought back into the investigation a month later as a street agent by someone who told me they needed people with the kind of "fire in the belly" I had shown working the suspect we had discussed at the Washington meeting. I got written up for having an "anti-management" attitude, but I also got a commendation letter from the Director of the FBI praising me for my efforts on the case. I framed both letters side by side in my office cubicle. They were like a living epitaph for my career as an FBI agent. I was never going to be someone who would go along to get along in hopes of pleasing my superiors and advancing my career. I had no grand ambitions; it was all about the cases for me. If I thought an investigation was headed in the wrong direction and precious time and effort were being wasted, I was going to speak up no matter whose feathers got ruffled, no matter what it would cost me. As I saw it, my sole obligation was to the victims.

My supervisor in the Sacramento office in the early 1990s, Don Pierce, was not your typical spit-polished, squeaky-shoe type of FBI manager. He was a crusty old New York guy, a man you definitely did not want to displease—but he had a huge heart. In order to transfer to Sacramento with his wife, who was also an FBI supervisor, Don had agreed to voluntarily step back down to a street agent position. Within a year he had moved back up to being a supervisor. As someone who feuded to the point of insubordination with managers who put their ambition over all else, I was deeply touched by Don's humility and selflessness.

Of all the supervisors I had during my career in the FBI, it was Dale Anderson and Don Pierce who had the biggest influence on my life, making me the person I am today. Don was what we call an agent's agent, incredibly perceptive and intuitive. He had a gift for recognizing what the people who worked for him were capable of, and I think he saw me as someone who could understand the emotional upheaval people go through when a child is hurt or goes missing because of what I was going through with my own son. So Don began channeling all the cases involving missing children to me, beginning with the kidnapping at gunpoint of a seven-month-old boy named Frankie Proctor.

At a quarter after 10 on the morning of April 19, 1993, two men knocked on the door of a South Sacramento home and pushed their way past one of the children who answered the door. One man had a bandanna wrapped around his face bandit style and wielded a sawed-off shotgun. The other wore a ski mask and brandished a large hunting knife. Kenneth Proctor was sitting in the living room when the men forced their way in. His infant son, Frankie, was lying nearby on the couch; Carol Gustin, Frankie's mother, was in the kitchen but came out into the living room when she heard all the commotion. There were a total of ten people in the house when the men arrived, including five of the couple's children and other relatives.

The intruders seemed to believe the Proctor home was a drug house and kept asking, "Where's the dope? Where's the money?" When the occupants denied that they had any drugs one of the men became more agitated, stating he was "sick" and needed his "medicine." As all this was going on the phone rang and one of the men ripped both landlines out of the wall and put them into a bag, which they would take with them. The intruders herded everyone into a bathroom in the back of the house and locked them inside. As they left the living room, Kenneth Proctor reached down to pick up his baby son but the intruders ordered him to leave Frankie where he was.

After a few minutes, not knowing what was going to happen to them, the family members began searching for a means of escape. Some of the children slipped out a bathroom window, one breaking her arm in the fall to the ground, and ran for help. The adults eventually managed to break down the bathroom door. By the time they reentered the living room the intruders were gone—and so was Frankie.

We learned about the kidnapping from the police-band radio. The Sacramento Police Department was handling the case, and Don Pierce initially sent a different agent from our squad down to offer our assistance, but the Sacramento authorities declined our help. I was not that surprised to hear this. A lot of local police agencies are understandably leery of the FBI coming in and running roughshod all over their investigation. Some simply view agents from local field offices, most of whom are not natives and—with frequent transfers—often brand new to the area, as outsiders with little to offer in the way of street sources to tap. Factor into that charitable interpretation the Bureau's inherent secrecy and reputation for taking credit when a case is solved and you can understand the distrust when the FBI shows up uninvited and starts sticking its nose into a case that doesn't necessarily fall within its jurisdiction. There was actually a joke in Sacramento law enforcement circles that went like this: There is an armed drug dealer holding out in a building. The Sheriff's Department sends its dog in, which brings out the drugs. The Police Department sends its dog in, which brings out the suspect. The FBI dog brings in a podium to hold a press conference.

But Don Pierce was not going to take no for an answer and neither was I. Frankie had only been gone for a few hours when I got to the scene. I checked in with Sacramento Police Detective Greg Stewart, and I got the same response as the first agent: thanks, but no thanks. I knew local police agencies might not have ready access to things we had to offer, so I advised Greg that one of the things we in the FBI could arrange was to polygraph the parents. In any kidnapping scenario involving a child, it is essential to rule out any involvement by the parents as quickly as possible so you can broaden your focus to other potential suspects. It is also crucial for nailing down pertinent facts and a timeline that will help shape the investigation. Greg agreed and I arranged for both parents to be polygraphed the following day at our FBI office. After the examination and subsequent interviews, we believed they had nothing to do with the crime and did not know the subjects who had taken their child. A canvass of the neighborhood further backed up their version of events, with one neighbor recalling seeing two men in dark clothing carrying a baby down the street around the time of the kidnapping—a baby who was light-skinned mixed-race like Frankie, whose father was black and mother was white.

Frankie

Unsure what to do next, this being my first missing child case, I simply stuck by Greg's side and tried to inject the Bureau's resources wherever they seemed useful. Don eventually assigned every agent on the squad to the case as well as everyone on the fugitive task force to assist the Sacramento police. Don had recently created the fugitive task force, which was a joint operation involving personnel from the FBI, Sacramento Police Department, Sacramento County Sheriff's Department, the California Department of Corrections, and the California Department of Justice. I thought that this would be a good opportunity to get the task force working together and build our relationship with the SPD.

Over the course of my time with Greg I learned that he had lost a son in a tragic accident. I shared with him the fight we were still waging with my boy's disease. We instantly understood each other's pain and formed a bond. The thought of a child alone and scared, suffering at the hands of a stranger, someone intent on doing him harm, was beyond horror. We desperately hoped that Frankie Proctor was okay and vowed to do whatever it took to find him and return him to his family.

The case appeared to be a home-invasion robbery committed by two individuals to satisfy a drug debt, or maybe the assailants were just two guys desperate to feed a habit and targeted what they believed to be a drug dealer's home. It was not unheard of for a family member or an associate to be kidnapped and held for some period of time to extract cooperation from the victims. But for someone to take a baby as collateral? That was beyond the pale even for the most hardened criminals. Collectively we pursued every lead we had but came up with very little. A search of the surrounding area by foot, motorcycle, and CHP helicopter yielded no baby and no other clues. Some neighbors of the Proctors who were, in fact, drug dealers were also interviewed as we wondered whether the intruders had simply hit the wrong house. Tracking dogs were brought in but did not detect a scent we could follow. A tap was set up on the Proctors' phone in case the kidnappers called demanding a ransom but no such call came. With a child's life in the balance and investigatory leads dwindling, I felt a level of frustration unlike I had ever experienced before.

During an interview after his polygraph, Kenneth Proctor reported that word on the street was that the two guys who took his son went by the names Bobo and Ray-Ray, and that one had just recently gotten out of prison. Sacramento Police were able to locate these two individuals who both were members of the violent street gang the Crips. They were brought down to the Hall of Justice, where Greg and I interviewed them. They were these massive, hulking guys who clearly hit the weights that were allowed at that time in the California prison system. I've worked out my whole adult life, but I literally looked like a lump of molten flesh next to these two.

Although I was case agent on the FBI side, it was still primarily a Sacramento PD case, so Greg took the lead in the interrogation. The guys were tough customers. It was difficult to tell whether they really weren't involved or simply were not going to admit it to us. We kept at it for a long while and then Greg made clear that we weren't interested in them for some drug deal gone bad or stash-house rip-off; this case was about an abducted baby and nothing else they might have done mattered to us. At that point Ray-Ray looked at us with eyes full of fury. He was clearly disgusted by what we had just told him and said that in prison he was someone who meted out justice to those who harmed children. We became convinced that these were not our guys.

We were back to square one again, our frustration mounting, when a strange phone call came into the FBI from a guy named Leonard Padilla. As one of those newbies to the area I had never heard of Leonard Padilla. He said he was well known to the FBI and gave me the name of an agent he said could vouch for him. I spoke to that agent and learned that Leonard was a bounty hunter based in Sacramento who was something of a legend in those parts. A son of Mexican immigrant farm workers who once toiled in the fields himself but found his calling bringing fugitives to justice, Padilla was a self-styled character who liked the limelight and often inserted himself into prominent cases. But he was also a guy with a big heart who really cared about victims and wanted to see the right thing done. He dressed like a cowboy straight out of the Old West: always in black, with a leather vest, oversize belt buckle, and a ten-gallon hat to which he added the flourish of a feather Cyrano de Bergerac style. Leonard had recently been released from a year in prison for failing to pay taxes, something the agent who had worked with him said he was proud of because it was based on principles that he believed in. The agent told me Leonard could be very hard to control but could also be an effective ally.

It was the type of call some would dismiss outright as not worth following up on. Was Leonard someone trying to insert himself into a case for notoriety or to press some personal agenda? I didn't know, but I was willing to give him a chance. When a child goes missing, the urgency of the mission and the commonality of the goal breeds a spirit of camaraderie unlike anything I had ever experienced on a case before. It seemed like Leonard genuinely wanted to help. He had met with Frankie's parents and put up a $1,000 reward for information leading to the return of the child.

"A thousand dollars on the street is a lot of money," Leonard explained, hoping it would encourage someone to talk. He also hit up other bail bondsmen in an effort to beef up the reward. But his involvement didn't end there. Leonard asked me to meet him at 9 PM that night at a bus station in downtown Sacramento. I brought along my partner from the fugitive task force, Tony Alston, a former DEA agent.

After brief introductions, Leonard nodded in the direction of a man at the bus station and said that he was one of the guys we were looking for. Tony and I turned to look and locked eyes with a man who took off running. We gave chase. Tony was fleet-footed and he and the suspect were soon out of my sights. Despite all the dedication I had put into running since surgery corrected my defects, I was still not very fast. One time a suspect told me he had actually slowed down to catch his breath during a foot pursuit because I was so slow. Not knowing how dangerous the guy Leonard pointed out might be, I had to buckle down and I caught up with Tony and the guy he had taken into custody. When I got there, Tony was collecting the drugs the guy threw away as he ran. Unfortunately, this man was just a guy, like Ray-Ray and Bobo, who thought he was being fingered for a drug offense and we determined he had nothing to do with a child kidnapping. Leonard had been adamant that his information was good, but I didn't know what to think.

The next day Leonard called again and asked me to meet him for coffee. Leonard moved around Sacramento like he owned the place.

He drove a big black SUV and when he showed up somewhere he wanted his presence known. Leonard had a cassette tape of a guy talking to his mother. In the conversation, the person could be heard telling his mother that he and another guy had rescued a baby from a family that had stolen the child. I wanted to get my boss's opinion and took the tape back to the office for Don Pierce to hear. Don said that we needed to follow up on Leonard's lead. The individual talking to his mother had details that were too accurate not to be involved in our case.

The Sacramento Police agreed and we pursued this new lead full force. The male on the phone was identified and it turned out he was just seventeen years old. Since he was a juvenile at the time of the crime, I will use the pseudonym Peter Wright for the minor suspect and the name Sally Wright for his mother, who played a crucial role in the resolution of this case. In the phone call, Peter said he and a friend had rescued a baby that had been abducted from a female friend of his. If this were true, the case was not at all what it seemed: not a botched stashhouse robbery, not a rash or incidental kidnapping to enforce payment of a debt, but a carefully planned child-snatching staged to look like something very different to throw off the cops to its true motive. Now the driving question was, who was the person claiming the Proctors' baby to be her own, and why?

Peter Wright was located and brought in with his mother to be interviewed. Many crimes are solved through appeals to the relatives of a perpetrator, who by virtue of their moral authority may hold more sway than a detective and be able to convince a loved one to do the right thing. Mrs. Wright was small in stature but stood tall in her ability to appeal to the consciences of both her son and his accomplice, a friend of Peter's who had been living with the Wright family until he fled town. Peter identified his twenty-year-old friend, Ethan Allen Walker, as the man who helped "rescue" Frankie Proctor at the behest of another friend, a young woman named Melody Rushton. It was actually Walker whom Leonard Padilla had been trying to point out to us when Tony and I took off after the running man, who had absolutely nothing to do with our case. While we literally were chasing the wrong suspect, Walker quietly boarded a bus headed out of town.

Frankie

My usual partner in the Sacramento FBI office was Ken Hittmeier. Ken and I were friends from the New York office. He got his transfer first and was offered South Lake Tahoe, which he turned down. To the rest of us aching to get out of New York, Lake Tahoe sounded like heaven, but "Hitman," as we all had taken to calling him, said there was too much snow. Instead, he transferred to Sacramento. When my chance finally came and Lori and I decided on Sacramento, I called Hitman to see what he thought about the area. In his inimitable understated way, he said it was OK, which really meant he loved the area. He and his family took us around on our house-hunting trip and it was one of the Hittmeier clan who suggested looking at Rescue. Hitman lived fairly close by, so we commuted together when I first moved to Sacramento. Unlike in New York, in the Sacramento office every agent was issued a Bucar, so people in the office thought our commuting together was so weird that we must be up to something. We were friends who became partners and we were virtually inseparable.

Hitman was working the case with us. At his request, Mrs. Wright called Ethan Walker at the San Jose residence where he was holed up. In one phone call, this mother accomplished what we had been unable to do. She told Walker that she was calling from the Sacramento Police Department and calmly questioned him about his involvement in the disappearance of Frankie Proctor. Then she passed the telephone to Hitman to get Walker's story.

Walker hedged when he first talked to Hitman. He initially denied involvement in the kidnapping, but then told the following story. An eighteen-year-old friend, Melody Rushton, had asked for his help getting back the baby she said had been stolen from her. She claimed she had a bad relationship with her sister's boyfriend, whom she said she knew only by the name "Easy." Stating that she was in fear that Easy would harm her, she entrusted the care of her baby to a friend, but Easy ran into the friend with the child at a shopping mall and took the baby away from her. She said the baby was staying at the home of Easy's grandmother, which was the Proctor house. Melody asked Walker to help get back her child, but he said he declined to get involved.

Mrs. Wright got back on the phone. After a heated exchange between the two, it became clear from hearing her end of the conversation that

Walker was one of the two men who had invaded the Proctor house and took Frankie. He still resisted giving up his accomplice, claiming not to know the identity of the other man involved and saying he only saw him wearing his mask.

Hitman got back on the phone and eventually Walker admitted his involvement but still refused to give up Mrs. Wright's son. He said he took Frankie from the house to a car where Rushton was waiting for them. He said Rushton dropped him off and left with the baby and the other masked accomplice. At the end of the phone call he agreed to return to Sacramento and turn himself in. When Walker arrived, Greg and I interviewed him and the story lined up with what Peter Wright had already confessed to us. Now we just needed to find Melody Rushton and Frankie.

The air felt charged with electricity. Each FBI agent involved in the investigation partnered up with someone in the Sacramento PD, including my boss Don Pierce and Sacramento Police Lieutenant Joe Enloe, and we turned over every rock looking for Rushton. By the end of the fourth day of Frankie's disappearance, our forces working together had developed information that Rushton might be at a location in north Sacramento.

Neither Greg nor I had slept since the case began, but I did not feel tired. I felt excited and buoyed by the bond that had developed between all of us. I could not have been prouder to be part of the FBI and specifically part of that FBI/Sacramento PD partnership working together toward such a worthwhile goal. The most satisfying part of being an FBI agent was always, for me, the bonds of friendship and mutual respect forged from working with various police agencies as we each brought our respective expertise to a common mission. The connection I shared with other likeminded investigators working crimes against children is perhaps something like that experienced by soldiers who go into battle together. There is an unspoken understanding that no one outside that world can ever fully share.

Eight of us showed up at the apartment where we believed Rushton was located, which belonged to her boyfriend. We were vested, armed, and ready for whatever might unfold. We knocked and as soon as the door was cracked open we rushed in behind the SWAT team, who quickly and efficiently secured the scene. On a mattress on the floor of the bedroom lay Rushton and her boyfriend. Between them was a small child. Everybody was crowded into the room, guns drawn, but there seemed not to be a sound as we all held our breath. Greg leaned down and gently lifted the child to examine him. I felt a sinking feeling in my stomach as the child appeared not to be Frankie. But slowly we realized that his appearance had been altered to make him less recognizable. His hair had been cut and dyed and he was dressed like a girl. Greg removed some of the infant's clothing and we could see that not only was he a male but he also had the telltale scar on his hip that Frankie's mother had described to us.

It was a surreal scene. Eight strapped and armored men passed the baby around to make sure he really was the one we were looking for, our eyes pouring over Frankie like a long-lost treasure. The disappointment I had momentarily felt morphed into an incredible adrenaline high. Other than the birth of my own children, finding Frankie Proctor alive was the most amazing moment I had ever experienced. After years of doubting whether I really was cut out to be an FBI agent, I could not believe I was a part of something so emotional and meaningful. The sense of belonging to something bigger than myself, of mattering, of making a difference was such a high it became like an addiction to me. The best part of that day was going home afterward and sharing it all with Lori, Joe, and Jordan. I felt as if what happened was in some way a testament to my own family. Anything I was able to accomplish in my life and career was because of their love and support, and so the pride I felt in helping find Frankie was an extension of the pride I felt for my own loved ones.

Greg found an infant car seat in the apartment and we decided that we would use it to transport Frankie to UC Davis Medical Center in the Bucar. That way we could get him past the clamoring media that had gathered to see the recovered baby. It worked. While Rushton was taken into custody and transported by others in our team to the Hall of Justice, Greg and I snuck Frankie out of the apartment and took him to the UC Davis emergency room to get him checked out. Greg and I stood over him like we were his parents. Here I was, back in the very same hospital where Lori and I had brought our son Joe when we finally made it to California—this time with another child who was getting a new lease on life.

While Greg and I were in with Frankie, a nurse told me there was a man waiting outside who really wanted to see the baby. When she refused to let him enter, he asked for me. I went out, and there was Leonard Padilla standing just outside the door of the exam room. I could see that, like me, his eyes were full of tears. Leonard was a big part of that rescue, too. I brought Leonard inside and in his face I could see the relief of a mission completed, the satisfaction of a wrong having been righted. All I could do was marvel at what we had done together. It was the beginning of a long friendship between the three of us, like a gift we all shared. Recovering that child gave my life meaning and helped sustain me through all the cases that did not end with a joyous reunion.

Greg and I could only linger with Frankie for a brief time, as we had to get back to the Hall of Justice to interview Melody Rushton. We had the baby back, had the offenders in custody, but still didn't really know why the crime had happened. It was hard to believe an eighteen-year-old girl was behind all of this. Since this was going to be a Sacramento County prosecution, Greg again took the lead in the interview. Greg has a patient demeanor and established a sense of calm in what might otherwise have been a very charged interrogation.

The truth was even sadder and more heart tugging than the tale the girl told her two friends to enlist their help. Melody associated with gang members in an environment rife with violence. She became pregnant by a guy who beat her up so badly that she miscarried. Unable to accept this fact, she maintained the appearance of being pregnant. But as time went by, she knew she would have to produce a baby—and not just any baby but one that was half-white and half-black, as Melody was white and her boyfriend black.

Melody was friends with the Proctors and knew they already had seven kids. She rationalized in her mind that she would be a better parent to Frankie. At times she told friends she was sexually assaulted by one of the Proctors, which produced Frankie. At other times she claimed they wrongfully accused her of being a drug addict and thus forbid her to have custody of the child.

Frankie

The stories she spun for Peter Wright and Ethan Walker and others she tried to induct into her baby-stealing scheme may seem far-fetched to you or me, but in the circles in which Melody Rushton traveled, they were not that preposterous. I believe the two young men who helped her were honestly duped and believed they were doing something heroic by returning a baby to his rightful mother. Except for Frankie's sister getting hurt trying to escape out the bathroom window, the intruders did not physically harm anyone and did not take anything other than the phones to prevent the family from calling for help while they were still there.

Still, the crime was terrifying for the Proctors. Frankie was ripped from his family and might never have been found. Wright and Walker brought weapons with them that could have led to a loss of life if things did not follow the plan they had imagined. So this was in no way a victimless crime and needed to be punished no matter anyone's intentions. At the conclusion of Rushton's interview, Greg had her write a letter of apology to the Proctor family. I had never thought of doing anything like that before and it seemed like such a great idea that I adopted the practice throughout the rest of my career. A letter of apology is useful in many ways. It helps cement a perpetrator's admissions in writing. It may provide a measure of healing not only for the victims but also for the perpetrator, who by apologizing must reckon, at least while writing that letter, with the pain they have inflicted.

The Proctor case was my entrée into the world of crimes against children and the portal through which I found my passion. It was also an important wake-up call for me as an investigator to never take anything at face value. This was not a crime motivated by money or drugs or revenge, but by simple human need. Fixating on the obvious, adhering to typical theories about drug crimes or home invasions would have been disastrous. A detective needs to be flexible and open-minded and allow an investigation to evolve—especially when investigating crimes against children, which often have deeply complex psychological motivations.

Rushton pleaded guilty on the eve of trial and was sentenced to eight years in prison. It was less than the maximum eleven years and eight months she could have gotten. Apparently the judge took into account the fact that she had no prior criminal record as well as perhaps some of the facts of her life that led her to act out her obsession with having a baby. Rushton said she had suffered multiple miscarriages prior to the death of the fetus due to the beating at the hands of her boyfriend. A psychiatric report prepared for sentencing revealed that she had suffered a brain injury in a fall as a child. It also stated that she had been the victim of childhood sexual abuse, leaving her with low self-esteem, which she sought to counter with a child's unconditional love.

A couple of weeks after we returned Frankie to his parents, the Proctors, along with their neighbors and friends, got together and threw a barbecue for the officers who had worked the case. When Frankie was taken, the Sacramento PD had painstakingly gone door to door throughout that neighborhood searching for anyone who might have seen something, following up on anything that didn't look right, checking anywhere a baby might be hidden. Those neighbors did not resent our intrusion into their lives; they rejoiced that a missing child had been found safe and sound and returned to those who loved him. The parents did not mind being polygraphed. They understood what was at stake and they knew that the sooner we could eliminate any involvement by them the sooner we could find who really did this. Still, a thank-you party was unexpected and a perfect happy ending to a case that meant so much to all of us who worked it. I didn't know at the time how rare it would be that cases I worked would end in happy resolution.

Leonard Padilla's notoriety would continue to grow over the years. He bailed out Casey Anthony, a Florida woman accused of murdering her two-year-old daughter and claiming instead that the girl was kidnapped by a babysitter who turned out not to even exist. According to Leonard, he did so in hopes of getting Anthony to confess to him and lead him to the girl's body. When she refused to even talk to him and she and her family instead sent him on what he viewed as wild goose chases based on imaginary leads, he went public with his suspicions of her and even offered his own reward to help find the missing girl. He has run quixotic campaigns for public office seven times to date: five times for mayor of Sacramento as well as for governor and Congress. Most recently I saw Leonard at a funeral for the victim of a serial killer, a case I have been working since retirement from the FBI. For once Leonard didn't make a production of entering a room. During the service I noticed him sitting silently in the back, quietly grieving.

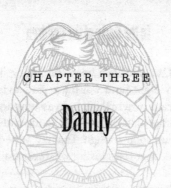

CHAPTER THREE

Danny

LESS THAN SIX MONTHS after the kidnapping of Frankie Proctor, Louis Freeh took the helm of the FBI as just the fifth director in its history. Freeh was one of those types prized by the FBI, a straight-arrow overachiever who had two different law degrees and had also been an officer in the Army Reserve and an Eagle Scout. After seven years as a special agent, he left the FBI to join the U.S. Attorney's Office and then served as a federal judge until President Bill Clinton appointed him FBI Director in 1993.

A father of six, Freeh took a particular interest in crimes against children and spearheaded a number of initiatives and policy changes aimed at taking a more proactive approach to investigating these crimes. I worked under five different directors during my thirty years with the FBI, and from my perspective Freeh was extraordinary in his passionate commitment to those who are truly society's most vulnerable. Even after his tenure with the FBI ended, Freeh has continued to stand up for abused and exploited children. He led the independent investigation of Penn State in the wake of the Jerry Sandusky scandal, issuing a blistering report that found that some university officials had known and looked the other way while its assistant football coach was molesting young boys he was purported to be mentoring, thus enabling the abuse to continue for over a decade.

When Freeh became Director, he ordered the FBI to insert itself directly into cases of reported or suspected child abduction. This was an especially important change in strategy because when the kidnapper is a sexual offender, the time for recovering the victim alive can be a very narrow window. All field offices were instructed to reach out and offer help to local police agencies within their geographical jurisdiction in cases involving missing children under the age of twelve rather than waiting to be asked, as had long been the policy. There would be no twenty-four- or forty-eight-hour waiting period, as is common in many missing person bureaus, where there is an assumption the person is not really missing but simply late or avoiding an unwanted confrontation at home and will turn up soon enough. That is a very dangerous assumption in my book, one that risks losing whatever trail of clues might be out there to follow.

Under this new directive, we were to make contact immediately with local authorities and offer the full array of expertise and services the Bureau had at its disposal to help find children and bring to justice those who had taken them. This included everything from polygraphers to profilers, from testing at the FBI's forensics lab to assistance in the field from our newly constituted Evidence Response Teams. The ERTs— made up of criminalists, forensic specialists, and other experts—are based in each field office and are able to deploy at a moment's notice to preserve and gather physical evidence at crime scenes before it is lost and then analyze this evidence. A new unit was also set up at the FBI's training center in Quantico, the Child Abduction and Serial Killer Unit (today known as the National Center for the Analysis of Violent Crime), or CASKU, to serve as a specialized rapid-response network, through which FBI field officers could tap experts in forensic analysis, interrogation strategies, behavioral profiling, and other case assistance. Bill Hagmaier, who ran CASKU at that time and was the profiler who got Ted Bundy to finally confess his crimes in the days before his execution, was also critical in pushing through changes in how we worked cases involving missing children, like dropping the twenty-four-hour waiting period.

After one particular ten-year-old boy in Maryland, George "Junior" Burdynski, went missing and suspicion fell on a ring of child pornographers who were believed to have befriended and molested two of George's friends as well as the missing boy, Freeh launched a pilot program in the Maryland office that eventually spread to FBI offices nationwide and was franchised to state and local police agencies as well. The Innocent Images initiative came out of the Director's recognition that the Internet was the ultimate "dark alley" where sexual predators, hiding in the shadow of anonymity, could meet kids to molest or obtain sexually graphic images that they then purveyed around the Internet to others with their same proclivities. Rather than waiting for crimes to happen and children to be victimized, FBI agents set up stings *To Catch a Predator* style, going into chat rooms, posing as children, and arresting those who tried to arrange assignations with kids.

"Our main goal was to rope in what are called travelers, predators who after a few cyber chats want to meet a child in a mall or at a motel," Freeh explained in his autobiography, *My FBI*.

Freeh mandated that every field office have at least two agents dedicated to investigating crimes involving child victims. I was named the Crimes Against Children Coordinator for our office and directed to offer our assistance in any child abduction case within our jurisdiction. In addition to working newly unfolding investigations, I was assigned to review every unsolved missing child case in our geographical area no matter how old the case was to see if there was anything the FBI could do to help solve it. Cold cases involving children are particularly heart wrenching, and working them set me on a personal journey that became an obsession. To not know for years or decades what happened to your child is a pain beyond imagining, and I vowed to do whatever I could to find these children and provide their parents with answers.

All together, these policies marked an incredible shift in priorities for a fairly hidebound agency, a breathtakingly humane initiative of which I was proud to play a part. With money and manpower in the FBI today understandably but sadly consumed with fighting terrorism, drugs, and government corruption, I mourn for the children—snatched, stalked, exploited, and murdered—who will pay an incalculable price for this shift in attention and resources.

Before newly enacted statutes and guidelines gave the FBI authority to immediately investigate child abductions, the Bureau didn't generally work sex crimes unless there was a violation of federal law involved, such as the belief a child may have been kidnapped and taken across state lines. So I started working the cases that would become my life's mission not as sex crimes but as missing person cases, only to discover that the suspect would usually turn out to be a sex offender.

In addition to Don Pierce's sense that I would have an affinity for this work due to the fight I waged for my own son's life, he may have selected me for the role due to the lengths I was going to in order to educate myself about the kind of person who most often commits these crimes. Once a month in California, the state Department of Corrections allows parole agents and criminal investigators to come together and interview a sex offender who has recently been released to reenter society. As a condition of parole, the offender is required to attend this meeting and answer every question posed. This provided an unparalleled opportunity to hear from the horse's mouth, so to speak, how a sex offender thinks and operates.

There is no other scenario where an offender has to answer questions put to him by law enforcement. During a criminal investigation or upon arrest, a suspect can simply remain silent, request a lawyer, or refuse to answer questions. Only in this unique setting could we ask them about how they found their victims, how they groomed kids, how they outfitted their homes to make them places that would attract children—and the offenders had to tell us. We could even make them show us identifying marks or tattoos on their bodies, things a victim might recall that would tie the offender to other past or possibly future cases. We could also be tougher and more adversarial in questioning these parolees in a way we couldn't be when working a case of our own and didn't want to risk the suspect shutting down and refusing to answer any more questions, which I have to admit was a cathartic experience. At the same time, just getting angry and yelling at a guy would defeat the whole purpose of being there. Instead, we wanted to extract whatever useful piece of information we possibly could from these encounters.

Each meeting would open with the parole agent for the particular offender who was getting out that month reading from a packet handed out to all of us describing the offender's MO, criminal history, and the crime for which they were currently being released. The first question the parolee was always asked was whether everything that was just read was accurate. Most offenders would try to deny or minimize. Their answers revealed their sick and distorted thinking. If we asked how they felt when they were around the child they molested they would say they loved that child more than anyone else could ever love them, that the child enjoyed what they did together, that they shared a "special bond." We would challenge their assumptions, asking if they thought it was really possible to have a mutual and consenting relationship with a five-year-old boy or seven-year-old girl. Yes, many would insist.

Every once in a while we would get someone who, at least for that particular moment in time, was able to break through his own denial and would admit, "I can't be around children. If I'm around a kid, I'll want that child." Others were so unrepentant they wouldn't even pretend to sound rehabilitated. One guy actually said: "When I get off parole I'm going to move to Arkansas and find an eight-year-old girl and marry her." He seemed to genuinely think there was something wrong with us that we did not share his type of thinking. His parole agent considered what he said so threatening that he rearrested him right there at the meeting for violating his parole.

The first time I attended one of these meetings I felt very uncomfortable. As the only FBI agent there, I wasn't sure if I would be welcome. At the end of the meeting a detective from the Sacramento County Sheriff's Department named Steve Hill introduced himself to me and offered to help me get acquainted with others in the group and to identify resources that might help me with my own cases. He explained that there was a special camaraderie among sex offense investigators and everyone always tried to help each other out. We were the soldiers on the front lines, thrust together in the trenches of a most unpleasant war. We needed each other's help, insight, and emotional support. No one outside our particular line of work would ever truly know or understand the things we saw and heard. The friendship and assistance Steve was offering me seemed too good to be true, yet he turned out to be the real deal, and he and I and our families are close friends to this day. He has a passion for working missing person cases that is as strong as anyone I have ever known. Steve opened doors that allowed me to learn from some of the most qualified professionals in the field, and it became my goal as an investigator to be worthy of being counted among them.

One month I showed up at the meeting only to discover that the guy being released was someone I helped put behind bars. He had molested a boy he met on the Internet, the son of an expert I had worked with on some cases. I was so outraged when I heard what had happened to this man's son that I got an agent in the FBI office where the crime occurred to open the case, and this man had been arrested and convicted of the crime. Years later, here I was, staring the guy in the face. I told him that I knew the person he molested and that I got the case going that ended in him being locked up. I promised him that he would never be rid of me and that I was going to be checking up on him for as long as he lived. At every meeting the offenders would be asked what they were going to do when they got off parole and invariably they would say that they were going to leave the state. I would make a point of saying that I was with the FBI and that we were in every state and that if they re-offended there was no place they could go that we wouldn't find them.

I kept attending these meetings throughout the rest of my career. And in all those years, I'm sorry to reveal, I never encountered a true pedophile (someone with a fixed sexual attraction for children who acted on that attraction) or a sexual sadist (someone for whom sexual excitement is tied to inflicting pain, suffering, and humiliation on others) who was rehabilitated. One guy, who ended up re-offending and going back to prison, used words very similar to what an alcoholic might use to describe his disease: "It's something that you have to realize is in you, and you have to deliberately avoid temptation at all times."

Pedophilia is like a switch that, once clicked, cannot be turned off. Among the investigators attending those meetings, our rule of thumb was that perpetrators typically understate their number of victims by 50 percent. We had a defrocked priest at one of the meetings who said he had molested 350 kids. He told us how he used the church to get access to kids by deliberately getting involved in youth activities, just as Sandusky apparently did by founding a charity for at-risk youth that was really just a gateway to vulnerable kids he could invite home for sleepovers and to shower with him in the university locker room. When we asked the priest whether the number of kids he abused was actually much higher, like 700, he said yes.

What I learned in these meetings helped me in every sex crime case I worked. With just the rudimentary two weeks of interrogation training I had received during my time at the Academy, it was by going to these Department of Corrections meetings and watching experienced detectives and parole agents interview extremely wily criminals that I learned how to be a sex crimes investigator. And when things got really dark for me, after years of working these emotionally draining cases, the comfort and support of the people that go to these meetings was one of the things that helped me through. I gave back by inviting all these investigators to take advantage of the services the FBI had to offer.

Any law enforcement officer could attend these Q&As. Yet I was the only FBI agent that I ever saw frequent these meetings. I tried to recruit other agents from my office to go, but no one else stuck with it. I can only guess it was because they didn't see these cases as necessarily having federal jurisdiction. But as the FBI took on greater involvement in cases of missing and exploited children, these sessions provided unparalleled insights into the psyche and modus operandi of sex offenders and served as a real-life practicum on how to draw information out of them during interrogations.

The case of Daniel David Hohenstein was one of the first cold cases I was asked by Don Pierce to go back and review in hopes of reigniting the investigation. Danny was just six years old when he disappeared on the cold, gray afternoon of December 1, 1992. He lived with his mother in Magalia, a small rural town in the northernmost part of California's Central Valley, on a bluff that dropped off into a big yawning canyon. Like so many of the bergs in this area of California, including my own town of Rescue, Magalia was a Gold Rush–era mining camp that had long since run dry. The town was originally called Mountain View because of its setting on the western slope of the majestic Sierra Nevada Mountains. It was also known near the time of its founding as Dogtown because of a dog breeding business located there, a fact that carried added poignancy when I learned more about Danny Hohenstein's life.

Danny was dealt a rotten hand even before tragedy befell him. Such is the case with many child victims whose life circumstances help place them in harm's way and make them especially vulnerable to abuse and exploitation. His mother's time and attention was so consumed by her own alcoholism that Danny was left to largely fend for himself and would sometimes show up at the homes of neighbors begging for food. His mother, Jackie Carter, was so deep in the grip of her addiction that she had once lost Danny for three days, forgetting that she had left him with a friend.

In the Name of the Children

Jackie had two other children, a twenty-year-old daughter named Shannon and an eighteen-year-old son named Brandon. But she had left them to fend for themselves in the apartment she had rented and moved in with an elderly man in failing health who was a drinking buddy at the bar she frequented. She was on welfare and the man had some financial means, so Jackie agreed to move into his house and serve as his caretaker, and she took only Danny with her. Brandon and especially Shannon had really been the ones to take care of Danny, so at the new home the boy was more on his own than ever. He was so alone in the world that his only friend and playmate was a cocker spaniel that had been abandoned in the neighborhood when its owner was sent to jail. Dogtown indeed. The boy and the dog were frequently sighted around the neighborhood together, soul mates in their abject neglect.

Danny was last seen in the late afternoon by some neighbors and workers at a construction site down the block where Danny liked to play. It had begun to rain and a construction worker told Danny to go home and put on a jacket. His mother said he came in at 4:30, put on a jacket, and then immediately went back out. Jackie was in the process of making dinner for Danny when he came in, so twenty minutes later, when the food was ready, she went out to look for him. She searched for almost an hour to no avail and then called 911.

The Butte County Sheriff's Department received Jackie's 911 call and immediately responded. Conditions that night turned from rain to snow and authorities worried that even if Danny had not been kidnapped but simply run away or gotten lost, he could be at risk due to the worsening weather. A massive search and rescue operation on the ground and by helicopter was mounted over the next three days throughout the neighborhood and into the adjacent canyon where the terrain grew quite rugged and dangerous.

I'd like to point out that law enforcement relies on help from unpaid volunteers when conducting large urban and wilderness rescue operations: pilots; backcountry climbers; scent dog handlers; searchers trained in using heat sensors, metal detectors, night-vision goggles, and other specialized technology; and people who train and equip themselves at their own expense and are willing to respond to calls for mutual aid at a moment's notice. They are a crucial and often unsung part of any search and rescue effort. When you put these skilled volunteers together with expert Sheriff's personnel, their success rate at finding missing persons or at least clues to their disappearance is very high. I would venture to say that when a search of the quality and magnitude of the one mounted to find Danny yields not a single piece of evidence, that itself is an important clue. Or, as they say in the forensics world, the absence of evidence is evidence.

Three days after Danny went missing, the cocker spaniel Danny played with was found on the opposite side of the canyon. At that point, the search and rescue effort was called off. The consensus seemed to be that Danny and the dog had wandered into the heavily wooded canyon, where the boy had succumbed as the result of an accident, predatory animals, or the elements. Investigators looked hard at Jackie, especially in light of the fact that she had failed an initial lie-detector test. But after she passed two subsequent polygraphs, they resolved that she probably wasn't involved in her son's disappearance.

Working a cold case is challenging, even under the best circumstances. Beginning an investigation years or even decades after a crime has occurred, it is too late to visit the crime scene or attend the autopsy where essential clues can be gathered. Time has passed and the memories of loved ones and witnesses have faded. Evidence may have been lost, misplaced, or destroyed forever before it could be discovered. All you have to go by is what is in the police file or in the evidence locker and whatever leads you can turn up on your own. You have to hope that the original investigation was thorough, that evidence was properly stored and accounted for, and that statements of witnesses and potential suspects were locked in so you can look for changes or discrepancies that the passage of time may uncover.

When your cold case involves a missing person who has simply vanished, you are at an even bigger disadvantage. Most criminal investigations begin at a known crime scene, either where a body is found or where there is evidence (blood, sign of a break-in, a ransom note left behind) that a crime occurred. In Danny's case, we had no corpse to tell us the cause or manner of his death or upon which we might find hairs or fibers or semen that could help us identify a perpetrator. We had no crime scene whatsoever where we could look for fingerprints, DNA, or signs of a struggle. In fact, we had no proof that Danny was even dead or had fallen victim to any kind of foul play. All we had was the timeline provided by his mother and those in the neighborhood of when he was last seen alive and the information that was in the file. Everyone would have to be reinterviewed, every statement and alibi double-checked, every memory refreshed and challenged, every clue analyzed anew.

Danny's case was about a year old by the time it was given to me and I began combing through the file. I did not pretend to be an expert after such cursory scrutiny, but I had a problem believing either of the main working scenarios. Jackie had reported Danny missing right away, awfully soon if she was attempting to cover up a crime she committed. As negligent a mother as she appeared to be, the tightness of that time frame made her look, in that moment at least, pretty responsible and like someone who did care about her son. And the scenario of Danny disappearing on his own in the woods also did not seem likely to me. I could not see how a child could vanish so completely in such a short window of time and no trace of his clothing or scent or anything else would be found in a search as comprehensive as the one conducted to try and find him.

Don Pierce decided that we should invite the lead Butte County detective and his supervisor down to our office and suggest we partner with them to take a fresh look at the case. I had my usual worries about how FBI involvement would be viewed by local authorities, especially because the FBI agents who had responded immediately after Danny's disappearance had not been really welcomed into the investigation. When the day for the meeting came I feared I might embarrass myself and give credence to the distrust many police agencies felt toward the FBI. I went out to the lobby to greet our two guests and brought them into a meeting room. The detective's name was Vern Kelch, and his supervisor at the Sheriff's Department was Perry Reniff. Vern was six foot five, with huge vise-like hands and a voice that rumbled like thunder. It felt like I was meeting John Wayne or a country-western version of *The Godfather's* burly henchman Luca Brasi.

Don joined us and got things going, and then asked me to offer my opinions on the case. I told Vern and his boss how impressed I was by their search and investigation and for that very reason had a hard time believing that Danny could have gotten far away on his own in such a short time period. I expected that our guests both believed that Danny had simply gotten lost and perished in the woods, but Vern immediately agreed with me. Don and Perry both thought Danny had died somewhere accidentally in the canyon, but to their credit they agreed to let Vern and me work together to see what we could find. I had no idea what I was getting into. It was the beginning of a marathon, years-long journey, full of ecstatic highs and dispiriting lows.

Not long after that first meeting, I traveled to the Butte County Sheriff's office in Oroville to meet with Vern and begin to sketch out a plan for our investigation. I had only seen the FBI files on the case, which were fairly limited, and Vern wanted me to review his department's files. I was taken aback when he handed me several thick volumes that were immaculately labeled and organized down to the smallest detail. The effort and dedication Vern had expended documenting every aspect of the investigation was truly a lesson to me. It is a common trope on police shows to depict cops bitching about having to write reports and keep up with paperwork, rather than "getting back out on the street." But a successful prosecution is dependent on the quality and thoroughness of the investigative file.

Because Vern and I were operating under the assumption that some person or persons had forcibly taken the boy, we would have to look at everybody who might have had contact with Danny, from family members to known sex offenders in the area. We would reinterview everyone, looking for details that didn't match up and also checking for any changes in behavior or lifestyle since Danny went missing that might indicate involvement in a terrible crime. We decided we would start our work together by meeting with Danny's mother and trying to conduct a less adversarial interview than the ones undertaken, by necessity, at the time he went missing. An added difficulty when investigating cold cases involving missing persons is that family members may lose trust in police and even become antagonistic to authorities as days turn into weeks then into years and the case remains unsolved. Maintaining the lines of communication is fraught and emotionally draining for both those who loved the missing person, desperate as they are for answers and resolution, and for the detectives who, try as they might, may be unable to deliver those things. It is crucial as an investigator to be able to distinguish whether any reluctance or hostility from a victim's family is simply the result of grief or frustration with the case remaining unsolved or of annoyance at being looked at as a suspect versus actual guilt and purposeful deception.

We drove to Magalia and Vern walked me up to Jackie's door. She answered and greeted us not with anger or suspicion but with warmth. I could immediately tell that she really liked Vern and that he had done an excellent job establishing a relationship with her. He gave her a bear hug and she genuinely hugged him back. Vern introduced me as an FBI agent assigned to Danny's case and described me in a way I thought left him plausible deniability in case I pissed her off. I came there expecting to find a woman at loose ends, a late-stage alcoholic living in chaos and squalor, but Jackie was nothing like I expected. She presented herself well and the house was neat and clean. She really appeared to be concerned about Danny and excited about what the FBI could do to help find him. I explained that the Bureau wanted to be more involved in cases of missing children and that I was here to help Vern and the Butte County Sheriff's Department. I asked her if we could sit down and go over as much as she could remember. I did not think we were going to get to talk to her at that very moment, but she agreed. Before we sat down she showed me where Danny slept and I saw some of the things he held dear, including the Nintendo game he liked to play. It was the first time I had ever been in a place so intimate: the bedroom of a child who had gone missing. My heart ached for Danny and the moments of happiness, however fleeting, he must have felt here.

The three of us sat down and started going over everything that happened the day Danny disappeared. I tried not to be judgmental, but I admit I came in angry at Jackie from all I had read about her in the files. I wasn't so much bothered by her failing the first polygraph she was administered. Polygraphs measure emotional reaction, and I expect parents to be emotional when their child goes missing. I also suspected she felt some responsibility for what happened to Danny—even if she had nothing directly to do with it—because of how she neglected him. Vern didn't believe she was involved, but I hadn't yet made up my mind and I was annoyed at Vern for being so nice to her.

Danny

My way of expressing anger in an interview is not like what you might see in TV or the movies. I don't play good cop/bad cop. I don't hit anybody or try to bully or intimidate a suspect. If I don't like you, I'm not friendly. I'm official; I'm FBI-ish. But it's a fine line. You can't be a complete asshole and then try to be nice later; the suspect will never trust you and you can kiss good-bye any chance of that person ever opening up to you. With Jackie I wasn't overly friendly or warm or comforting. I told her straight out that I was angry at her for how Danny lived and she knew that meant I would ask her questions she wouldn't like, but she still answered them without any apparent artifice or attempt to make herself look better. That was a sign to me that she was telling the truth.

I was stuck on the fact that the same person who once misplaced her son for three days had started looking for him within twenty minutes of last seeing him and then called in authorities within an hour. Jackie admitted that her diligence that day was initially self-motivated. Danny was supposed to stay with his dad the night he disappeared. Jackie was trying to get Danny fed and then over to his dad's house because she had plans to go out to the bar that night. When Danny came in momentarily to get his coat, she was in the process of making macaroni and cheese for him. It took her another twenty minutes to finish preparing the dish, then she went outside to call him in. Motivated to get him over to his dad, she searched for about an hour before calling the police. The honesty of that admission was heartbreaking, but it made sense considering how she lived her life. I asked a lot of hard questions, but she never backed off or got defensive. Over the course of the interview, and even more so over the time we spent working the case, I came to realize that Jackie would have welcomed anyone who was trying to find her son, even if they did suspect her.

After the interview with Jackie I drove home, emotionally wrung out but also exhilarated that I had not done anything to make Vern turn away my help. I called him a few days later and suggested that we start everything over from scratch and he agreed. Throughout all the years I worked with Vern on Danny's case, I had a caseload of ten to twenty other active investigations I had to juggle at any one time, including some of the other cases described in this book. But every few weeks I would make the two-and-a-half-hour drive to meet with Vern, and we systematically went about identifying anyone who might have had access to Danny the day he went missing and then tried to eliminate each person as a suspect. The process we fell into was to identify someone we wanted to look at and have that person come into the Butte County Sheriff's Department for an interview. If we could not rule out the suspect's involvement through our own interview, we would arrange for a polygraph.

As the years passed, a deep friendship developed between Vern and me. As hard and disappointing as the work often was, I looked forward to each day I spent with Vern. He was a practical joker who loved to take advantage of my naïveté and lack of knowledge about anything outside my city-centric worldview. Vern would always provide tidbits about rural life that were deliberately misleading, but I believed them, and he knew it. On one occasion as we drove by a herd of cows grazing on a hill, Vern "explained" how cows that grazed on slopes developed a "longer side" that enabled them to stay upright. I blindly accepted this as fact and never questioned it. I eventually shared it with Lori, the fish and wildlife expert, just to look smart. After she got done laughing, Lori explained that Vern had fooled me.

To be able to bust your partner's chops without rancor is the way we in law enforcement express our affection for each other. Vern had initially been wary of working with the FBI, but the delight he took in pulling one over on me let me know that he accepted me as a true partner. And I respected him so much that if he told me something, I believed it, even if I should have known better.

From having been exposed to an FBI-administered polygraph in the Frankie Proctor case and now experiencing them again in Danny's investigation, I learned that a polygraph is a valuable investigative tool but that its usefulness is directly related to the quality of the person administering the test and interpreting its results. During my career, I have seen guilty people pass polygraphs and innocent people fail them. Because what the test is measuring is the physiological signs of stress, the so-called lie detector can be particularly unreliable in heavily emotion-laden cases involving crimes against children. It is up to the polygrapher and the detectives working the case to find out what may be causing stress during a polygraph and determine whether it has anything to do with that person actually being responsible for the crime being investigated. In one case I worked regarding the possession of child pornography, a suspect failed a polygraph. But when my partner and I interrogated him, we believed him to be innocent. It later turned out that there was a screw-up with the forensic examination of the man's computer. In fact, no child pornography was found on the man's computer and he was exonerated.

Two years into my work on the case, three years after Danny disappeared, Vern and I traveled to the Los Angeles area to interview one suspect. He was a guy with a really violent reputation who traveled in some of the same circles as Jackie and had sadistic sexual predilections, according to interviews we conducted with some of his sexual partners. He was not happy that we had come all the way to LA looking for him, but he agreed to be polygraphed. We were so convinced the guy had taken Danny that we got the polygrapher, the esteemed and experienced Jack Trimarco, believing it, too, when we briefed him before the test. The polygraph lasted three hours and we were sure it was going to end in a confession. As we waited outside, the suspect suddenly burst out the door and stormed past us in tears. Jack trailed a short distance behind him, but he made no signal for us to stop the guy, so we reluctantly let him go. Jack proceeded to tell us that the suspect passed the test with flying colors but Jack continued to interrogate him because we had gotten him so fired up for it. Vern and I finally caught up with the guy a few blocks away and offered him a ride home, but he wouldn't come anywhere near us, preferring to walk the several miles home.

Vern was better at keeping his emotions under control, but for me the experience was brutal. I was so sure we had our man and now we were back at square one. It was like an endless roller-coaster ride and I vowed to keep my hopes in check, but it was an impossible promise to keep. This experience showed once again the importance of not getting too wedded to any theory or suspect or polygraph result.

We looked hard at one of the construction workers who had been doing a job down the block from Danny's house. He had been one of the last people to see Danny and seemed to know more about the boy than a stranger would likely know. But we ultimately concluded that he had simply taken a paternal interest in the lonely, friendless boy who often hung around the construction site after school, recognizing the deprivation in Danny's life that was obvious to any observer.

One guy came to our attention after his daughter-in-law called and suggested him as a suspect. We interviewed all of his kids and every one of them said that he had molested them. His son told me that he used to stay up at night to try to prevent his father from sexually assaulting his sister. All the kids were grown now, in their thirties and forties, but they worried that their father still had such an appetite and might have been on the prowl for someone else's kid to molest. It was excruciating to do these kinds of interviews, to take in so much pain, to hear how someone could betray his children's trust without any thought of the wreckage he was leaving behind. We wanted this guy to be our man just for the pleasure of putting him away, but he was ultimately ruled out by alibi.

Each day when I got up, no matter what case I was working on that day, I thought of Danny and Vern. We had to entertain every possible scenario. We even had tipsters claiming Danny had been murdered and cannibalized by a Satanic cult. Leads as crazy as that still had to be checked out. One soul-shaking thought was the possibility that someone had taken Danny not to hurt him but in the belief that they could offer him a better home. As nice as it was to hold on to any hope that Danny was alive, it was horrible to think that someone might attempt to save Danny by destroying all those who loved him.

Early on, Vern and I had made a decision to make Jackie and her daughter aware of our renewed investigation and seek their help. Shannon clearly loved her brother and wanted to be a big part of the effort to find him. I asked both Jackie and Shannon to tell us about anyone they could think of who might have had contact with Danny. I gave them every number I had and asked them to contact me if anything new occurred to them, no matter how crazy or insignificant it might seem.

Weeks turned into months and then into years and everything seemed to lead to a dead end. Yet we kept visiting Jackie and Shannon. It was hard to see them knowing we had no answers to give them. But realizing that we cared, that we were working together and constantly doing something new to try to find Danny, seemed to offer them comfort. It got to the point where Jackie and Shannon would hug me, too, but I always teased Vern that they hugged him harder.

One day three years into our joint investigation, four years after Danny's disappearance, Shannon called me and said that her mother was friends with a woman whose son might be a child molester. He was a minor who also had a severe intellectual impairment, and I worried what that might mean for our ability to prosecute him if he did turn out to be involved. But Vern and I would leave no stone unturned. We had become bound to each other and to our common mission, and even though years had gone by with little to show for it, the drive to keep going never flagged within us. I immediately called him and relayed what Shannon had said. After much effort Vern managed to locate the boy, who was living in a state facility for developmentally disabled and mentally ill minors. Vern also had found information indicating the boy may have molested multiple kids. The most shocking news: the boy was just fourteen years old at the time Danny disappeared. He was still a minor at the time we learned of him, just about to turn eighteen.

I'm going to call the boy Jonathan and his mother Diana. I have made the decision not to use the real names of anyone who has not been charged or convicted of the crimes I was investigating, even if it pains me to do so. Some cases are unsolvable because of lack of evidence. Other times you are sure you know who committed the crime but the perpetrator cannot be charged for reasons completely beyond your control. Because everyone deserves a chance to challenge the case against them in court, I will give "Jonathan" and "Diana" anonymity. But Danny deserves better. And so does Shannon, whose devotion to her brother broke the case wide open and who is the real hero of this story.

By the time we located Jonathan, Vern had developed a fairly complete profile of him. Jonathan was apparently born with developmental disabilities and had an IQ of just 65, which is in the range of mild retardation, possibly as a result of fetal alcohol syndrome. He spent much of his young life in state mental facilities, bouncing from one placement to another because of behavioral problems the staff members were unable to control. However, he had been released into the custody of his mother for about a year and a half, a period that coincided with Danny's disappearance. Three months before Danny vanished, Jonathan had lured a six-year-old boy behind a Dumpster in the apartment complex where he was living with his mother in Oroville and attempted to sodomize him. Fortunately, a man at the complex saw what was happening and intervened before things went too far. At that point the family relocated to within two miles of where Danny lived with Jackie. Then, just nine days after Danny went missing, Jonathan again was reported to authorities for groping a six-year-old hearing-impaired boy on the bus special needs kids rode to school.

In the facility where Jonathan was currently housed, he continued to act out both violently and sexually toward other young boys, necessitating he be kept under constant supervision. Jonathan was so physically powerful that he seemed to get what he wanted even in the midst of other dangerous offenders. One day he was found with the toughest patient in the facility sitting in his lap. He described his sexual urges as all consuming, stating that he cannot stop himself when presented with a sexual opportunity.

Even if Jonathan had molested Danny, it was hard for me to imagine a child killing another child. But Jonathan's history revealed other disturbing characteristics. He was known to have tortured and sexually assaulted animals. FBI profilers have discovered that cruelty to animals is a trait often found in the backgrounds of homicidal individuals. Was it a sign that, in addition to deviant sexual compulsion, Jonathan was capable of murderous violence?

The big question was whether Jonathan had access to Danny on the day the child disappeared. We knew Jonathan and his mother, Diana, lived very close to where Danny and his mother were staying with the elderly man for whom she was providing care. Vern found out that Diana also had a drinking problem and hung out at the same bar as Jackie. Shannon had described her mother and Diana as friends, but when Vern asked Jackie about Diana she said that she did not know the woman well, although she believed that Diana had been to her house once about a month before Danny went missing.

It was hard to know if Jackie was telling the truth. I don't believe she was deliberately obstructing our investigation, but she may have been holding back, reluctant to acknowledge the role her own unsa-vory lifestyle played in exposing Danny to danger. It was also possible Diana and Jonathan had been to Jackie's house without her knowledge. A suspicion we had is that Diana may have known the owner of the house from the bar and wanted to become his caretaker, to share in the pay he was offering or the possibility of inheritance when he died. She and Jonathan might have come around when Jackie wasn't there and Jonathan might have befriended Danny.

While not conclusive proof that the boys had contact with each other, one fact we uncovered gave us both pause. Jonathan's records indicated that he chronically suffered from scabies. Scabies is a para-sitic infestation that is commonly passed among children in close set-tings. Eradicating the condition requires, among other things, shaving off or treating the hair with medicated lotion and thoroughly cleaning all clothing and bedding where the mites that carry the disease may be lurking. On the day he vanished, Danny was suffering from scabies, and his mom kept him home from school to treat it. Jackie shaved Danny's head and spent the day cleaning the house and doing load after load of laundry. In fact, the picture used on the missing person poster was of Danny with a buzz cut, not the way he usually wore his hair.

Don gave me authorization to go with Vern and try to speak to Jonathan. We asked one of the counselors at the hospital where he was institutionalized to sit in with us. When Jonathan came into the room I was taken aback by how big and strong he was—not the "boy" I had imagined. He would certainly have been able to overpower Danny, who was three and a half feet tall and weighed just around forty pounds when he disappeared. It was even more shocking to see how intellectu-ally challenged Jonathan was. He answered our questions and would ask one of his own if there was something he did not understand, but he seemed to have the comprehension of a twelve-year-old.

Vern started the conversation by saying we were looking for a little boy named Danny. Jonathan said he knew Danny and had been to his house. Vern showed him a couple of pictures and Jonathan identified the one used on the missing poster as Danny. He then picked out Danny with longer hair in a group picture with other kids, saying that was how Danny looked "now." We also had a picture of the dog found in the canyon and Jonathan described it as "Danny's dog." When Jonathan accurately stated the color of the T-shirt Danny was wearing when he disappeared I could see the blood rush to Vern's face and felt the flush in my own. Nobody outside law enforcement and Danny's mother knew that piece of information.

What Jonathan went on to tell us was shattering. He said his mother had taken the boys to the park. When Danny went into the restroom to pee, Jonathan followed in behind him and tried to sodomize him. He said Danny started to scream and that he covered the boy's mouth to stop him from screaming. He eventually let Danny go and the boy fell to the floor, blood dripping from his nose. After a while, his mother came in looking for them. He said she asked him to help her put Danny in their car.

It was like listening to a child who doesn't know right from wrong. He seemed to be confessing to sexually assaulting and killing Danny, although he didn't use those clinical terms, without realizing what he had done. And he had no understanding of the concept of death. There was the comment about how Danny looked "now" with his hair grown out. He described him and his mother dumping Danny's body in the woods but said they did it so Danny could "sleep" and said he removed the child's shoes and socks so he would be more comfortable. Jonathan's mother, however, was a nurse and would have been able to determine that Danny was dead.

As the day went on, Jonathan got tired and he began to make less and less sense. At one point he said Danny fled the bathroom and hid in the bushes and that Diana took Jonathan home, told him to wash up, and then she went to look for Danny but was unable to find him. We couldn't tell what was the truth and what was fantasy. It seemed, however, from the identifying facts he had given us, that Jonathan did know Danny. At the end of the day, Jonathan began crying and said what happened to Danny was his fault. He said he wished Danny were there so that he could apologize to him.

Vern and I wanted nothing more than to get back to Butte County and find Diana. The day was so draining that three hours into the drive we had to stop and try to sleep. But neither of us could sleep a wink because we were too wired. So we resumed our journey, talking the whole way about how we should approach Diana and what we could expect from her. We were convinced that after what Jonathan told us, Diana would certainly agree to help us and share everything she knew. We could understand how a panicked mother might do something rash in the moment to protect her child, but now it was time to do the right thing. That was our hope, anyway, but it was a fantasy.

Diana denied everything. We still hadn't been to bed when we found her and we tried for several hours to convince her that it was best for Jonathan to resolve this now. But she insisted that she had never met Danny. She stated that she hadn't even met Jackie until after Danny disappeared. She said she had been to Danny's house with her own son once after the disappearance and a lot of news clippings were laying around. She suggested that when we questioned Jonathan he was making up stories based on what he read in those clippings—which seemed highly unlikely due to his comprehension difficulties.

I felt we needed specialized help, the kind I thought expert minds in the FBI could provide. As I began handling child abduction cases I became familiar with the work of the profilers in the FBI's Child Abduction and Serial Killer Unit and was particularly impressed by Roy Hazelwood and Ken Lanning, who were among the first to use behavioral science as an investigative tool. Hazelwood had retired from the FBI and was on the road teaching, but I had attended some of his seminars and had a sense that he was passionate about cases like Danny's. I called him and he advised us to go back over and over again to see Jonathan in hopes that we could obtain enough consistency in his statements to prove what was accurate. He said it would be one of the most difficult things we would ever have to do, but if we could devote the time and effort we would have the best chance of solving the case and finding Danny.

Mike Morrow, a profiler from CASKU, was assigned to work on Danny's case and he opened up all the resources of the Bureau to us. He made himself available any time I called, gave me insight into how to interview Jonathan and how to try to gain the cooperation of his mother, and calmed me down when I got too worked up about the case. I can't think about Mike without getting emotional about what a special person he is. At one point he put me in touch with one of the biggest non-FBI experts in the field of forensic psychology, but when I called, unlike with Hazelwood, I was told by the person who answered the phone what the expert's hourly rate would be and that he may or may not "take the case." I decided I would rely only on those who really cared: Vern and myself and those at CASKU.

We still had no idea where Danny was but thought the backyard of the house where Jonathan had stayed with his mother was a good place to start. To help with the search, Vern contacted forensic anthropologist Turhon Murad, who founded the program in forensic anthropology at California State University at Chico and had worked on many prominent cases, including the kidnapping and murder of twelve-year-old Polly Klaas. He also worked to help identify the remains of unknown soldiers from the Korean and Vietnam wars. We showed up at Diana's house with a team of forensic anthropologists from Murhad's department and volunteers from Vern's and my offices. I had never been involved in a search for a body before and I learned that day how long, T-shaped hollow poles are used to carefully probe the earth in hopes of finding a clandestine gravesite.

No trace of Danny was found. The anthropologists located an area that was used as a burn pit. They painstakingly excavated bones from the pit with brushes and scrapers, but they turned out to be animal, not human. The most curious thing we discovered during the search was what appeared to be a shrine. There was a statue of a little boy with wings, which perhaps represented an angel. Another ceramic statue held a set of car keys. We did not know what to make of that.

Those car keys haunted Vern and me and we decided to look for the car Diana had owned at the time of Danny's disappearance. Again, it seemed like a long shot that anything incriminating would be memorialized this way, but we had to follow it up. The car had been sold, but we located its new owner, who not only readily agreed to allow us to search it but also handed over the vacuum cleaner he had used to clean the car and that might have preserved forensic evidence. The Butte County Sheriff's Office and the FBI's Evidence Response Team processed the car and submitted their findings to the FBI lab. We knew Jonathan's words would never hold up by themselves; we needed some kind of hard evidence, and the car was perhaps our last hope of getting it.

Danny

Vern and I went back to Diana, but she continued to insist that neither she nor her son had ever known Danny. She was polygraphed and the results were inconclusive.

She passed a voice stress test but in a subsequent interview was deemed to be lying, making us question the results of the voice stress analysis.

Vern and I looked further into the backgrounds of Diana and her son. We learned that Jonathan had been sexually assaulted himself by one of Diana's boyfriends when he was six—Danny's age. I suspect the abuse may have continued over a protracted period of time. Then Jonathan, in turn, began offending against other boys. Jonathan's siblings knew about his predatory behavior and took steps to stop him from hurting other kids. On one occasion they took him to a sporting event and tried to prevent him from using the public restroom. After he caused a scene they eventually relented. But when he seemed to be taking too long they went into the restroom to investigate and saw that the light had been turned off and found Jonathan approaching a young boy. The siblings described Jonathan as having an unusually close relationship with his mother. At the facility where he was housed, staff members came to believe Jonathan was having sex with his mother in the bathroom when she came to visit him. On one such visit they were caught in the act.

Vern and I went back and talked to Jonathan. On our second visit he alternated between making damning admissions and then denying everything he had just said. When making these retractions he said he was following his mother's instructions—he said straight out, "My mother told me to tell you that I didn't know Danny"—and after calling his mother during a lunch break remained resistant. But then he changed course again, telling us he had sodomized Danny so roughly he "hurt Danny really bad" and caused him to bleed. After the second visit, the story he related remained pretty consistent. We reality checked what he told us about Danny by asking him about other molestations he committed that could be verified by police reports and everything he told us about those crimes turned out to be true.

Jonathan said he had been to Danny's home many times. He thought the old man who owned the house was Danny's father and said he came over with his mother when she helped take care of the man. He talked about playing with Danny in his room. He even described the video game device Danny had in there. Once again, Jonathan had accurately described something about Danny that no one outside the family and law enforcement knew. We'll never know for sure, but I suspect he had already begun at least touching Danny inappropriately on visits to his house—Jonathan himself described taking even greater liberties at Danny's house. On the day Jonathan admitted hurting Danny, Jonathan said he and his mother were driving by and saw Danny playing outside with his dog and invited him to go to a park with them. He said Danny got into the car along with the dog.

I don't believe Diana participated in killing Danny, but she clearly knew about Jonathan's proclivities and allowed him to have access to Danny and other young boys. And according to Jonathan, she engineered and participated in the cover-up. Jonathan said he and his mother actually made two trips to the woods before dumping the victim's body: the first time getting spooked and driving away when some people walked up to their car and asked them what they were doing. This would explain why Danny was not found during the intensive search of the canyon. Vern had organized his files so well that he was able to pull up a report in which some members of the search and rescue team recalled seeing a car in the area when they were looking for Danny. As two of the searchers approached the car, the driver pulled away. Could that have been Diana and Jonathan fleeing with Danny still in their car?

After turning eighteen, Jonathan was transferred to one of the state psychiatric hospitals for adults and was later moved to a different hospital. In each of those facilities, he made the same admissions to Vern and me and also in separate sessions to his caregivers. Following Roy Hazelwood's advice, Vern and I visited Jonathan eight or nine times over a period of several years. Every time we uncovered a new piece of information we went back and interviewed him again. We kept going back because we wanted to know exactly what had happened to Danny and hoped there might be some way to hold his killer accountable. We kept going until we felt we had gotten everything we could out of him and we couldn't wring out the rag anymore. I believe Jonathan probably smothered Danny to death while assaulting him. During one visit Jonathan acted out on his psychiatrist how he held his hand over Danny's mouth to quiet his screams and Vern and I both noted how his hand was covering both mouth and nostrils. It was terrible listening to him describe over and over again what he did to Danny and to see him actually get sexually excited as he recounted it.

In my opinion, the FBI lab is the best in the world at analyzing evidence. But because of the number and magnitude of investigations the FBI handles, it can take a long time to get results back on a case not considered an immediate priority. The evidence we had submitted was pretty speculative—hairs from a car that may or may not have been used to transport a dead child years ago and had changed hands and presumably been cleaned countless times since then. We wanted those hairs checked against a blood sample taken from Jackie. A DNA profile cannot be generated from hair alone unless the root is still attached to the hair, where nuclear DNA is found. A new technology was emerging at that time, however, for analysis of rootless hair for what is known as mitochondrial DNA (mtDNA)—molecules present in the hair shaft itself as well as in bones. Mitochondrial DNA does not yield the unique individual profile or "genetic fingerprint" that nuclear DNA analysis does. Instead, this type of DNA, solely inherited from the maternal line, links all those with a common mother. In other words, Jackie and all of her children would share the same mitochondrial DNA profile and a hair from Danny analyzed this way would match a profile developed from his mother.

This scientific advance would mark a great leap forward in solving cases where no body is ever found and in cold cases where the remains are so old and degraded that a conventional DNA profile cannot be generated. But my case had not yet risen to the level where such a test could be ordered. This was during the Clinton presidency and as I waited I tried not to go ballistic wondering whether the lab was having to spend time testing Monica Lewinsky's blue dress instead of working on Danny's case.

In January of 1998, five years after Danny was last seen alive, a stunning break occurred in our case. Hikers traversing a wooded area of the canyon about a mile from Danny's house came upon a child-sized skull and some tattered fragments of clothing. The skull was provided to Dr.

Murad and his staff at CSU Chico for analysis. Dr. Murad and his anthropology department had developed computer software that enabled a picture of a missing person to be transposed onto a skull to see if the bone structure matched. Using this technology, Murad believed there was a good possibility the skull was Danny's. The Sheriff's Department and the CSU forensic team searched the area and found more bones uphill from where the skull was discovered. Ultimately, about 40 percent of the skeleton was recovered, including the long bones of the leg, which retain DNA longer than other bones that have decayed due to exposure to the elements.

The most chilling part of the discovery was that the lower leg bones were not found encased in shoes and socks, as they often are when someone is dumped or buried while shod. Instead, shoes and socks matching those Danny was wearing when he vanished were found nearby. Did that mean Jonathan was telling the truth about removing Danny's shoes and socks to make him "more comfortable" before he and his mother left him to "sleep" forever in the forest? Vern and I took Jonathan out to the canyon one day and asked him to point out where they had dumped Danny's body. The place he pointed to was very close to where the skull was found.

Confirmatory tests could now be run. Danny's case was one of the first in FBI history to employ the new form of DNA testing. One day I got a call from John "Jeb" Stuart, who pioneered mitochondrial DNA testing in the FBI and established a national missing persons DNA database. He told me that testing revealed that both the bones and the skull matched the mitochondrial DNA profile of Jackie Carter. He also said they were testing hairs collected from the search of Diana's car that looked most like they could be from Danny and that at least one also matched Jackie's mtDNA profile.

It took me ten minutes after hanging up to take in the magnitude of what Jeb had just told me. Because Danny was the only unaccounted for child in Jackie's maternal line, the bones could belong to no one but Danny. And the hair was almost certainly Danny's as well. What possible innocent explanation was there for Danny's hair being found in Diana's car, because both Jackie and Diana denied being friends and Diana claimed that she had never even met Danny or been to his house

Danny

before his disappearance? I called Jeb back to confirm that I had heard correctly what he said. Then I called Vern to tell him the thunderous news. I could feel adrenaline pumping through my body. My heart was pounding and I suddenly felt a sensation of tremendous restlessness, like I was jumping out of my own skin.

"Vern, I think they may have identified Danny's hair in the car," I croaked into the phone. There was silence on the other end of the line and I could hear him draw in his breath. After several long seconds he said that he would call me back in ten minutes. Just as I did, Vern needed time to regain his composure before he could take in this information. After we both collected ourselves, I told Vern how proud I was of what we had done together, and I suggested that he be the one to advise Jackie, Shannon, and Brandon of the news.

By the time we got the news about the hair, the statute of limitations for being an accessory after the fact to a felony—the only thing we thought we could charge Diana with—had passed. Jonathan was still incompetent to stand trial for what he had done. And while there is no privilege in California law protecting a child from having to testify against a parent, as there is between spouses, it is unlikely his statements would be admissible in court due to his intellectual deficits. Even with that piece of physical evidence, we couldn't prove that Diana had dumped Danny's body and covered up her son's involvement in his death because Jonathan was known to take the car sometimes. Solving a case and getting justice are two very different things, and the likelihood that no one will ever be held responsible for taking Danny's life and keeping his fate hidden for many long years is something I still have a hard time accepting. It's also hard to live with the sad reality that Danny was victimized by someone who had been victimized himself, someone who had been dealt an equally rotten hand in life, someone so utterly vulnerable to the predations perpetrated on him before he became a perpetrator himself.

For reasons I don't understand, the county sheriff hung on to Danny's remains for several more years. Shannon had to go to court to get them released. By the time they were finally turned over to his family, Jackie had died, succumbing to her alcoholism. Danny was laid to rest next to his mom in a small mausoleum not far from where he lived and died.

Shannon arranged a memorial service and several people from the community who had been moved by his plight attended. Vern and his wife, Vera, and Lori and my sons attended the memorial service. I was so grateful for my family's support through all the years it took to bring Danny "home," and I was moved that they wanted to be there to honor Danny and his family. I was proud to have them with me and to have others get to know them.

In the years he was on this earth, Danny had a life that was so dismal that his family had hardly any pictures of him. It was a problem during our investigation; one of the few pictures we could find was taken by a dentist after repairing his teeth, which due to neglect were all rotted out by the time he was just six. Vern and I wanted Danny's siblings to have something to remember their brother by, so I had an FBI technician edit out the protective napkin the dentist had chained around his neck before taking the photo. We framed the picture for Shannon and Brandon and attached a small bronze plate below it with a note from Vern and me. A different image stays with me, however—that of Danny standing on a neighbor's back deck, wearing pajamas and shivering in the cold, asking to be let in to get something to eat. To this day I live with the face of that little boy beseeching a stranger for some simple human kindness. It has never faded in my mind's eye, even after more than twenty years.

Both Vern and I stayed in contact with Shannon, and Vern's family and mine remained close until he passed away in 2012. Shannon came to Vern's funeral, and the image I carry with me from that day, one that I treasure, is of Shannon and Lori and me all holding one another and offering each other comfort and strength.

CHAPTER FOUR

Michael

NO CASE HAS HAUNTED ME MORE than the murder of eight-year-old Michael Lyons. The memory of finding his body—savagely tortured, mutilated, and thrown away like trash along the banks of the Feather River, in hopes the rising tide would carry away all trace of his killer's dastardly act—is seared forever in my mind. Nearly two decades have passed, yet that murder scene is the last thing I think of each night before I fall asleep and the first to flood my thoughts when I wake in the morning. It has apparently taken up permanent residence in my subconscious as well. In the years since his death I have had to undergo several surgical procedures, and each time, hospital personnel have told me, as I begin to lose control and slip under the spell of anesthesia, I call out Michael's name, scream in horror at his fate.

A fellow detective named Jeff Gardner, whom I confided in about the Michael Lyons case, told me there is always going to be the "one"—the case you cannot let go of, that you carry with you to your own grave. For him, the one was a toddler who was subjected to inexplicable sadism by his own mother and sister, who tied the boy by his penis to his bed and then beat their captive prisoner for days on end. The boy was so badly injured that he fell into a coma and was not expected to live. Gardner sat by the boy's bedside in the hospital until he passed away, not wanting the child to die alone.

I understand that need to stand vigil, driven by respect for life and to honor a child that suffered so much. Long after Michael Lyons's case was solved I continued to visit his grave, feeling a sense of loss that went beyond bringing his killer to justice. Perhaps because Michael was the same age as the son I nearly lost, and also because his crime scene was the first I had been to involving a child, his case had the most profound impact on me of any I worked in my career. But he is far from the only one who haunts me. There is also Danny, of course—and Alexia, Salaam, Silvina, Juli, Courtney, and so many others. Their faces and stories remain present in my mind like Russian nesting dolls, each waiting its turn to be brought to the surface, to be revealed and examined anew.

Their cases were never to me just names stamped on a file, or scrawled on a whiteboard, or typed on the recipe box–style index cards the FBI used to assign cases when I started at the agency. Outside of my family, these victims were the people I cared most about in the world. I feel blessed and heartened to have some of their loved ones, and even some victims who managed to survive the horrors inflicted upon them, still in my life. At my darkest moments I have wanted to join these kids in death, feeling a perverse sense of envy that for them the pain and horror has mercifully ended, while for me those feelings continue unabated by confessions or convictions.

Being a criminal investigator means living every day in fear that you might have missed something, overlooked some essential clue, forgotten to ask the question that might have solved a case or saved a life. When the victim is a child, every second that passes and every decision you make comes with a heightened sense of responsibility. I'll never stop second-guessing myself, wondering if I did everything I could have done or should have done to get the best result possible under the circumstances. Like the tales of Scheherazade, the stories of these children spin out, cross over one another, loop back and forth in my memory, as if by constantly reworking them in my mind, the kids, like Scheherazade, can somehow make it through the night and stave off execution. But the cold reality of their deaths is always there in the morning, like an ice bath flooding my senses.

On May 16, 1996, in Yuba City, California, Michael Lyons never made it home from school. His parents last saw him when they dropped him off that morning at his elementary school, where he was a third grader. Yuba City is situated at the confluence of two rivers, the Feather and the Yuba, in Northern California's Gold Country. The day Michael disappeared, his family was preparing for a move to a new house in Marysville, a neighboring town just across the Feather River. His mother and stepfather were painting and doing some repairs at their current house that day, so they told Michael to go stay with his grandparents after school until they could pick him up. The grandparents lived just a block from his school and Michael was looking forward to seeing them. Visits with his grandparents were considered a treat for good behavior. But unbeknownst to Michael and his parents, the grandparents weren't home that day, so presumably Michael started making his way back to his parents' house on his own.

A family friend reported seeing him walking on a street near the school at 3:15 PM. Another person would later report seeing a man driving a truck in the area stop abruptly alongside a walking boy, call him over to the vehicle, pull him inside, and then speed off. Unfortunately, the witness did not report this suspicious sighting immediately, assuming the man she saw was just the boy's father. After we discovered that this sighting occurred along the route the boy would use to walk home, we came to believe that this was in fact how Michael had been kidnapped.

When Michael's mother and stepfather found he was not at his grandparents, they spent a couple of hours searching for him, and then called the police. The next day the Yuba City Police Department requested assistance from other agencies, including the FBI. The FBI has fifty-six field offices in major cities around the country, like Sacramento, and within those larger geographical areas there are what is known as resident agencies in smaller cities that have jurisdiction over a specific area. Steve Broce from the Auburn Resident Agency was assigned as the FBI case agent. I drove to Yuba City and was paired up with the lead Yuba City PD detective on the case, Mike Green, to interview Michael's mother, Sandra.

I believe in conducting very extensive interviews with victims, witnesses, and suspects. You never know what seemingly extraneous fact might turn out to be important, what question might prompt a crucial revelation, what detail might break a case wide open. To explore every potential scenario that might explain a person's disappearance, we have to ask their loved ones very personal and painful questions. Family members with things to hide, including potential involvement in the crime, will lie or refuse to answer these questions. Some just don't want to dredge up family secrets. Sandra was admirably forthcoming. She told us that when Michael was just three years old his uncle sexually assaulted him and that ever since then the boy had been acting out. I believe that Sandra sharing this information meant that she was prepared to do whatever it took to find her son. I was really impressed by her honesty and thankful for her telling us everything she could in hopes of identifying potential suspects.

The revelation that Michael had been previously victimized made us wonder if the uncle should be the first suspect to consider. Another possible suspect his mother mentioned was a neighbor in their apartment complex who was always inviting young boys into his apartment. But before we could begin down those roads we got a call that the body of a child had been found about two and a half miles from the school along the shores of the Feather River in an area locals referred to as the "river bottoms"—a forbidding place where homeless people lived in whatever they could muster together for shelter and where drug use was rampant.

Some utility workers who wanted to help with the search that authorities had mounted had walked the area along the river and discovered the body. The head of the newly formed Evidence Response Team in our field office and an uncommonly sensitive soul, Todd Drost, immediately rushed out to secure the scene and make sure it remained as pristine as possible. Mike and I headed over and met up with a group of FBI agents and police officers at the head of a trail leading down to the river. It was decided that six of us would go in: Todd and two other members of the ERT, the deputy coroner, and Mike and I. We walked carefully, scanning the terrain to make sure we did not miss or disrupt anything of importance. After a short distance we could see what appeared to be the pale, waxy flesh of a decomposing corpse. The body was not buried but so obscured by thick brush that we could not tell it was actually a person until we got up close. We found the body lying face down near a tree, naked except for a shirt pulled inside out over the deceased's head and upstretched arms, obscuring his face—as if his killer literally wanted to make him faceless, less than human. We knew from interviewing Sandra that Michael was wearing a Batman T-shirt on the day he disappeared, but it wasn't until we gently turned his body over and carefully pulled down the shirt, revealing the boy's

Michael

face and the iconic Batman logo on the T-shirt, that we felt confident this was indeed Michael. Still, the coroner asked us not to say anything to the family until tests could be run to confirm the identity.

I had seen many dead bodies at the mortuary where my dad worked, but nothing could prepare me for the experience of encountering the corpse of a murder victim at a crime scene. In a funeral home, the dead are dressed and made up to look their best, to appear serene, at peace with their fate. At a crime scene, the dead have no dignity. The savagery inflicted on them is visible. They are often naked, sometimes posed in provocative and degrading positions that provide their killer prurient delight. As if their killing was not punishment enough, their bodies are abandoned and subjected to further depredation by scavenging animals and the indifference of Mother Nature. There is no peace at a crime scene, no serenity. There are no happy memories, like at a memorial service, to draw upon to leaven the horror of death—only stark, brutal reality. There is no forgetting what one sees at a crime scene and I will never recover from seeing this particular one.

There were what would eventually add up to be more than seventy shallow puncture wounds all over Michael's body, indicating a prolonged period of torture. As if that wasn't ghastly enough to contemplate, the boy's throat had been slashed nearly down to the spinal chord. The neck wound was not visible until we pulled his shirt down, and to see his throat gaping open made all of us gasp. Considering his pants had been removed, it seemed likely that he had been sexually assaulted as well. In fact, it would be determined that he had been sodomized so brutally he suffered internal injuries. Off to the side of his body was a blanket on which I presumed he was assaulted and killed. It was so saturated in blood it would take three days for the blanket to dry out for testing in the FBI evidence room.

It was clear that Michael had not been dead for long, maybe just a few hours, because rigor mortis had not yet set in. But it was already too unconscionably long for a child to have been abandoned in such an inhospitable environment. I can still see ants crawling up and down Michael's lifeless body and I wanted desperately to swat them away but had to resist that impulse so as not to alter any evidence and simply observe while the forensic experts processed the scene. I don't know how long it took for them to do their job, but it felt like forever, and I remember standing there feeling utterly helpless, struggling not to betray the emotions I was feeling, like a pilot trying to remain calm and think logically as his plane goes into a tailspin. When you see something like this, your blood is boiling and you want to immediately rush off and follow up every clue, but instead you have to control yourself and let the experts do what they do best while you wait to determine the next step. I tried to take in everything the evidence team was saying, because what these experts see and report at the crime scene is critical in shaping where the investigation should go. But it felt like time had stopped for an eternity while I looked at that boy and thought how much he reminded me of my own.

My belief in the importance of good evidence collection, and that case agents and detectives go out to crime scenes to see for themselves what is being collected, was underscored when what would turn out to be a damning piece of evidence was uncovered. As the deputy coroner and Evidence Response Team members pulled down Michael's T-shirt and freed his upstretched arms, they found clutched in one of his fists a cheap piece of jewelry: a woman's bracelet. My mind went racing. Did his kidnapper dangle this shiny trinket out of the window of his truck to lure Michael over, asking him if it was his or offering to give it to him as a gift, as some child kidnappers do with the promise of a puppy? Or did he give it to the boy in the truck to mollify him, a little toy to keep him happy and absorbed until he was able to drive somewhere safe enough to carry out his nefarious plan? Or did the boy simply grab the piece of jewelry on his own inside the truck and clutch it for dear life like some talisman he prayed would bring him luck, or to which he clung for comfort like a stuffed animal, as he endured horror after horror? Something powerful made him keep clutching that trinket even after death. It was as if he were trying to preserve this important clue, pointing us to his killer.

Finally, the crime scene experts had completed their work and we were allowed to remove Michael's body from the scene. The whole time we were there a news helicopter was buzzing overhead just above the height of the tallest trees in the area. The whir of its blades was so loud we could barely hear each other on the ground and the air it was

MISSING

JULIE SUND   CAROLE SUND   SILVINA PELOSSO

1999 PONTIAC GRAND PRIX
CALIFORNIA LICENSE 4BMV025

ANYONE WITH INFORMATION SHOULD CALL
THE FEDERAL BUREAU OF INVESTIGATION
AT 1 800 435-7883
TOLL FREE

A missing persons flyer for the three tourists—Carole Sund, her teenage daughter Juli, and family friend Silvina Pelosso—who vanished in 1999 while visiting Yosemite Park. It initially seemed most likely that their rental car had skidded off an icy road and become buried in a snowbank or river. In fact, all three were murdered at the hands of a serial killer who sought to act out his very particularized sexual fantasy.

Juli Sund (left) and Silvina Pelosso (right) practice gymnastic moves in their room at Cedar Lodge before settling down for bed. Tiny fabric cuttings found in their abandoned room were later matched to Juli's blue flannel pajamas.

The last photo of the victims alive, recovered from their camera, shows Carole Sund and Silvina Pelosso getting ready for bed at the Cedar Lodge, just outside Yosemite Park. About twenty minutes after this picture was taken, hotel handyman Cary Stayner knocked at their door, insisting he needed to come in to fix a leaky pipe.

In happier moments on their excursion, Juli (left) and Silvina (right) take a whirl on the park's outdoor ice rink.

Silvina and Carole pose along the Merced River, which runs through Yosemite Park. Carole met Silvina's mother, Raquel Pelosso, when she spent a high school semester abroad, living with Raquel's family in Argentina. Carole wanted to return the favor, and in the winter of 1999 Silvina came to stay with the Sund family in Northern California and spend a term at Juli's school.

Silvina and Juli on a hike to Yosemite Falls. The girls became friends, like their mothers, and Juli hoped to visit Silvina in Argentina the following summer.

An aerial view of where the missing tourists' rental car was eventually found, tucked into a heavily wooded area off a dirt logging road, leading the FBI to believe that their killer was a local who knew the backwoods well. The car remained obscured for more than a month, despite a massive search by ground and air, until a man out target shooting came across it.

The tourists' rental car, abandoned and burned in an attempt to destroy evidence. Two of the three victims' bodies were found in the trunk and an ominous inscription was carved into the hood.

The search and rescue team amassed at the site where the missing tourists' rental car was found: a group effort involving many law enforcement agencies. The FBI's Evidence Response Team carefully processed the scene while search dogs sniffed in vain for any sign of the third and still missing tourist, who turned out to be Juli Sund.

The picturesque structure known simply as the Green House, where the serial killer's next victim, naturalist Joie Armstrong, lived in Yosemite Park.

The washed-out bridge where Cary Stayner stopped his car on a drive through the park and noticed Joie Armstrong packing her car for a visit to friends. The Green House can be seen a short distance down the road on the left.

When Joie failed to show at her friend's house, park rangers went out to the Green House to perform a welfare check. They found Joie's white Toyota truck parked outside full of her belongings but no sign of Joie, indicating she never set out on her trip.

Cary Stayner's International Scout. Its distinctive paint job matched the description of a vehicle a neighbor recalled seeing outside Joie's house the day she disappeared.

Michael

churning up was in danger of blowing away microscopic evidence. The team had placed Michael's body on a blue tarp so that as they removed his remaining clothing any evidence that might come off would be captured by the tarp and not get lost. Then they covered him lightly with the tarp until a body bag could be brought in. Fortunately, a canopy of trees had prevented the media copter from getting a shot of the child. But I was terrified that at any moment the churned-up wind would blow the tarp off the boy, and his grieving parents, who still did not even know his fate, would see what no parent should ever have to see—on TV, no less. I could barely contain my fury at the insensitivity of the media at that moment and at how blithely unconcerned they seemed to be with our need to preserve a delicate crime scene.

It was spring and the river was rising, lapping ever closer to our crime scene. In fact, if we hadn't gotten there when we did, Michael's body and all the other evidence we found would have been washed into the river and potentially lost forever. Because Michael's body was located closer to the water than to the closest road, our original plan had been to float his remains out on a river patrol boat. But I couldn't bear the thought of his family seeing footage of their son being floated down the river in a body bag. So I talked the deputy coroner and the lead detective into letting the three of us carry the boy out in our arms, back down the trail and out to the road where the coroner's van was parked. It was the most dignified way I could think of to remove his body from the scene, and I felt it was the least we could do for a precious child. In the gallows humor of cops, a coroner's van is commonly referred to as the "meat wagon," and it shamed me to think I had ever thought of it that way as I loaded this young boy's body inside.

Years later I ran into the deputy coroner who was at the scene that day and helped carry Michael out of the river bottoms. We were at a conference and when we encountered each other we both immediately had to rush outside before losing our composure. Moments like what he and I and Todd Drost experienced that day, so grim we can barely express them to each other, bond those of us in law enforcement forever in some kind of silent compact. They also bond us to the dead. Like the boy with whom my friend Jeff Gardner sat vigil, I hope that on some cosmic level, Michael knew that he was not alone at that horrible scene and that his life was valued. I hope that if he could sense anything it was not the dampness and the ants and the slicing blades of that helicopter but the embrace of our protective arms.

The river patrol boat we decided not to use to ferry the victim's body away ended up playing a crucial role in apprehending his killer. The Sutter County Sheriff's Department had dispatched the boat to the river after receiving the report that a body had been found. As the boat made its way downriver looking for the crime scene, the two deputies on board caught a glimpse of something white on shore. They decided to head toward the object, thinking it might be the murder scene, but as they got closer they could see the white-colored object was actually a truck. As they got even closer a man who had been sitting in the cab got out and told them he had gotten stuck in the mud. The officers were automatically suspicious of encountering anyone this close to the crime scene. In addition, the man made some comments that raised their hackles, asking them what was going on in the area, even though from the location of the man's truck there was no way to know anything out of the ordinary was happening. They asked to see his ID, and when he said he had no identification with him they detained him on their boat until they could verify who he was. They soon determined his name was Robert Rhoades and when they ran his record they discovered he was a convicted sex offender. Their fast acting helped save the day and prevented Michael's killer from slipping away.

Robert "Rocky" Rhoades, 43, was on parole for the molestation of his four-year-old step-granddaughter. For that crime he served eighteen months of a three-year sentence and had been released in 1993. He had previously served time for the 1985 kidnapping, robbery, and rape at knifepoint of a female realtor, whom he abducted after making an appointment to see a house she was selling. As they drove away from the property in his vehicle he made it clear to the woman that he planned to kill her.

"This is going to be just like in the movies, except you're not going to survive," he told the terrified woman. Rhoades was cocky, bragging to her about how smart he believed he was and declaring that "smart people are the ones who get away" with their crimes. Instead, it was his intended victim who outsmarted him and managed to get away.

Michael

Believing she would otherwise certainly die, she hurled herself out of the moving car and lived to testify against him.

The jewelry clutched in Michael's hand and the fight the boy put up in the man's truck would end up being Michael's way of testifying against Rhoades.

It was late by the time we finished following up leads and I headed home for the night. I must have been in some kind of emotional black-out state, because I remember nothing of the drive until I was pulled over by a California Highway Patrol officer, who clocked me going 115 miles per hour. I told him what I had done that day and he spent some time talking me down, and then he insisted on following me for several miles to make sure I had regained my wits. It was a gesture of compassion I will never forget and an example of the supportive bond we in law enforcement share. When I got home I hugged my sons for a very long time, then climbed into bed and held Lori and told her about the horrific sight of finding the boy in the Batman T-shirt. I didn't find out until after I retired that Lori went through the house the next day when I went back to work and got rid of every Batman T-shirt my kids owned, somehow, with her remarkable sensitivity, understanding that seeing one of our boys in Michael Lyons's death garb would be more than I could bear.

My younger son, Jordan, could also tell something was wrong with me in the aftermath of Michael's murder. Even when I was home I wasn't really there, staring off into space, consumed with thoughts and images of the case. Jordan asked me what was wrong and I didn't know what to say. I didn't want to lie to him, so I told him I had seen a bad thing, a boy that was killed, whose neck was cut, and it really affected me. Jordan was just six years old, far too young to handle even that sketchy amount of information. The next day he recounted what I said to his teacher and I had to go down to the school to explain myself. It would be a long time before I would share anything like that again with my kids.

Our investigation fanned out on several fronts, with various teams and experts following up different leads and carrying out different tasks. Some people were looking into Rhoades's background; others were making contact with his parole officer and searching his home. Forensic experts were examining physical evidence gathered from the crime scene and from Rhoades's truck, which they had to use heavy equipment to extricate from the swamped-in area where it had gotten stuck. A pathologist was performing an autopsy on the victim, trying to determine what exactly had happened to Michael. Still other investigators were canvassing the neighborhood around where Michael's body was found to see if anyone saw or heard anything—although in this case the neighborhood was not an urban street or rural road or manicured subdivision but a loose conglomeration of homeless encampments where people were living off the grid, either by choice or by circumstance, and didn't welcome inquiries by police.

We learned from our investigation that Rhoades was married but separated from his wife and lived alone in a home they had purchased in the area. He worked ostensibly as a barber but spent much of his time down at the river bottoms hanging out with some of the people living there and doing copious amounts of drugs. It was rumored that one woman living in the river bottoms had gone to his house with him one night and had sex, but when approached by the officers canvassing the area she refused to answer their questions.

I felt this woman might have important insight into Rhoades. From what I had learned on the job working the child sex cases and going to the Department of Corrections parolee meetings, I knew that sex offenders act out in some way with all their sexual partners in an effort to satisfy their dark fantasies. I accept that under our legal system a defendant has a constitutional right to remain silent and not incriminate himself if he so chooses. But I'm not about to let witnesses, who have no liability whatsoever in the crime, hold back potentially important information without doing everything I can to get them to share it with us. Jokingly referencing the stereotype that local law enforcement often has of FBI agents as arrogant showboats who swoop in and think they know better than everyone else how to run the case, I told the team that I was going to show them how the FBI would get the woman's story and went down with Mike Johnson, a sergeant with the Yuba City PD, to see if we could get her to open up.

She lived in a tent pitched between some bushes with a whole passel of cats and dogs. She was only in her forties, but the ravages of methamphetamine addiction and living outdoors made her look like a living cadaver. I went through this elaborate preamble, saying a little boy was brutally murdered nearby and that we thought she might be able to help us and that there is nothing anyone should be unwilling to do to help a child who was killed. She went into her tent and motioned for us to come in and sit with her on her bed, which was a filthy cot. It was complete squalor inside the tent and we didn't know whether this woman might be crazy or have weapons in there. Mike just shook his head, but there was nothing I was unwilling to do to find out what this woman might know, so I went inside and sat with her. I told her that I thought she knew the man who may have killed the boy and that she might have information that could help Michael and his family. She was reluctant to say anything and only spoke obliquely. She indicated she knew Rhoades and said she may have "spent time" with him. I just kept talking to her, bringing it back to Michael, and told her I needed to know if she and Rhoades had sexual relations. I explained that the little boy had been sexually assaulted and that any sexual experience she had with Rhoades might help us understand what happened to the boy.

I could tell she was really fighting with herself over whether to say anything. Finally, she blurted out, "Yeah, I fucked him," in a tone that indicated she was testing me, trying to shock me and see if I was judgmental. Instead, I responded in a way that she was not expecting.

"Was he a loving and caring partner?" I asked. She looked stunned and her defensive walls collapsed. She told me she went in his truck with him to his house one night and they did crank (methamphetamine) together. After using the drugs, Rhoades turned into a monster. The scene she went on to describe was bizarre and horrific. The sex they had was rough and violent. At one point, in full erection, he took his penis in his hands and bent it in half. As a man, I cannot imagine doing something so painful to myself, but it seemed as if that was precisely why he did it, that he liked pain. He was not only a masochist but also a sadist. He grabbed a hammer and started smashing things in the house. Then he jumped on top of her and pounded the hammer all around her body, like how a gunslinger in an old western would make his victim "dance" by shooting all around him. The woman feared she would not survive her time with Rhoades, but eventually he drove her home and she was overwhelmed with relief to have gotten back to her tent alive. She was in such a rush to get out of his truck that she left behind a piece of jewelry—the bracelet we found clutched in Michael Lyons's hand.

She had given us so much—the bracelet alone was damning, irrefutable proof that Rhoades was Michael's killer—but I still pressed her for more. In my experience, interviewing a victim in a sexual assault case is more difficult and requires more delicacy and skill than getting a confession from a perpetrator. The victim feels like you are asking them to recount how they were humiliated, how their dignity was taken away from them, forcing them to recall being in a position they want desperately to forget. It was clear this woman was also a victim of Rhodes's sexual sadism, and it pained me to have to ask her these uncomfortable questions. But at that point I felt it was important not just for Michael but for her, too, because her violation mattered to me as well and the full ramifications of what she had been through needed to be acknowledged.

I asked her if Rhoades had sodomized her. She didn't know what that was, so I had to explain that it meant putting his penis in her rectum. She denied it, but I felt she was holding back. I said that I understood how humiliating that experience could be but that if it did happen she needed to tell me because it could be very important to Michael. I explained that forced, violent sodomy is something sexual sadists may do because they enjoy inflicting pain on others, that the suffering they inflict on their victims is sexually arousing to them. She just kept saying no, that this had not happened, and I didn't believe her, but it seemed like a bridge too far for her to acknowledge this final indignity. When I felt she wasn't going to say any more, I thanked her for all she had shared with us and praised her for having the courage to do so. I told her she didn't deserve what happened to her and urged her to take care of herself and be safe. Then I got up to leave. Mike and I were no more than fifty feet from her tent when she came running after us and blurted out that Rhoades did sodomize her. She ended up being a crucial witness, her lost bracelet virtually cuffing the hand of Robert Rhoades to Michael Lyons.

The forensic and evidence teams also turned up clear and convincing evidence of Rhodes's guilt. Michael's blood was found on a fishing knife in Rhoades's truck, and the child's footprints were detected on the inside of the truck's windshield as he undoubtedly fought against his attacker. It was an unbearably long struggle. It is believed that Rhoades tortured the boy for ten hours—some denizens of the river bottoms said they heard a child screaming all night—as Rhoades methodically inflicted those seventy-something shallow stab wounds, twisting and turning the knife to inflict even greater pain, before slicing Michael's throat. DNA evidence also confirmed that Rhoades was the person who sexually assaulted Michael.

With an overwhelming amount of evidence amassed against Rhoades, there did not seem to be anything more for me to do on the case. I said my good-byes and headed back to Sacramento, not knowing if I would ever see anyone from the team again but feeling bonded for life by what we did together in pursuit of such a noble cause. Yet the following weekend I was asked to come back. The Yuba City police had located Rhoades's wife, Lynette, and wanted me to interview her. I partnered up again with Mike Johnson and we drove to Stockton, where she was living with her parents. The whole family greeted us with hostility. They denied Rhoades had anything to do with the crime, claimed we had framed him, and said that his attorney had told them not to talk with us. As with the woman in the river bottoms, I was not about to walk away without trying my damnedest to find out if there was something important Rhoades's wife knew that would help the case.

"We've driven a long way to speak to you," I said, controlling the anger that had risen inside me. "I won't ask you any questions, but I'm not leaving until you hear what I came here to say." They agreed to hear me out and I proceeded to give the most horrid, detailed description I possibly could of the crime scene I had witnessed a few days earlier. I told them about every cut I had observed on the boy's body, about the slashing of his throat. I described every drop of blood, every repulsive detail I could think of to emotionally hurt them. I ended by saying, "That little boy's footprints were found on the inside of the windshield of your husband's truck, which was found stuck in the mud close to the site where the boy was murdered."

My reasoning was that if she still refused to talk to us after hearing all of what I had just said, then I would have to accept it. But the minute I finished, Mrs. Rhoades appeared to have some type of seizure and collapsed. I was horrified and wanted to call 911, but her family said that she experienced these episodes all the time and would be fine in a few minutes. Mike and I looked uncomfortably at each other and I prayed that he knew more than I did about first aid in case we had to intervene. But as her parents predicted, she quickly regained her composure and as soon as she could speak she promised she would tell us anything we wanted to know.

She led us downstairs to another part of the house where we could talk in private. She met Rhoades, inauspiciously, as his prison pen pal, corresponding with him while he was doing time at the Deuel Vocational Institution in Tracy, California, for the kidnapping and rape of the real estate agent. They first laid eyes on each other in August of 1987 and just over three months later were married, allowing them to have conjugal visits. When he was released in 1990, they moved in together. Two years after that she turned him in to authorities after learning that he had molested her four-year-old granddaughter.

Despite his violation of her granddaughter, and her role in sending him back to prison, they resumed their relationship upon his release from his second prison stint. However, the marriage was rocky, largely due to his drug abuse. He had graduated, or perhaps I should say devolved, from cocaine to crank and would disappear for days on end. His routine was to use drugs at the river bottoms, and then stay away from home and hide out from his parole officer until he had cleaned up enough to pass a urine test. She was so troubled by his drug usage that she kept a daily record of his intake and actually gave the calendar to us. She also said that when he was "coming down" from meth he would have a strong sexual urge but was unable to achieve satisfaction. Ironically, many sex offenders struggle with various levels of impotency. Only when acting out their deviant fantasies can they reach, or get close to reaching, a satisfying sexual release.

In the last six months leading up to Michael's murder, the marriage further unraveled and the couple lived together only intermittently. She knew nothing about Michael's killing but gave us information that tightened the connection between Rhoades and Michael even further. A few days before the murder she had cleaned her husband's truck and found a piece of jewelry wedged into a fold in the seat, which she pulled out and left on the dashboard. When we showed her a picture of the bracelet Michael had clung to for dear life, she identified it as the piece of jewelry she had found in the truck. She also recognized the blood-soaked blanket we found at the scene. She said it was the same one she and her husband used when they went camping and fishing. Before we left I wrote up her detailed statement and had her sign it and also had her sign the backs of the photos of the bracelet and blanket, acknowledging her identification of those items. She agreed to testify against her husband, but by the time of trial she had again fallen under her husband's thrall and attempted to recant. Her statement and the signed photos, however, prevented her from doing so.

I never interviewed Rhoades, but I was present when an attempt was made to polygraph him. I had recommended to the Yuba City police a polygrapher named Pat Flood, whom I had worked with before on some cases with the Sacramento County Sheriff's Department. The first question he asked Rhoades was, "Did you kill that boy?"

Rhoades simply responded, "Where's my truck?"

That was all he said and then he refused to answer any questions. Flood considered this deflection, this nonresponse, as tantamount to an admission. I was surprised at the time that Flood felt that way because I didn't hear anything from Rhoades I would have considered a confession. But over the years I have found that when people refuse to answer specific questions, when they refuse to even acknowledge the question being asked, it is because they have no good answer to give.

If I had had the opportunity to interview Rhoades, I would have given it my best shot, but I do not think he would have ever confessed. I believe he is a remorseless psychopath, someone devoid of any genuine emotion or empathy, the kind of person psychologist Robert Hare described in his seminal book on psychopaths, *Without Conscience*. Hare developed the test that is used for diagnosing psychopathy and is the world's foremost expert on this very dangerous and completely untreatable form of pathology. I was introduced to *Without Conscience* at a training seminar I took from Roy Hazelwood. I had read the book after the training seminar because I wanted to be a better investigator, and I read it again while working on Michael's case to try to make sense of such a senseless crime. The success I have had in getting criminals to confess is by appealing to whatever good still exists in them. I did not see that kind of humanity in Robert Rhoades.

In the Name of the Children

Rhoades was charged with capital murder for the rape, torture, and killing of Michael Lyons and took the stand on his own behalf at trial. He admitted he was at the river bottoms the night Michael was killed but said he had nothing to do with the crime, basically ignoring all the evidence against him. He claimed that after getting his truck stuck in the mud he had walked and hitchhiked back home to get a portable winch to use to extricate his truck and had only returned to the vehicle shortly before he was spotted by the river boat patrol. He was convicted in June 1998, but the jury could not agree on the question of what penalty he should receive, splitting 10–2 in favor of execution. A second penalty phase jury was impaneled at the end of the year and voted unanimously for death.

Under California law, juries in capital cases can only recommend a sentence, which after conviction of a death-qualifying special circumstance must be either life in prison without the possibility of parole or death. It is the trial judge who decides between those two options and imposes the sentence, choosing whether or not to follow the jury's recommendation. The weekend before Rhoades was to be sentenced, his lawyers said they received a handwritten letter signed "Raymond," claiming Rhoades was being set up by someone with whom he once served time. The defense counsel asked for a continuance to investigate the mystery letter, then for a new trial. Both requests were denied and on September 10, 1999, Judge Loyd Mulkey Jr. sentenced Robert Rhoades to death. A collective "yes" went up from Michael's extended family as the judge revealed his decision.

"Michael is finally free," his mother told the press after sentencing. "You have to have justice before you can be set free."

Her sister, Tina Lyons Icenbice, in urging the judge to sentence Rhoades to death, said, "I only pray that there will never be another family or another child that will have to endure what we have gone through."

I hope that Michael is at peace, that he is indeed free and that his soul is at rest. His family must live with the pain of never having him back in their lives, but I hope that they find some comfort in the conviction of

Michael

his killer. As horrible as things were and are for them, they were fortunate in only having to wait two years for the justice of a guilty verdict. Julie Connell's family had to wait twenty-three agonizing years.

Beginning in the 1990s, the state of California began collecting DNA samples from everyone convicted of a serious felony. Those samples were analyzed and the offender's DNA profile was entered into a database administered by the state Department of Justice. DNA profiles generated from evidence collected from crime scenes where the perpetrator is unknown, in both current and cold cases, are also entered into the database and the computer looks for matches. This system is a tremendous tool for law enforcement, especially for working sex crimes, and has resulted in many cold cases being solved. But until recently, massive backlogs in processing DNA evidence in order to generate a searchable profile meant that it might take years or even decades to find a match.

In 1998, a cold DNA "hit" revealed that Rhoades had raped and killed an eighteen-year-old girl in the San Francisco Bay Area in 1984, twelve years before he murdered Michael. Julie Connell was a straight-A student from San Lorenzo who was excitedly looking forward to her high school graduation. She was such a serious student that on the day she disappeared, she went to study in a Hayward park while her mother and sister took in a movie at a theater across the street. When the movie ended and they came out, Julie was gone. Five days later, her body was found in an animal corral in a canyon about nine miles away from where she was abducted. She had been tied up, raped, and like Michael, was killed by having her throat slashed. Also like Michael she was discarded in a most dehumanizing way when her killer was done with her—as if she was, in fact, an animal.

Rhoades, who was living nearby in San Lorenzo at the time Julie was killed, was never considered a suspect and the case went unsolved for fourteen years until the databank matched Rhodes's profile to DNA from semen recovered from Julie's body. For a dozen years he was free to rape and kill again. It was Michael who pointed the way for Julie's murder to be solved, just as he had fingered his own killer by clutching that bracelet. The sacrifice of his life was a horrible price to pay, but the fact that he was able to help Julie's family gives his death even greater meaning for me. I hope it provides some comfort to his loved ones.

A grand jury indicted Rhoades for Julie's murder in 2000, but the case did not get to trial until 2007. It was also a capital case, with the special circumstance of murder during the course of a rape making Rhoades potentially eligible for a second death sentence. The jury deliberated for just over an hour before convicting him of Julie's rape and murder. When they filed into the courtroom with their verdict, several jurors gently touched an empty chair that the prosecutor had told them symbolized the absent girl.

The jurors were not told that Rhoades had already been convicted of murdering another child until the penalty phase, and the jurors appeared stunned by the news. Some were in tears as they heard how similar the two crimes were—even the judge noted during sentencing that the deadly wounds on Michael and Julie could have been interposed. Cuts on the shirts Michael and Julie were wearing when they were abducted were almost identical. The prosecutor also pointed out how in both cases Rhoades chose isolated locations to torture and kill his victims, where he could take his time and believed no one would hear their screams. The jurors also heard from the real estate agent who very nearly became his third murder victim.

The fact that Rhoades had already been convicted of murdering Michael was an additional special circumstance the jury could find to make him eligible for the ultimate punishment. The jury did so and recommended he be executed. On June 19, 2007, with Michael's mother in attendance along with the Connell family and most of the jurors from Julie's case, the judge handed down a second death sentence. Rhoades was fifty-four years old, twenty-three years older than he was when he ended Julie's life. The Lyons and Connell families can now be certain Rhoades will never be able to hurt another child. What none of us knows for certain, and what nags at my conscience and keeps me up at night, is the possibility that there might be more victims of Robert Rhoades who have yet to be discovered—kids with the supreme misfortune to have crossed this predator's path, whose parents are still waiting to find out what happened to their missing loved ones.

CHAPTER FIVE

Alexia

THE MOST FUN I HAD as an FBI agent was working on the Fugitive/Violent Crimes Task Force that Don set up in the 1990s. It was great because of both the camaraderie and the excitement of going out and pulling bad guys off the street. It was more like what I imagined the job to be back when I was a kid watching *The FBI*. We had a ton of equipment at our disposal, long guns, bulletproof vests, and the latest technological wonder: cell phones. It did mean spending quite a bit of time away from my family. But I realized that if I couldn't be home with Lori and the boys, then being with my "other boys"—Glenn Walters, Ken Hittmeier, Tony Alston, John Boles, Tom Roloff, and all the other task force guys—was a good place to be. Although I was so proud and grateful for the training, experience, and access that had been afforded to me by the FBI, I realized from working with the members of the task force that I had a lot more to learn.

Tony Alston was primarily my partner in those early days and he was the man I wished I were except for one thing: he was a couple of inches shorter than me. My dad was six feet five inches tall and I always struggled to be considered six feet. Tony had everything else. He was handsome, athletic, and had a great head of hair. He was also smarter than me, dressed far better, and had a sharper wit. I can admit all this now because I am too old to have any competitive jealousy. Tony's dad had been an agent as well and was one of the case agents on the Patty Hearst case.

One day I was called out to help round up a fugitive who was wanted out of South Dakota. The day happened to be my wife's birthday, and Lori was not happy that I had to run out on another special occasion. We caught the fugitive and Tony and I ended up transporting him back to the office in our car. I pulled out my new cell phone to call and tell

In the Name of the Children

Lori I would be home soon and then the thought hit me: let this guy explain to my wife why I was missing her birthday. I told him to tell her why I was not with her and to apologize. I dialed the number and handed my phone to him.

"Mrs. Rinek, I'm sorry your husband is not home for your birthday and I promise it won't happen next year," he said.

Tony was a new agent at the time and wanted to interview the guy about the crime he was wanted for, even though all we needed to do was make sure he got back to the authorities in South Dakota. I mock-whined to Tony that we should only interview guys wanted in Hawaii or some other nice vacation spot because doing an interview would inevitably get us drawn into the case. Like all new agents he ignored me and interviewed the guy. Sure enough, he had to go out to South Dakota six months later to testify. When he got back he told me that the first question he was asked on the stand by defense counsel was whether it was normal FBI policy for people arrested to have to apologize to agents' wives.

I was unchastened and had a few more arrestees call home to apologize to Lori for my missing family time. I once had a bank robber call Lori's aunt to apologize for causing me to be late to Thanksgiving dinner. The humor is what got us by, the camaraderie carrying the day. Tony always got his revenge for whatever stunt I pulled. On one occasion he recruited the SAC's administrative assistant to call me up to the boss's office. Whenever I was called up there, it was never for a good reason. I got the call, asked what it was about, and was told, "Just get up here!"

I went into the bathroom, splashed water on my face, and resigned myself to accept whatever was about to come at me. As I arrived, the secretary just waved me on into the SAC's office. Tony was coming out of the office, saying, "I don't know what Jeff meant, I am sure it wasn't like that," or something to that effect. Our SAC at the time was bald and all I could see at first was a bald-headed man in a chair turned away from me waving an angry finger at me to sit down. As I walked fully into the office I could see it was actually not the SAC but another agent who had been recruited into the prank. He fooled me so well it took several minutes for me to stop sweating and for my heart to calm down to a normal rhythm.

Alexia

As I got into working crimes against children, the days of pranks and levity fell further behind me. I was lucky to always have good partners, but there are some things that are hard to talk about even with your partner. I had one partner tell me he couldn't work with me anymore. There was no problem between the two of us; the cases were just too hard for him to take. I understood. These are not cases you can leave behind each night at the office door. They nag at your conscience, weigh on your soul, follow you home. These victims live inside of you and what they endured becomes a permanent part of you.

On September 25, 1997, the Sacramento County Sheriff's Department received a call from a woman in Pennsylvania requesting a welfare check on a six-year-old girl named Alexia Reale. Alexia and her thirteen-year-old sister, Jessica, lived with their mother, Barbara Carrasco, and stepfather, Larry Carrasco, in a quiet middle-class neighborhood in Elk Grove, a suburb of Sacramento. The woman who called identified herself as a friend of the girls' maternal grandmother, Margaret Reale. She said the grandmother had lived with the family until earlier that year and had witnessed incidents in which the parents physically abused Alexia and had seen injuries on the girl as a result of those beatings. She had not heard from her granddaughter in more than a month and was afraid something terrible might have happened to her.

Sheriff's deputies went out that very day to check on Alexia. Barbara and Larry claimed that Alexia had moved to Chicago to live with her father, Chun "Charles" Chang. The deputies made several disturbing discoveries. They found Jessica sleeping in a filthy shed in the backyard that had been used for Barbara's dog-breeding business. The shed was sparsely furnished with a lounge chair, a TV, and a bucket the girl apparently used as a toilet. There was no sign whatsoever of Alexia ever having lived in the Elk Grove home. In fact, in every family photo that looked like it might have included Alexia, the face of what was clearly a young child had been cut out. I've known people, after a particularly painful breakup, who cut the image of a former lover or ex-spouse out of a picture. But excising a child? It was like someone was trying to erase Alexia from family history.

In the Name of the Children

Deputy Steve Hill, a missing persons investigator with the Sacramento County Sheriff's Department, called me to see if the FBI could locate Alexia's father in Chicago and confirm whether or not he had the girl. Through work on many different cases I had become good friends with Steve, the guy who had welcomed me so warmly to the monthly meetings with paroled sex offenders, and his partner, Mona Feuillard, a detective assigned to the department's Child Abuse Bureau. The Sacramento County Sheriff's Department and the Sacramento FBI office had long had a strained relationship dating back to the killing by parcel bomb of computer rental storeowner Hugh Scrutton in 1985. When the FBI linked that case to the Unabomber, they took the information uncovered by the Sheriff's homicide investigators and then cut the department out of the case. I had endeavored to heal that divide and wanted to aid Steve and Mona any way I could. As Steve said at that first meeting where we met, those who investigate sex crimes and missing persons cases know what we are up against and always try to help each other. Now it was my chance to help them find this little girl.

I requested an agent in our Chicago office make contact with Alexia's biological father and find out if she was with him. It took a while to find him, but Charles Chang was eventually located in Chicago and said there had been no plans for Alexia to move in with him. In fact, he had not heard from his daughter since April.

Five days after the welfare check at the Carrasco home, before we had been able to find and interview Alexia's birth father, a major development occurred in the case that increased our fears that something very bad had happened to Alexia. The Sheriff's Department was called to Jessica Reale's school after the girl revealed to a teacher that her stepfather had come into her room the night before while she was sleeping and poured bleach on her. The chemical had actually burned her skin and was causing her a great deal of pain. When she raised the tail of her shirt, burn marks were clearly visible on her back. Jessica was taken into the custody of Child Protective Services and Larry and Barbara were arrested.

Mona said Jessica had backed up the story of Alexia going to live with her father. I suspected she knew more than she had let on but had been afraid to speak up and suggested my FBI partner and I try to reinterview her. Mona agreed and Bill Nicholson, a newly assigned agent that I had invited to work the case with me, and I went down to the county's Children's Receiving Home, where children are taken when they are removed from their homes by CPS. Jessica agreed to meet with us, and the facility provided us a room where we could talk.

We started by asking Jessica about her own life and what it was like for her growing up. She confessed that her mother was heavily into drugs and that it was her grandmother who had really raised her. She expressed great affection for her grandmother, who had lived with the family until earlier that year. When Jessica was eleven, her mother said she wanted to take a more active role in parenting but due to her meth addiction was unable to attend to the needs of her children.

We then asked Jessica about the incident that caused her to be removed from her home. She said that her mother and stepfather had become fixated on a belief in vampire-like demons. They believed these evil forces were in their house and inside their children and the only way to get rid of them was with bleach. She said her mother restricted her to the backyard shed and told Jessica she was going to die. It broke my heart to hear this young girl say that she was actually relieved to move to the shed because it gave her some separation from her parents—the people who should have been protecting her, not predicting or wishing for her death. It was while sleeping in the shed that Larry came in and doused her with bleach.

We had a lot more we wanted to know about Jessica's own treatment, but we had a missing child potentially in great peril and were afraid that at any minute Jessica might clam up and refuse to talk anymore. So we needed to bring the conversation around to Alexia. Jessica described how she was the one to care for her sister, to get her up in the morning, help her get dressed, feed her. One disturbing fact she described was how Alexia was always very sweet and compliant in the morning, but when Jessica would return home from school the girl was angry and profane and disruptive. We wondered what was happening to Alexia when her sister was not there to protect her that was causing the child to act so aggrieved. But when we asked Jessica where her sister was, her demeanor changed. She stonewalled and then claimed that Alexia was with her birth father, possibly in Hong Kong.

In the Name of the Children

I could tell Jessica loved Alexia, not just as a sister but also as the de facto mother she had become for the girl due to Barbara and Larry's drug use. To break through her fears and defenses and get her to reveal all she knew I needed to tap into the feelings Jessica had for Alexia so that she would feel compelled to stand up for the little girl—to speak for someone who literally could not speak for herself. I asked her to tell me about her sister, to recall the best times they spent together. Larry and Barbara spent most of their time holed up in their bedroom getting high and then sleeping off the crashes between the highs, so for Jessica the good times were when she and Alexia were by themselves watching TV together—free, at least for a while, of the folie à deux that had consumed their parents.

As Jessica talked about her sister she grew more and more emotional. I could sense we were getting to something important, so I kept pushing her. She expressed fear for herself and her grandmother and began crying so hard that social workers who were observing from outside the room wanted to come in and end the interview. They were actually banging on the door and I told Jessica they were going to make us stop the interview. At that point she said there was more to tell and that she wanted to continue. It was one of the most courageous acts I have ever observed from anyone, much less from a child.

The dam had burst and there was no going back for Jessica. What she proceeded to tell us was a story so horrific it still causes me nightmares. To rid the children of "demons," Barbara and Larry made the girls drink bleach. For the final eight days of Alexia's life, three times each day, her mother mixed up an eight-ounce milkshake made of bleach and ice cream and forced her daughters to drink it. The first time Jessica refused and Larry punched her in the eye and forced the mixture down her throat. After that, she was afraid to refuse. Barbara and Larry both claimed they, too, were going to drink the concoction, but Jessica never saw them do so.

The drink made Jessica sick to her stomach and when she got a chance she would sneak into the bathroom and try to throw up as much of it as she could. Alexia was unable to make herself throw up, so Jessica put her own finger down the girl's throat to induce her sister to vomit. After the third or fourth dose, her parents found out what Jessica was doing and locked her in her room, letting her out only for the few minutes each day it took to administer the next drink. I can't even imagine the level of fear, dread, frustration, and helplessness Jessica must have felt each time she heard the whir of the blender, knowing it was time for the next poisoning and there was no longer anything she could do to help her sister.

On the eighth day, the last time Jessica was brought out to drink the toxic cocktail, she found Alexia collapsed in the hallway, pale and unconscious. Barbara kneeled over the girl, looking as if she were trying to revive her. But neither Barbara nor Larry called for medical assistance. Instead, after determining she was dead, they placed Alexia's body in a large freezer in the garage. Then after a few days they brought her frozen corpse into a walk-in closet in the master bedroom and cut her body into pieces with a pruning saw. Larry escorted Jessica into the bedroom to watch her sister be gruesomely dismembered. Jessica tried to avert her eyes, but Barbara made her stay in the room and began drilling her daughter on what was to be their cover story: that Alexia had gone to live with her father. They then gathered up the remnants of Alexia and burned them in the fireplace, one handful at a time. I could scarcely believe what we were hearing, but we would later find a neighbor who recalled a strange smell around the time of the incident and saw black smoke coming from the Carrascos' chimney. It stood out in the person's mind because it was so odd to see someone burn a fire in the summer in the Sacramento Valley, where nighttime temperatures range from the high 80s to the low 90s.

What Jessica was describing was so unspeakable it seemed indecent to ask her to continue, but we did because we had to. Jessica recalled how Larry ate ice cream while he fed his stepdaughter to the fire—the same ice cream he used to make the poison he forced the girls to drink more palatable. Jessica said she fled to her room in disgust. But later, deep in the night, they brought her out again. They had gathered up the ashes and bone fragments into a garbage bag and placed it inside an empty ice chest. Then the three of them drove down to the Sacramento River looking for a place to dispose of all that was left of Alexia. At one point, while scouting out dumpsites, they actually locked themselves out of their car and had to break a window to get back in. They eventually decided on a spot. Barbara dumped the ashes into the river, and then threw the bag, the cooler, and the saw in as well.

"They were kind of relieved she was gone," Jessica recalled. "I didn't see any remorse or anything." Jessica believed Alexia died on June 19, 1997—meaning she was actually still five years old when she was killed—because that was the day her mother wrote down on the calendar that Alexia went to live with her father. For much of the rest of that summer, Jessica said, Barbara "started acting like Mommy again." Jessica returned to school, which she had stopped attending regularly when she took on full responsibility for caring for Alexia. But then her mother and Larry started up again with the stuff about demons. The talk grew crazier and crazier. Barbara said Jessica was a vampire sucking electricity out of the wall sockets and was going to suck the life out of the "baby Jesus" Barbara imagined she was carrying through immaculate conception. That's when Jessica was banished to the backyard shed. She had tried blocking out the memory of what happened to her sister, but her denial ended on that night in late September when Larry came into the shed and doused her with bleach.

The thought of parents devising their own Auschwitz-style crematorium made me apoplectic. I did not want to believe anyone could be capable of doing what Barbara and Larry had done to their children. But Jessica had lived it and the unvanquished love she felt for her sister had given her the strength to survive and bear witness. Bill and I were now obligated to be her witnesses and do everything we could to put her parents where they could never hurt her or any other child again.

Jessica's biggest fear in letting the truth come out was the effect it would have on her grandmother, who had heart problems and was in precarious health. That was why she had held back even after she was removed from her parents' home. All we could do was assure her that no matter how painful it would be for her grandmother to hear what had happened to Alexia, she would certainly want Jessica to be free of the hell she had been forced to live in.

In interviews and in her testimony at trial, Jessica's grandmother had her own tale of horrors to relate. Margaret Reale told us that Barbara had given away two other children, two boys born prior to Jessica and Alexia, to a friend because she didn't want them. She had also talked about getting rid of Alexia, a claim backed up by friends and acquaintances on whom she had tried to pawn off the girl. Margaret believed Barbara may have been abusive to one of the boys and witnessed abusive behavior toward both girls while she lived with the family in Elk Grove and did her best to protect the children. Barbara seemed to take a particular dislike to Alexia, whom Margaret said she always hated. Barbara and Larry referred derisively to Alexia as a "motherfucking bitch" and that "ugly Chinese bitch." One of Barbara's former husbands reported seeing Barbara hold a lighter flame close to Alexia's feet. Margaret saw Barbara and Larry yank both girls by the hair and at one point they installed a lock on Jessica's bedroom door and even nailed her windows shut. This left Jessica without access to a bathroom and Margaret threatened to call police over it, which led to them kicking her out of the house a few months before Alexia was killed. According to Margaret, Barbara was the dominant figure in the relationship and it was she who dragged Larry into rampant drug use, which fueled their collective paranoia. They complained that the house was bugged and that people were after them. They claimed that demons had possessed the girls and their grandmother as well.

We had another bodiless murder case to attempt to prove. We had an eyewitness statement from Jessica, but we needed evidence to back it up. And in this case, unlike Danny's, we had the additional burden of proving, in effect, that Alexia actually existed and was with her parents when she died—because Barbara and Larry had done everything they could to erase all trace of her from their lives. I believe we served five different warrants on the Carrascos' property and we never found one single thing proving Alexia had ever lived at the Elk Grove home: no clothes that belonged to her, no toys, no photos with her image except those with the child-sized head eerily cut out. Like the holes in those pictures, I felt there was a hole in the world, a hole in me, a hole in all of us who knew what had happened to Alexia but were never able to find her.

Jessica did not think she would be able to find the place where her parents dumped Alexia's remains, but she agreed to ride around with us and try. She remembered crossing a bridge and then going several more miles but was not able to pinpoint an exact spot. We sent divers into the water, but finding anything months after the fact in a cloudy, fast-moving river that flows for hundreds of miles was a near impossibility. Mona and I stood for hours at opposite ends of the search site directing traffic while divers risked their own lives in frigid, boulder-strewn waters looking for evidence of a child's death but found nothing. We did find broken glass at one of the pullouts by the river that looked to be from a car window, but tying that to the Carrascos' car was impossible.

Larry and Barbara had a large number of dogs, perhaps as many as ten, and as with all the humans in their life they also came to believe their dogs were possessed by devils. Around the time Alexia disappeared, they killed all of the dogs and buried them in the backyard. It was such a curious fact that we wondered if parts of Alexia might have been hidden inside the corpses of the dogs. It was a thought so terrible none of us wanted to entertain it, but it was a hypothesis we had to check out. With the help of personnel from the Sheriff's Department, forensic anthropologists with excavation equipment and ground-penetrating radar, and a group of furloughed inmates from the county jail, we dug up and examined each one of those dog carcasses but found no remains belonging to Alexia. At one point, however, we thought we did. As we dug up the yard we had cadaver dogs at the scene that alert, by making a designated signal, when they detect the smell of human remains. They did not alert when we dug up the dog carcasses, because they could differentiate animal from human. But the next day the cadaver dogs started hitting like crazy. Our hearts rose in anticipation until we figured out that the jail inmates that had helped dig up the dogs had discarded their rubber gloves into the dog graves when they refilled them. It was the smell of the diggers' skin cells inside the rubber gloves that they were reacting to, not any remains of Alexia.

The smell of death at a crime scene is always horrific to experience. It stays in your nose for days even if you wear a protective mask or smear Vicks under your nostrils to try to block its stench. It clings to your skin and clothes like a shroud, causing you to feel nauseated and retch even after you leave the scene. I can't even begin to describe how overwhelming the smell of so many decomposing dogs was and how it seemed to permeate every cell of my body. Anything that even remotely resembles that smell triggers a cascade of memories and sensations in me even today, inducing the same sickening feeling I felt in the Carrascos' backyard.

The family had installed an alarm system in their home, which seemed to me less about keeping potential criminals out and more about keeping anyone from getting in and finding out about the crimes going on inside. Every time we came with a new warrant we set that alarm off. I felt so much anger toward the Carrascos for what they had done to these two innocent girls that even that alarm enraged me, and one day in a fit of pique I cut every wire that ran to that alarm box.

The entire house had been scrubbed down with bleach, and as we searched the home the smell of that chemical still permeated the air. We literally peeled back the wallpaper, paint, sheetrock—every layer of that structure looking for biological evidence. Bill almost single-handedly dismantled the fireplace brick by brick and turned over the masonry to the FBI lab for analysis, but still we found no trace of the little girl, since even the fireplace had been washed out with bleach. New carpeting had been installed in the master bedroom and new linoleum laid down in the walk-in closet where Jessica said the disarticulation of her sister had occurred, much newer than any floor coverings in the rest of the house. Barbara and Larry may have acted like crazy, delusional people plagued by phantoms of their imagination, but they had taken meticulous care to clean up after their crimes and cover their tracks.

The effort to find proof of Alexia's life and death was massive and unrelenting. There was no such thing as weekends or days off. Mona's entire Child Abuse Bureau was brought in to help, but we never found a single piece of physical evidence confirming that Alexia had lived in that house, much less that she had been slowly and painfully murdered there. That failure has been one of the hardest things for me to live with. I just can't accept that anyone can be erased from the face of the earth and made to appear as if he or she had never even existed. But I know that Alexia lives on in the memory of her sister and grandmother who loved her and in the hearts of all of us who felt her life mattered and tried to bring her justice.

Mona worked hard and long to get the Sacramento District Attorney to charge Barbara and Larry with Alexia's murder. When Assistant

In the Name of the Children

Chief Deputy DA Marv Stern finally gave the go-ahead, Mona allowed Bill and me to serve the arrest warrants on the couple in jail, where they were already in custody awaiting prosecution on other charges. When we served Barbara in the women's jail, she immediately started blaming Larry, which for me was an acknowledgment that Alexia did exist, that Barbara knew she was dead, and that Alexia was killed while in the custody of her mother and stepfather. Each concocted stories laying responsibility on the other. At one point Barbara claimed her husband tied Alexia to her highchair and drowned the girl and at another time claimed Jessica had killed her sister. Larry, in turn, said his wife smothered the girl while performing an exorcism.

Barbara and Larry Carrasco were each charged with the murder of Alexia and assault, torture, and other charges involving Jessica. Barbara initially pled not guilty but then agreed to plead guilty by reason of insanity to second-degree murder in exchange for the state dismissing all the other charges against her. That required a mini-trial to determine if she was, in fact, insane.

The question was whether Barbara suffered from a methamphetamine-induced psychosis or some other mental illness that rendered her insane as defined by law, which would mean she was unable to understand what she was doing or distinguish between right and wrong at the time of the offense. An expert retained by the prosecution found her to be sane at the time of the killing. The defense submitted three reports by mental health experts who had evaluated her. Two of the experts did not really address the issue at hand; the third did find her to be insane at the moment the crime was committed but sane immediately afterward when she clearly recognized the wrongfulness of her action and began to take steps to conceal her involvement in Alexia's death. The court determined Barbara to be legally sane at the time of the murder and sentenced her to fifteen years to life in prison.

While the trial judge believed that Barbara was addicted to methamphetamine and did suffer delusions from time to time as a result, he explained that "legal insanity requires far more than mental illness. And it requires more than transitory hallucinations or delusions, whether drug induced or otherwise." The judge pointed out Barbara's long history of disliking her daughter—"a festering loathing of this particular child" that preceded her addiction—and her many attempts to get rid of her, which included trying to talk friends and even strangers into taking the girl off her hands. Just as we who had worked the case viewed it, the judge believed Barbara's methodical conduct leading up to Alexia's death and her elaborate cover-up in the immediate aftermath belied her claims of insanity and demonstrated that she knew the difference between right and wrong. The judge also rejected Barbara's attempts to shift the majority of the blame to Larry.

"I am more persuaded by the less biased testimony of her surviving daughter, Jessica, than I am the defendant's rendition of her stories of dismemberment and cover-up which followed," the judge stated in his ruling. "I find that her role was much more than the defendant has chosen to convey to this Court. She was a leader and active participant throughout."

The California Court of Appeal affirmed the decision, outlining many of the facts before and after Alexia's death that showed awareness that Barbara knew she was committing a crime and attempting to get away with it: her failure to drink the bleach mixture herself, her forcible separation of the girls to prevent Jessica from saving her sister's life, her failure to seek medical assistance for Alexia after she collapsed, her obliteration of Alexia's remains and sanitizing of the crime scene, and her repeated efforts to program her daughter into sticking to an arranged cover story to explain Alexia's whereabouts.

Larry pleaded not guilty and decided to roll the dice before a jury. His defense, in essence, was that the devil made him do it: he was not intending to harm either of his stepdaughters but to help rid them of demons. To prove his good intentions, he pointed to the fact that he stopped making Jessica drink the bleach after Alexia "unexpectedly" died. The jury was not persuaded and found Larry, like his wife, guilty of second-degree murder. They also convicted him of assault resulting in Alexia's death and of torturing, unlawfully punishing, and willfully inflicting great bodily injury on Jessica. Larry was sentenced to a cumulative sentence of forty years to life in prison: fifteen to life for the second-degree murder conviction, twenty-five to life for assault resulting in the death of a child under the age of eight, and an indeterminate sentence for the torture of Jessica.

He, too, appealed and objected to, among other things, the torture conviction. The crime of torture is defined as "the intention to cause cruel or extreme pain and suffering for the purpose of revenge, extortion, persuasion, or for any sadistic purpose." Larry objected to the notion of sadism, claiming he drew no pleasure from what he did to Jessica. But the Court of Appeal found otherwise, pointing to his own words—"Do you like this?"—uttered to Jessica when he burst into the shed where she was sleeping and doused her with bleach. That occurred months after Alexia had died, after any possible belief that bleach was helping and not harming his stepdaughters was no longer tenable.

If Jessica had not spoken up to her teacher and been removed from her home, who knows if she might have met the same fate as her sister. It is interesting to note that the last thing the family did before embarking on the bleach regimen was to take a trip back east to visit the two sons Barbara had given away. Barbara had said she wanted the boys back because she believed they could help save the world from being taken over by demons and vampires. Was that a drug-induced delusion, or part of a plan to subject all of her children to the "treatment" she administered to Jessica and Alexia? She did, in fact, meet with the boys but for whatever reasons they did not return to California with her. For that twist of fate, I am grateful.

We don't know the exact, proximate cause of Alexia Reale's death. At Larry's trial a forensic pathologist testified about the effects of ingested bleach on the human body. Dr. Robert Anthony stated that because bleach is so harsh and corrosive, it causes hemorrhaging in the esophagus or stomach. Because its fumes are chemical irritants, the lungs would fill with liquid, which could cause heart failure. The chemical is also toxic to the bloodstream, leading the lungs, liver, and kidneys to fail. Sodium and chloride levels in the blood would mount to the point where the victim would eventually fall into a coma. It would also wreak havoc on the pH balance of acids and alkalines in the blood, causing the nervous system to shut down. Considering Alexia weighed just forty pounds at the time of her death, her body would have been overwhelmed quickly by the poison. Death was inevitable. If what Larry and Barbara Carrasco inflicted on that little girl is not the very definition of cruel and unusual punishment, I don't know what is. Fifteen years in prison, or even forty, is no comparison.

Jessica's strength continues to amaze me. She is in her thirties now and still speaking up on her own and her sister's behalf. Her mother has twice come up for parole consideration, but Jessica has helped persuade the Board of Prisons to deny her parole. Parents are supposed to love and protect their children, but Barbara was never a true mother to her, she told the parole authority, and deprived her of the sister that she loved. She remains committed to pulling back the cover on her parents' lies, as are all of us who refused to allow a five-year-old girl to be erased from the book of life and worked to bring justice for Alexia and her brave sister.

CHAPTER SIX

Alexander ("Salaam")

LIKE ALL CULT LEADERS, Ulysses Roberson espoused a bizarre, megalomaniacal philosophy. He claimed to be Muslim, but the beliefs he adhered to were singularly his own. He seemed to think that if he had ninety-nine sons and each of his sons in turn fathered ninety-nine sons, he would be able to rule the world. He was surprisingly good at recruiting women to help him toward that goal, and not the kind of seekers and lost souls you might expect to be drawn into a cult, but intelligent, accomplished women who had fully functioning lives until they fell under his sway. Once he had them in his thrall he kept them there through abuse and intimidation, breaking them down until they seemed to have no will of their own. He beat them for infractions as small as asking a question. He carried a gun and threatened to kill them and their children. He shaved the hair of one of his "wives" into the shape of devil horns, then expelled her from the family for breaking the cardinal rule: opening the door when police came knocking.

Maybe the philosophy he espoused was all a lie, a scam he perpetrated to give himself an aura of messianic authority. Maybe it was really all about sex and money, as almost every cult is at its heart. His harem of wives existed to serve him sexually and produce his children. And he made them work, ostensibly to support the children they bore him but really to support him so he didn't have to work. In fact, he would seek out new women to add to the family whenever finances ran low. Having children with him also served to bind the women to the family, making it harder for them to leave. He kept his offspring in line, as he did his wives, through fear and violence. And if he wanted to hurt those children or rid himself of one altogether, he could couch his sadism in the trappings of religion. The child was a bad seed, who needed to be cast out.

Alexander ("Salaam")

After working Alexia's case I wanted to hear no more talk of God and demons as an excuse for inflicting suffering on children. But investigating the kind of crimes I did required spending most of my time in worlds where every noble human impulse—the desire to be loved or to be cared for, to follow, to admire, to believe in someone or something—is perverted in service to the twisted needs of those who abuse, exploit, and murder children.

The disappearance of Alexander Olive was another cold case I reviewed as a result of the Freeh directive to see if there was anything the FBI could do to help find the boy. Salaam, as he was commonly known, was last seen in 1985, when he was just four years old. That twelve years had already passed without resolution at the time I was assigned the case filled me with a sense of overwhelming sadness and enormous responsibility. Little did I know that it would take another thirteen years before his killer would be brought to justice.

Alexander's parents met in a most unusual way. Rosemary Judith "Judy" Olive was a twenty-three-year-old nurse working in a Texas hospital when Ulysses Roberson brought in his wife, Raj, to deliver their baby. He didn't introduce Raj as his wife, however, but as a sister he was helping out. Roberson, who was going by the name "Tony Rich" at the time to duck a warrant for check fraud, was a smooth talker who seemed more intent on impressing the young nurse than on the birth at hand. He called himself a mystic, a psychic, and a "hermetic scientist" and offered to cast Judy's astrology chart, which he promised would empower her to make good decisions in life. He had her fill out a form detailing her history and goals and told her to come by his house for her astrology reading. It was a clever ruse that enabled him to quickly ascertain her dreams and desires, her strengths and weaknesses, and then use that knowledge to control and manipulate her. When she came over, he told her he could predict even more about her future by "reading" the moles on her body. He gave her a blue-colored drink and told her to take a bath. The next thing she recalled was waking up to Roberson having sex with her.

He convinced her that this was not a rape but that they had connected on a physical and spiritual plane. When she discovered that she was pregnant he asked her to move in with him. But as it turned out, she wouldn't be living just with him but with Raj and his child by Raj and other women who would come later and the children he had with them. They would effectively be sister wives in a polygamous cult, although he did not actually marry any of them.

Roberson employed all the typical measures cult leaders use to erase his wives' preexisting identities and remold them according to his wishes. He gave them all new names of his own choosing. Judy became Ruby. He'd chosen Raj for "head wife" Renee Alyce Jones, an acronym of her initials. The names he came up with for the children had a faux-spiritual or mystical cast to them, befitting their status as children of a self-styled prophet: Yewaur, Uhrtiko, Invaka, Urenauld, Unkw. He claimed they were Muslim names, but like the rest of his well-honed spiel they were just words he made up.

For Alexander he chose Salaam, an actual word that means *peace* in Arabic. It is commonly used as a greeting in Muslim countries that translates roughly to "be safe." It also means to bow in respect and obeisance. The choice of that name was bitterly ironic, as Salaam would never know peace or be safe thanks to his father—but he would be made to obey him. A man who did nothing to deserve respect and obeisance would instead command it through the infliction of brutal punishment, especially with Salaam, the son he always viewed as different and defective and singled out for the worst treatment. Roberson claimed he named the boy Salaam to help him because of difficulties he would face as a result of being mixed race (Judy was white and Roberson was black). But his racial mix was something Roberson himself held against the boy and also used to manipulate his mother.

A second strategy employed by cult leaders is to separate and isolate members from their family and friends in order to become the sole figure of authority in their lives. Judy had been close to her family, but Roberson turned her against them, convinced her that her family would try to kill her unborn child because he was part black. Her family took the still-pregnant Judy to a deprogrammer and she gave birth while living apart from him. But the hold Roberson had on her was too strong, as it had been for Raj, who also returned to him after her family initiated deprogramming. Judy wrote to Roberson when the baby was about four months old, and Roberson and Raj came to collect them.

Alexander ("Salaam")

By the time she returned, some new "wives" had been added to the mix. Nearly a dozen different women joined the family during the years Judy was part of it. Roberson moved the group from house to house, city to city, between several different states, keeping the women off balance and the prying eyes of law enforcement and CPS at bay. Sometimes he rotated his wives between houses in the same city or kept the women and children in one house and had a separate one for himself where he could seduce and recruit new potential wives. He also made his current wives, including Judy, attract other women into the fold. The targets were nearly always women at some turning point in their lives, making them vulnerable to Roberson's entreaties. The sheer number of women willing to buy into the program helped enforce conformity within the closed society.

All these things are tactics used by cult leaders to ensure complete control and dominance over their followers. Every decision was made by Roberson because his professed spiritual and mystical powers meant that he and only he knew what was best for all of them. He even called himself God at times and made Judy meditate to images of him seated on a throne. He made all the women work and turn their paychecks over to him, depriving them of the financial means to leave the family. Judy worked two jobs and Roberson took all her money. He posted house rules and assigned each woman specific chores; any deviation from his rules was punished with beatings. He once began whipping Judy with a belt while she slept and laughed while he did it. The women were not allowed to question anything he said or did. They simply had to comply with whatever he instructed them to do.

To keep Judy from going back to her family, Roberson appointed his mother and his mother's boyfriend to guard her. He even made Judy wear dark makeup for a while so she would look black and be unrecognizable to her family. After a while, he began to separate her from Salaam and from the other family members. One day, without warning, he dropped her off in the San Francisco Bay Area, telling her it was a test to see if she could survive on her own in a new city. He had gotten a Social Security number for her in the name of Ruby Roberson and instructed her to get work at a hospital there and send her checks to him. He wouldn't even tell her where he would be living, just gave her the address of a post office box where she was to forward her pay. Then he drove away, taking Salaam with him.

Judy complied. Even without the daily presence of Roberson bearing down on her she seemed to have no will of her own. She visited the family from time to time and sometimes they would visit her. When she saw Salaam he was frail and withdrawn and had visible bruises. On one occasion, when she gave him a bath, she found deep scabs and swelling on his ankles. When she asked him what had happened, the boy said his father tied shoestrings around his legs and hung him upside down by the shoestrings. (Some of the other wives, who witnessed the incident, believed rope or wire was actually used, which cut into the child's skin and left scars.) Not long before that occasion, one of Roberson's older boys, Urenauld, had been removed from the family after fleeing his own savage beating and running next door to a neighbor's house. Roberson said that Salaam had the same demon in him that had been in Urenauld. He said to get the demon out he needed to get Salaam to the verge of death and claimed he had suspended the boy like that for three days.

The image of Salaam suspended in midair like meat on a hook is one I will never be able to get out of my mind no matter how long I live. The sadism of that act is beyond comprehension. It was a slow form of torture, like something out of the Spanish Inquisition. To imagine the helplessness and hopelessness this child must have felt, as so many adults saw what was happening to him but did nothing to help him, churns my stomach even today. Roberson went on deriding Salaam to Judy, describing him as a "bad seed." He complained about the boy's stutter (which he had tried to "cure" by withholding food from the boy) and said he wanted him out of the family. Judy said she would arrange a place for him but was so broken down she failed to act immediately and take him with her that night—a decision, or lack thereof, that would have fatal repercussions.

"I don't know if you would call it post-traumatic stress syndrome, post-torture syndrome, post-concentration camp syndrome, post-psychological manipulation, but I wasn't as healthy as I am now," she would explain later at trial, describing her inability to protect either herself or her child at the time.

Alexander ("Salaam")

The last time Judy saw her son was on December 19, 1985, at the home where Roberson was living in South Lake Tahoe with several of the wives and children. Salaam was being punished again on that day, forced to stand in the corner by his father. A few weeks later, Roberson came to see her and said he had sent Salaam away to a Muslim school "to teach him how to be black." He refused to answer any questions about Salaam and got angry with Judy when she tried to ask one of the other wives, a woman named Pamalar Lewis, about the boy.

A few weeks later he demanded Judy come to Tahoe and help deliver Raj's latest baby. When she got there, he told Judy he wanted to get her pregnant to "replace" Salaam. He forbade her to ask him anything about her son and when she persisted he punched her in the face so hard he broke her jaw, then stomped and kicked her for a long time as she lay cowering on the ground. When he finally stopped she tried to flee the house but he hauled her back. For several days he continued to berate her about the "lesson" he "taught" her with that beating. After a week he finally drove her back to San Francisco but warned her at gunpoint not to seek medical help or involve the police.

She told him she would claim she was mugged, but after he left she told the truth. The spell he had cast on her had finally broken. She spent two weeks in the hospital and had to undergo surgery. With her jaw wired shut she was barely able to speak, but she went to the police in both San Francisco and South Lake Tahoe, swore out complaints against Roberson, and got a court order demanding he return her son to her. Roberson had fled to Los Angeles after beating Judy, but police caught up with him there. He served a year in jail for assaulting her but claimed that Judy had taken Salaam with her in December 1985. Raj backed up his assertion.

As I looked over the file I found many letters from Judy begging the FBI to help find her son. But it was a letter from an unexpected source that stopped me cold. A year or so after Salaam disappeared, Pamalar Lewis wrote the FBI claiming she not only knew what had happened to Salaam but was also an eyewitness to the events surrounding his fate. This was amazing and unexpected because by the time South Lake Tahoe Police went out to the house looking for Roberson and Salaam everyone had cleared out except for Pamalar. After finding a large bloodstain in the closet of the upstairs master bedroom, the police came down very hard on Pamalar and she shut down and refused to cooperate.

Pamalar was just twenty years old and taking classes at UC Berkeley when she met Ulysses Roberson in the summer of 1985, six months before Salaam disappeared. At that time Roberson was calling himself "Dr. U" and even carried a doctor's medical bag. She fell for him and moved into the house in South Lake Tahoe where Roberson was living with Raj, a woman named Traci, and a half dozen of his kids by various mothers. Unlike the other wives, she was not expected to work outside the home but to help take care of the children. After that initial interrogation she left town and went back to school. Eventually the South Lake Tahoe police got a judge to issue a material witness warrant and went down to the Bay Area and pulled her out of her dorm room. They brought her back to Tahoe and put her in jail, but she still refused to talk. Eventually they had no choice but to let her go.

I was shocked to find that a woman who had adamantly refused to cooperate with local authorities had written the FBI detailing what she saw. While I could understand why the local police had taken such a hard-line approach with her, in hopes they could scare her into turning on Roberson, it was clear now that this was a mistake. None of the other women in his life had ever cooperated with the police against him. He had too strong a hold on them; they feared him more than they feared anything law enforcement might do to them. But something appeared to have shifted with Pamalar. She was clearly troubled by what had happened to the boy and was reaching out to help. The FBI had also made a mistake. Rather than reopening the investigation when they received her letter, the agent handling the case at that time simply put it in the file.

I took the letter from Pamalar and went to see an FBI agent I knew in the South Lake Tahoe office, Chris Campion. Chris would spend most of his career doggedly working leads trying to find Jaycee Dugard, who was kidnapped at the age of eleven while walking to her school bus stop in South Lake Tahoe by a convicted sex offender and held for eighteen years before being discovered and freed. Chris and I had become close friends working cases over the years, and I told him that I felt we needed to tell the South Lake Tahoe police about this letter. Chris agreed. We met with an SLT detective named Ken Hunt and asked for his permission to try to bring Pamalar back in. He consented, so I began calling her.

Interviewing witnesses and victims can sometimes be even more challenging than interrogating a perpetrator. All the adults who stood by while Salaam was victimized let that child down, and it is something that they will forever have to live with on their consciences. It is important to recognize, however, that Pamalar was also Roberson's victim, as was Judy, and both were bound to him. Like hostages brainwashed by their captor, their every thought and decision had been controlled by him for so long that it was hard to separate psychologically from him and recover any sense of their own agency. We see the same thing in what psychologists have defined as battered woman syndrome, a form of PTSD where women (or children) who live under the constant threat of fear and violence may develop "learned helplessness"—a state in which they resign themselves to a fate that seems inescapable. This makes it very hard for them to get themselves out of a bad situation. We've also seen this with kidnapped children who don't flee their captors even when they have a chance because they've lost the sense of having any control over their lives. This state has even been created in animals during experiments with electric shock. When the animal comes to believe shock is inescapable, it stops doing anything to avoid it, even when given the opportunity to do so. I also believe that some victims of domestic violence make excuses for and try to explain their abusers' behavior because they simply cannot believe someone who is supposed to love them really intends to do them harm.

The letter Pamalar wrote the FBI was from a woman finding her own voice again. She was taking back her control, feeling her way out of the fog that had enveloped her life. But like an alcoholic in recovery, coming back to full consciousness meant having to confront the wreckage of the past. She had witnessed terrible things and failed to intervene. She had kept a terrible secret. I had to help her feel safe enough and strong enough to stand up to Ulysses Roberson and do the right thing at last for Salaam.

For a long time Pamalar wouldn't talk to me. She'd tell me to call at an appointed time, then when I did she wouldn't answer. I knew I needed to be patient, to not demand too much of her before she was ready to give it to avoid scaring her off again. She had no reason to trust the FBI any more than she had the South Lake Tahoe police, as so many years had passed without response since she found the courage to mail that letter. I'm sure it was also very hard for her to reopen that part of her life again. Like many prisoners of war or Holocaust survivors, she was not eager to revisit the past. I just kept persistently calling her and eventually got her to start opening up a little bit. For ten months I kept at it. Finally, she let me come see her in San Francisco and we had dinner together. That led to several more meetings where we slowly began to build a relationship.

Each time we spoke I impressed upon her how important it was for her to follow through on what she had started so many years ago because Salaam was still missing. In the years since Salaam's disappearance, Roberson had been sent twice to prison in Washington State. In 1987 he was sentenced to five years for the assault on Urenauld. And in 1992 he was handed a fourteen-year stint for drugging and raping a thirteen-year-old girl he had lured to his home under a new ruse: promising to give her a job in the cosmetics company he claimed to run. Roberson's MO had not changed in the intervening years; he had merely tweaked it to suit the impressionability of his target. I had to make sure Pamalar understood that although he was at that moment in prison he would eventually be back on the streets, and with his proclivities there was no reason to believe he would not return to the life he had always lived: exploiting and brutalizing women and children. She could help prevent that.

Eventually Pamalar felt comfortable enough to tell her story and even agreed to accompany me to the Lake Tahoe house and take me, Chris Campion, and the South Lake Tahoe police detective, through what happened the day Salaam's brief and painful life came to an end. Being inside that house, where some new family lived blissfully unaware of what had occurred there, was surreal. It was not some backwoods hovel where one might expect a cult to hole up, away from civilization. The two-story home was just off the picturesque lake in a little lagoon. Inside it looked like a ski lodge, with an exposed beam ceiling and big rock-embedded fireplace.

Alexander ("Salaam")

Nine people were in the house the day Salaam died: three adults (Roberson, Raj, and Pamalar) and six toddlers and infants from assorted wives. As in all of Roberson's homes, there were strict rules about who did what and who could go where. The master bedroom at the top of the stairs belonged to Roberson. Only he and occasionally Raj were allowed in there. They also had exclusive use of the master bathroom, which included a tub.

At some point during the day, Pamalar found Salaam lying naked on the garage floor. His father had locked him in there to punish him, apparently for soiling his pants. It was a very cold day, with snow on the ground outside. The garage was unheated and the boy lay motionless, possibly in hypothermia, on the bare concrete slab. As she approached him she saw that his eyes were open but fixed off in the distance. She felt she didn't dare move him but brought out a blanket and draped it over him. Even that small act of kindness left her terrified. If Roberson found out that she had interfered to help the boy there would be hell to pay.

When Roberson discovered the blanket he was indeed furious. But he didn't think it came from Pamalar; he assumed the boy had gotten it himself. He flew into a rage, snatched the boy up by his ankle, and beat him viciously with a piece of firewood. Pamalar could hear Salaam begging, promising to never do again whatever his father thought he had done wrong. But his father showed no mercy.

"He was near dead and yet he got a blanket," Roberson said when he was done. He seemed astonished, saying that showed Salaam had spunk. But for a man who wanted absolute control over everyone around him, spunk was not a quality he either prized or condoned.

Later that night, Roberson came downstairs carrying a bundle the size of a small child under the same blue blanket Pamalar had used to cover Salaam in the garage. He loaded the bundle into their van along with Raj and all the children except the eldest boy still living in the home, Yeuwar, who was five at the time. As soon as they left, Pamalar and Yeuwar ran upstairs looking for Salaam, but he was nowhere to be found. What they did find was blood on the floor of the closet in the master bedroom. When the family returned, everyone was accounted for except Salaam. Pamalar never asked what happened to the boy. She was too afraid. She saw the damage he did to Judy when she came and asked about Salaam.

Pamalar recalled two previous incidents where Roberson hung Salaam upside down by his feet: once from the rail of his crib, which left rope burns around his ankles, and another time when he was suspended from a pole for several days. She described it as being like a lynching, a "slave scene." He also locked the boy in the closet, withheld food from him, and talked about getting "the devil out of him."

Pamalar's account was later backed up by physical evidence. In addition to the large bloodstain in the bedroom closet, blood was also found on clothing and a blanket in a U-Haul left behind at the South Lake Tahoe house. The blanket was blue, just as Pamalar had described. With no reference sample on hand from Salaam, there was no way at the time to tie that blood to the missing child. But as DNA technology developed, the FBI lab was later able to determine that the blood came from an offspring of Judy and Roberson. They only had one child together, so it had to be from Salaam. Yet even with Pamalar's testimony and the DNA evidence, the District Attorney was still reluctant to prosecute. There was no body, and although the blood evidence indicated Salaam was most likely dead, they would still have to prove that he had been murdered and that the murder was committed by his father and not by someone else in the house. Prosecutors only get one bite at the apple, and if Roberson was acquitted for lack of evidence, they would never be able to go after him again for Salaam's murder. This provided little consolation to me and Chris, and no doubt frustrated the South Lake Tahoe detectives who twice filed charges against Roberson, only to see them dismissed by the DA for insufficient evidence.

Our chances of making a case stick improved in 2001 when Chris tracked Raj down in Cleveland and got her to turn on Roberson. Raj confirmed Pamalar's account of the confinement and beating in the garage but took it a crucial step further. She could confirm that Salaam was dead; she had seen him with her own eyes and Roberson had made damning admissions to her.

Even then it would take eight more years—until 2009—to bring him to trial. Roberson fought extradition to California all the way to the U.S.

Alexander ("Salaam")

Supreme Court. He then tried to get the charges against him dropped, arguing that he had been denied his right to a speedy trial. That was particularly galling because the delay in prosecution was all due to him: his success in hiding Salaam's body so well that it still has not been found; his flight and lack of cooperation; his myriad lies and the lies he got his wives to tell on his behalf through threats and intimidation; and the tyrannical control he wielded to prevent so many eyewitnesses from reporting the disappearance and death of a defenseless child. He also engaged in various courtroom shenanigans to delay the start of trial, such as firing his lawyers and then asking for time to get his new defense team up to speed.

By the time he went to trial, many of the women who had been under his control and even some of his children came forward to testify against him. Raj described how Salaam and Urenauld were especially singled out for punishment. She recounted the incident in which Roberson hung Salaam by his ankles and the scars that left on the boy. She remembered another incident where Roberson held the boy up in the air with one hand and used the other to whip him with his belt. And she recalled the final terrible day when Roberson confined Salaam to the freezing cold garage.

At one point she went into the garage and found Roberson punching the boy in the stomach. He ordered her to get out and she retreated to her room. Later that day, Roberson woke her from a nap and told her that Salaam was dead and that he believed he had killed him. He went and got the boy and carried him upstairs in a blanket. She remembered that Yewaur called out as they passed through the living room, asking his father what was wrong with Salaam, but Roberson claimed he was just asleep. Once upstairs he put the boy into the bathtub and ran the water. Raj came into the bathroom and saw Salaam, clearly dead, floating in the water. Raj said that when she began to cry, Roberson pressed a gun to her pregnant belly and threatened to kill her and everyone in the house, so as to leave no witnesses, if she ever told anyone what happened to Salaam.

When they got into the van that night she said Roberson ordered her to keep her eyes closed, so she laid back in her seat. She had no idea where they drove but recalled that twice Roberson pulled over and took things out of the van. He told her to tell anyone who asked that Salaam was with Judy, and she complied.

Felicia Burns joined the family just after Salaam disappeared. She was only eighteen and introduced to Roberson by another of the wives, who was one of her coworkers. She testified that Roberson told her he didn't like Salaam because the boy was half-white and said he sent Salaam away because he was "incorrigible." He would threaten to send the other children "away" as he had Salaam when he wanted to keep them in line. He also threatened the kids by telling them they might end up in foster homes or with Satanists who would sacrifice them to the devil. She was there when Roberson broke Judy's jaw but said she was too afraid to do anything. Only when Roberson began calling himself God did she begin pulling away from him.

Another woman, an optometrist recruited into the cult by another wife who happened to be one of her patients, said Roberson told her that he had sent Salaam away and that he was never coming back. He said he wasn't going to let any other child tear the family apart as Urenauld had by seeking help from a neighbor and drawing the attention of the authorities. He also referred cryptically to someone dying in the South Lake Tahoe house.

A sixteen-year-old babysitter recalled the sad specter of the children having to line up and kneel before their father in order to get food. She also testified that Roberson told her that Salaam was "evil" like Urenauld and that he had to discipline him to get the evil out of him.

Urenauld, who may have met the same fate as Salaam had he not had the courage and strength to seek help and make his break from the family, came forward to speak up for the brother he had lost. "I am here because there is a four-year-old boy who . . . just vanished off the face of the earth," said Renauld Jones, having returned to his original name. He also wanted to send a message to the three sons he now had, to ensure they would never be treated the way he and his brothers were treated.

Renauld had managed to escape his father's clutches before Salaam disappeared but recalled his dad singling out Salaam for the most severe punishments, complaining that he was the devil or had demons in him because he was half-white. Renauld himself endured numerous beatings by his father, was denied food, and was locked in a dark closet for days at a time. The worst came when he was just eight years old and his father attacked him with the broken-off leg of a chair.

"I honestly believed I was going to die if I didn't get out," he said, describing the day he took refuge with a neighbor who called the police. Roberson threatened to kill Raj and Urenauld unless she took the blame and said she administered the beating as a "corrective action" for Urenauld playing with his brother's penis—when in fact his father had attacked him for the grave sin of eating a cookie.

Roberson did not take the stand. The man who claimed to be God and sometimes Satan, the final word on all things in what the prosecutor called "The World of U," remained silent. He dressed the part of a holy man in court, in a Muslim robe and kufi cap, but with the curtain finally pulled back exposing his sordid world it was like the phony Wizard of Oz yelling, "Pay no attention to that man behind the curtain!"

And while the defense succeeded in preventing the word cult from ever being uttered during the trial, the judge did allow a sociologist and college professor who had once been in a cult herself to talk about the mind-set of people in a closed "self-sealing system" dominated by a charismatic leader and how they could be rendered to a state of such submission that they would not immediately report something as horrendous as the murder of a child.

The prosecution asked the jury to find Roberson guilty of first-degree murder, which carries a sentence of twenty-five years to life, and would most likely have meant that he would never be released. However, the jury rejected that charge as well as a hate crime allegation and instead found him guilty of second-degree murder. On January 6, 2009, nearly a quarter century after Salaam's brief life ended, Ulysses Roberson was sentenced to fifteen years to life. That means he could be eligible for parole within a decade, although the District Attorney's office vowed to fight that. In a final indignity, Roberson asked to leave the courtroom during the sentencing hearing while Judy gave her victim-impact statement, but the judge denied his request. Instead, he had to listen to her and watch a slide show of the handful of photos that exist of Salaam.

Few jurors were willing to explain their verdict beyond saying they simply did not have enough evidence for the more severe charge, which requires a finding of premeditation. Undoubtedly the fact that so much time had passed since the killing worked in the defendant's favor, making the memories of those who testified against him seem suspect and faulty. I hope the fact that all the eye and ear witnesses were fellow cult members did not make the jury see them as less credible or sympathetic. That would be a tragedy beyond the already tragic death of Salaam, but I know it is human nature to reject things that seem so foreign and threatening to our own life experience.

I respect the jury system, but it saddens me that homicides committed by a parent or domestic partner rarely result in a first-degree murder conviction. This happens so often statistically that a law professor who studied the phenomenon dubbed this the "domestic discount." It's not just a problem of juries but also a prevalent attitude throughout the legal system, from how prosecutors charge cases of domestic homicide to how judges sentence defendants. Intimate-partner homicides are typically viewed as "crimes of passion," rash, spur-of-the-moment killings even when there is evidence of planning and premeditation. The same is true when a parent kills a child, which is typically treated as an insanity case or as discipline gone too far.

I think we simply don't want to believe that anyone would intentionally murder his or her own child, as I believe Ulysses Roberson and the Carrascos did. There was ample evidence that Roberson hated Salaam and wanted him out of the family. By his own admission, he brought him "to the verge of death" at least once before. He always viewed him as less than, impure, "a white snake" in the midst of his tribe, and he seemed to blame him for the loss of control he felt over the family after Urenauld was removed from the household. He stated repeatedly to many different people that he wanted Salaam out of the family, and then used his disappearance to intimidate the other children into submission.

While seeing Roberson finally pay for what he did to Salaam was deeply satisfying, it still gnaws away at me that we didn't get Salaam's remains back and probably never will. Roberson isn't telling, and Raj swears she doesn't know. Tahoe is surrounded by massive amounts of rugged, sparsely populated, and unsearchable terrain. There is the frigid lake itself, the second deepest lake in the United States, ringed by snow-covered mountains. A vast desert stretches to the east across Nevada. To the west lies California's massive Central Valley. There are

Alexander ("Salaam")

simply unlimited places to dispose of a body where no one would be likely to come across it. A cellmate of Roberson's while he was in prison in Washington State claimed that Roberson told him he had buried a child in the desert, which Roberson said was an acceptable and common practice under Islam. Could that be, I wonder, what happened to Salaam?

CHAPTER SEVEN

Carole, Juli, and Silvina

CAROLE SUND GREW UP in a well-to-do family that made millions in the real estate market, but her heart was always with the less fortunate. She married her high school sweetheart, Jens Sund, the son of Danish and Salvadoran immigrants, and after having a daughter together, Juliana, the couple decided they would open their home to kids in desperate need of a loving and stable family. They took in foster kids and ended up adopting three children of mixed African-American heritage, as Carole became aware that black kids are far less likely than children of other ethnicities to exit the foster system and find permanent homes. Carole also had adopted siblings, so expanding her family with Jens through adoption seemed natural and right.

She spent thousands of hours volunteering with groups that assist foster kids and abused and neglected children, those most vulnerable to victimization and least able to protect themselves. She joined the NAACP to better understand racial issues and keep her children in touch with their culture. She advocated for abused kids in the legal system, taught parenting classes, and also worked with developmentally disabled adults living in group homes who were trying to establish a measure of independence.

There was another person Carole considered part of her family: her "Argentinian sister," Raquel Pelosso, whom she met when she spent a semester abroad during her senior year in high school living as an exchange student with Raquel's family on their cattle ranch in the Argentine city of Las Varillas. Raquel had been an exchange student herself the year before in Michigan and the two became fast friends. By the end of Carole's six-month stay they were so close they exchanged friendship rings. They remained in touch for the next twenty-six years, as each married and had children.

Carole, Juli, and Silvina

At one point Carole traveled to Argentina to look into adopting there. Carole's daughter Juli and Raquel's second child, Silvina, were just toddlers when they met but they immediately began their own friendship. Just like their mothers, the girls wanted to expand their horizons. In 1999, when Silvina was sixteen and Juli was fifteen, Silvina came to stay at the Sunds' home in the Northern California town of Eureka and spend a term at Juli's high school. Juli, who seemed to have inherited her mother's adventurous spirit—and her passion for fighting against victimization, as Juli started an anti-rape campaign at her school after two of her teenage girlfriends were sexually assaulted—also hoped to visit Silvina in Argentina that summer.

The Sunds wanted to show Silvina as much of America as they could fit around her school schedule. They took her to popular tourist haunts like Disneyland and San Francisco's Fisherman's Wharf. But they did not want her to leave without seeing some of America's true national treasures: places of such incomparable beauty and serenity that the mere memory of them can provide balm to the soul. Carole decided to take Juli and Silvina to Yosemite National Park over President's Day weekend in February 1999. The park, lionized by John Muir and enshrined in the public imagination by the iconic photographs of Ansel Adams, had particular resonance for Carole, who had honeymooned there with Jens. At the end of the long weekend, Carole would bring Juli back home and Silvina would fly to Arizona with Jens and the younger Sund kids to visit the Grand Canyon. Two unforgettable places: the best sights the West had to offer.

Carole had the trip planned out like clockwork, as was her manner. She and the girls would fly from Eureka to San Francisco on Friday, February 12, then rent a car and drive to Stockton, where Juli, who was on the cheer squad at her high school, had a competition the following day at the University of the Pacific. On Sunday they would drive on to Yosemite. They would spend all day Monday touring the park, then drive back to the San Francisco airport on Tuesday, where Silvina would meet up with Jens for the flight to Arizona.

Carole and Juli were so impressed with the University of the Pacific that Juli thought she might like to go to college there. They made plans with another mother who attended the cheerleading competition to meet back there on Tuesday to tour the campus. Carole was confident that they could fit the stop in on their way back from Yosemite and still make it to San Francisco in time to catch their respective flights.

They headed out Sunday morning on Highway 140 for Yosemite. The route follows along the Merced River, one of the two rivers that wind their way through the park, and becomes increasingly twisty and treacherous as it climbs up the Sierra Nevada Mountains and then plunges down again to the floor of Yosemite Valley. The three checked into the Cedar Lodge, the hotel Carole had booked just outside the western entrance to the park in the town of El Portal. The lodge had an unusual layout, with more than two hundred rooms in a half-dozen separate buildings spread out over 27 acres. The one they were assigned, room 509, was so far away from the office and the amenities clustered around it that in bad weather you would have to drive over if you wanted to check out of the hotel, or eat at the lodge's restaurant, or swim in the pool, or sit in the Jacuzzi. In high season the rooms would have been packed with guests and the parking lot teeming with cars, but in the dead of winter the place was eerily quiet. Carole and the girls had no idea that they were the only guests in their entire building. The hotel, we discovered later, didn't employ daily maid service and would just keep renting fresh rooms further and further out away from the main office area until a crew came in and cleaned all the dirty rooms in one fell swoop.

Monday afternoon, after spending the whole day in the park, Carole called her husband from their hotel room. She told him that the girls had had such a good time exploring the park—hiking its trails and ice skating at the open air rink on the valley floor—that they hoped to go back into the park for a few hours Tuesday morning before heading to the tour at UOP and the meet-up at the airport. They rented some movies to watch in their room that night and were last seen around 7:30 PM eating in the diner attached to Cedar Lodge. The girls ordered burgers, mom a veggie burrito. Weight-conscious Carole ate only part of the burrito and had the rest wrapped up to go but ended up forgetting to take it back to their room. The waitress who served them held on to it, assuming they would come back for it, but they never did.

The trio never showed up for the campus tour on Tuesday. Nor could Jens find them at the airport. His flight into San Francisco from Eureka was delayed by five hours due to bad weather and he eventually decided to fly on to Arizona with his other children, assuming Carole had gotten tired of waiting and put Silvina on an earlier flight. But Silvina did not turn up in Arizona either. He repeatedly called home but got no answer. When he called the Cedar Lodge he was told that the three had left. Although they had not come into the office to check out in person (many guests don't, simply leaving their credit card on file to be charged), their luggage was gone and their room keys were left in the room. On Wednesday, February 17, Jens called the Sheriff's Department in Mariposa County, where the Cedar Lodge is located, and reported them missing.

A search was mounted, which greatly increased in intensity after a high school student found the plastic insert from Carole's wallet—with her driver's license and credit cards still intact—on February 19 on the median of an intersection in the city of Modesto, a two-hour drive from Yosemite. Due to the treacherous wintry driving conditions, most of those working the case presumed that the three had perished in a car accident, either by skidding into the river or plunging into a ravine, where their vehicle had become obscured by either the terrain or the elements. But the appearance of the wallet in Modesto pointed to foul play: most likely a kidnapping or carjacking. The FBI became involved and I was named case agent, because I was the usual person tasked with handling suspected kidnappings within our office's jurisdiction.

The quality and scope of the search for the three missing tourists, directed by the Mariposa County Sheriff's Department, was second to none. The park is so large—spanning over 1,100 square miles and three different counties—that personnel from multiple agencies came out to assist. Hundreds of officers and agents participated in the search by air in helicopters and reconnaissance planes, on the ground by foot and snowshoe, and on water in the many lakes and rivers surrounding Yosemite. Search dogs were employed, along with radar and sonar equipment. Because that area was home to the once-thriving Gold Rush, there were countless abandoned mining caves and tunnels that would make a great place to hide a car or body and we had to check all of them, a particularly eerie task. But we found no trace of the tourists or the fire engine–red Pontiac Grand Prix Carole had rented for the trip.

In the Name of the Children

On Monday, February 22, I was dispatched by my SAC, James Maddock, to Modesto and told to report to a command center at the FBI's resident agency, which was located within the DoubleTree Hotel building. I didn't even take a change of clothes with me, assuming I'd be back home that night. Tony Alston, whom I had worked with on the Frankie Proctor case and who was a former partner of mine, was in charge of the Modesto resident agency then, so it was like visiting an old friend.

Normally, when I would go to a resident agency's territory, I would work for, with, and at the discretion of the agents in that office, much like I do when partnering with members of local law enforcement. It is their backyard, and I believe it is important to respect that fact. But when I met up with the agent who should've gotten the case, Terry Scott, he told me that he was heavily involved in another case and that it was better for me to take the helm.

The victims' families had all come to Modesto and were staying at a Holiday Inn in town. Jens was there, along with Carole's parents, Francis and Carole Carrington. Raquel Pelosso and her husband, José, had also flown in from Argentina. Over the previous weekend, the Carringtons had posted a $250,000 reward for the safe return of their missing loved ones and another $50,000 reward to anyone who could locate the rental car. During the extensive search, nine vehicles were found abandoned on various roads around the park, but none was the car in question.

It was clear that Jens was nowhere near Yosemite or Modesto at the time Carole, Juli, and Silvina disappeared. But at that point we couldn't rule out any theory. In any investigation you start at the center and work out in concentric circles. Family members could have a personal or monetary motive for wanting to kill a loved one and always have to be eliminated, so we wanted to start with Jens. Terry and I convinced FBI management at the resident agency that we just wanted to introduce ourselves to the family, but we were really going in to interview Jens. We spoke to him for three hours. At the end of an interview I always ask the subject if there is anything important that I failed to cover.

Carole, Juli, and Silvina

"You didn't ask me if I did this," Jens said. So I did and he said no. We asked him to submit to a polygraph the following day and he passed. I never definitely eliminate anyone from suspicion based on a polygraph result alone. But based on everything we had gleaned from and about Jens, we believed he was not involved in the disappearance of Carole and the girls, and Terry and I were content to move him down the list of possible suspects to consider.

I also partnered with Modesto Police Detective Jon Buehler to interview Francis Carrington. I was really impressed with Jon. The Modesto Police, in my opinion, had their act together. I was always looking to try and make myself better by observing others who know the subject and area better than I do, and working with the Modesto PD was a good learning experience for me. When Jon and I talked to Mr. Carrington, it was clear that he was extremely concerned about his missing loved ones and was going to extraordinary lengths to help search for them—from putting up his own money for a reward to creating his own volunteer center and missing persons flyers to reaching out to every contact he had, including high-level politicians, seeking attention and resources to further the investigation.

We then turned our attention to the Cedar Lodge. With the discovery of the wallet insert, my bosses at the FBI were becoming convinced that whatever happened to the three women occurred in Modesto, but I was not so sure. When you have a missing persons case with no known crime scene, you start looking at the place the victim was last seen. Although the women's luggage was gone when the room was checked, a few things had been left behind: a bag with some souvenirs purchased on the trip, an apple, and a bottle of tomato juice in the fridge. A pink blanket from one of the beds was missing as well as a pillowcase. Some videos they had rented from the motel to watch were there, including the Tom Cruise movie *Jerry Maguire*. The towels in the bathroom were soaking wet and a soiled sanitary napkin was in the trashcan. Most curiously, little cuttings from fabric were found on the hotel room carpet, but nobody knew what the significance of that was at the time.

My game plan was to interview everyone at the Cedar Lodge who might have had contact with the missing women and then polygraph them. The first person on my list was the handyman, who, I learned, had changed the locks on room 509 the day the Sund-Pelosso party rented the room. Carole had requested separate room keys for her and the girls and to comply the hotel said they needed to change the locks. Anyone who had access to keys that could have opened that door needed to be looked at hard. I wanted to know everything I could about that man and found out that his brother was not only a registered sex offender but also that he had victimized the handyman's own daughters. The handyman passed a polygraph and we lowered him, too, on the suspect list. He wasn't completely out of the running, but we had to widen the net so as not to waste precious time and resources on a bad lead.

Next up on my priority list was a man named Billy Joe Strange, a graveyard-shift janitor in the Cedar Lodge restaurant. He didn't have any contact with the victims that we knew of but he had a record of violence toward women. He had also dated another employee whose husband died under mysterious circumstances. When I reviewed the report on the man's death I was shocked to read that he had been stabbed several times in the back with scissors and then drowned in a shallow creek but that his death was ruled as a suicide. That bizarre factoid made me interested in talking first with Strange. But ultimately the local authorities in that jurisdiction were convinced that the man's death was indeed a suicide. Strange not only failed his polygraph but also became so angry over the questioning that he almost attacked the examiner, Harry Sweeney. He was arrested for a parole violation—drinking alcohol—and stains that looked like blood were found during a search of his van. They tested positive in a presumptive test in the field, which meant they could be blood. But in confirmatory testing back at the lab they were determined merely to be rust, which is known to cause false positives due to oxidation.

While the first guy we looked at, the handyman, was in the midst of his polygraph, I found my SAC typing up a search warrant affidavit for the man's home. This seemed awfully premature, so I asked why.

"Because he's the one," Maddock said. After the guy passed his polygraph, Maddock decided just as quickly that the handyman was not involved in the case. Conversely, when Billy Joe Strange failed his lie detector, Maddock became convinced he was involved in the disappearance of the women, a belief only reinforced in his mind by Strange's violent anger toward the polygraph examiner. But I was far from sure that was significant. Strange might have been justifiably scared and outraged at being accused of something so heinous. I know that if I were falsely accused of murdering three people—two of them kids—I'd be very angry. And the fact that he got that emotionally overwrought during the interview would almost ensure that he would "fail" the test, because what a polygraph is measuring is not truth per se but physiological signs of stress.

I cannot overstate how inexact a science polygraphy is. It is useful in prioritizing suspects and helping to decide where investigators should concentrate their attention. But there is good reason polygraphs are not admissible as evidence in court. The examiner cannot read a person's mind or examine the contents of his heart to differentiate truth from lies. Instead, deception is inferred based on changes in the person's emotional response system to particular questions, as measured by sensors attached to the subject's body that detect changes in heart rate, blood pressure, respiration, and sweat. One time while I was working in New York, I had a suspect pass a polygraph who was accused of embezzling $17,000 from a federally funded health project. He had stolen the funds, but it turned out that he passed the test because he wasn't particularly worried about that theft. He was far more concerned by the fact that he had embezzled $80,000 in state funds, something he had not been questioned about.

Billy Joe Strange had done a lot of bad things in his life and might have overreacted during the polygraph in fear that he was being fingered for something he didn't do or that other bad acts he committed that were unrelated to the missing women were about to be uncovered. He was a volatile guy with a drinking problem, a history of violence, and sketchy friends. He looked like a good suspect, but so did a lot of people, including an alarming number of Cedar Lodge employees or locals who were regulars at the hotel bar, one of only a few places serving liquor near the park. Yosemite may be a special, sacred place for the visitors who gape in wonder at its splendors, but many of the residents and workers in and around its fringes are a hardscrabble bunch who struggle to make ends meet with low-paying and seasonal jobs catering to tourists. While most are hardworking and law-abiding, some people with less savory backgrounds are attracted to the area as a place they can live somewhat off the grid and where law enforcement is sparse. Drugs are a huge problem in the area, even inside the park. Ten years before this case a federal grand jury had heard testimony of rampant drug dealing by employees of the park's official concessionaire.

Confirmation bias is a problem in many investigations, especially in missing person investigations where there is no obvious crime scene or trail of leads to follow. You look at registered sex offenders in the area and, of course, they all look like viable suspects unless they have an airtight alibi that eliminates them from consideration. This was a huge problem in the Sund-Pelosso case because the investigation sprawled over so many jurisdictions and the potential number of felons, sex offenders, and bad guys of all stripes who potentially could have crossed the trio's path increased exponentially.

My approach was to have everyone polygraphed, and then puzzle through any possible reasons for the failure with the examiner, while at the same time looking for evidence that would either keep them under suspicion or exclude their involvement. But with Strange in custody I wasn't allowed to continue working my way through Cedar Lodge employees. The higher-ups were dead set on Billy Joe Strange and I was beginning to be marginalized from the investigation.

Still, I began running down another lead that seemed critical. Carole and her husband had an account at Wells Fargo Bank and, after contacting the bank, I learned that a slew of inquiries about the account had been registered in their system. Someone illicitly attempting to access a missing woman's bank account might very well be the person responsible for her disappearance. Calls regarding an account are not recorded. But because the bank pays for its 800 line, calls made to that number can be tracked to the number from which the call was placed. The bank actually had installed software that could automatically match the caller's identity to each transaction, but unfortunately that system had not yet been activated. So we had to go through a long and laborious process of running down the telephone numbers from which the calls had been made. A lot of the inquiries turned out to be from bank employees, looky-loos curious because of the notoriety of the case. Others were automatic entries generated by computerized system maintenance. There were two calls, however, that appeared worrisome.

Carole, Juli, and Silvina

The first was placed on February 19, the day Carole Sund's wallet insert was found on the street in Modesto. The caller, a woman, claimed to be Mrs. Sund and requested that a duplicate ATM card be sent to her. The employee taking the call asked for identifying information to prove this really was the account holder and when the woman failed to provide that information the bank employee ended the call, as per bank policy. Unfortunately, that meant that the address the woman had requested the card be sent to was not recorded. The second call came in on February 22, also from a woman claiming to be Carole. She was able to provide Carole's Social Security number and obtained balance information on the account. I wanted to interview the employees who took those calls to see what other information I could glean and trace exactly who made the inquiries. Within a day I had spoken to both employees and had established approximate time frames for when the calls were received. But because Wells Fargo is such a big institution, even after narrowing the window to an hour around the time we believed the calls were made, there were still 10,000 possible numbers in the phone records from which the calls might have come.

Media attention was reaching a fever pitch and, as with the Unabomber case, agents and managers looking to make their mark began flooding in. A manager who didn't much like me was brought down from Sacramento. He told me I was working too hard and arranged to have me sent back to Sacramento for a week. I was not given a choice, but I decided that no matter where he sent me he couldn't stop me from working the case. Instead of going to the office I spent the whole week at Wells Fargo's telebanking center trying to narrow down who made the two calls posing as Carole. I sat in the cubicle of a woman named Maria, the bank employee I had previously been dealing with by phone. She is one of the many generous souls I have encountered during my career in law enforcement who go out of their way to help when someone goes missing. By the end of the week, Maria and I had painstakingly winnowed down the list to 144 possible phone numbers. I returned to the Modesto command center with the list, divided up the numbers by city of origin, and began distributing them to the offices with jurisdiction over those areas.

In the Name of the Children

Media was descending from all over the world on Yosemite and the command center in Modesto. The Embassy of Argentina was asking for information, and Maddock began holding regular press conferences even when he didn't have any news to report. He was anxious for results and was frustrated that there was none yet to be had. He confronted me in a room full of people about my work on the bank inquiries, demanding an answer I couldn't yet give him. So he took the lead away from me. After all the work Maria and I had done to reduce the list to a manageable one, the SAC wanted all bank inquiries from the entire day of each call to be looked at—which increased the phone numbers to be tracked and traced to the millions. It was an impossible task and to this day the lead remains unresolved. I continued working on the investigation of Billy Joe Strange and other suspects, but it was ever more clear that I was case agent in name only because information was being deliberately withheld from me and I was being iced out of activities that would have enabled me to gather crucial facts.

On March 18, Chris Hopkins, the head of our office's Evidence Response Team, got a call from the California Highway Patrol that the car rented by Carole Sund had been found. A man who said he had been out "plinking"—target shooting with a rifle—discovered the burned-out hull of a vehicle on a dirt logging road in the Stanislaus National Forest near his hometown of Long Barn. The car had been driven about a hundred feet off State Route 108, a highway north of Yosemite, into an area nestled by trees, and then clearly torched. The man, a local carpenter named Jimmy Powers, thought this might be the car everyone was looking for, so to make sure he called it in correctly he removed the license plate and took it with him as he went to look for a phone. He would receive the $50,000 reward posted by the Carrington family.

I was back in Sacramento at the time and told to report to Sonora, the largest town close to where the car was found. I went home to get a change of clothes. Lori and the boys were away for a couple of days, so I was taking care of the animals and when I got home I found one of our dogs in the throes of dying. When I moved out to California with my family we had two Golden Retrievers we named Fred and Barney after the characters in *The Flintstones*. We had originally planned to get just one puppy, but when we arrived at the breeder's the two puppies were inseparable, so we agreed to take both. They were great dogs, and Barney had preceded Fred in death. Fred was now very old and I could see that day that things were dire. I had to get to Sonora, but I sat down on the floor and Fred rested his head in my lap. I sat there until he took his last breath and died in my arms. The vet arrived, whom I had called earlier because I was worried that Fred was suffering. We cried together and she took him away. I then gathered my stuff and made the two-hour drive to Sonora.

I had called Lori earlier that day to tell her I had to go to Sonora. She and my sons had put up with my sudden protracted absences from our family life that my work demanded. Now my family had our own little tragedy and I couldn't be there for them. I had to tell them over the phone that Fred had died, and it killed me. It took me a while to compose myself before I could even break the news to them.

I stayed the night at an inn in Sonora and tried to prepare myself for what we might find out the next day from the car. It was our first "scene," our first piece of concrete evidence, and I was anxious to go out with Chris and the Evidence Response Team. My view, that it is absolutely critical that the detective in charge of a case be present while the forensic specialists process the crime scene, was certainly crucial in solving the Michael Lyons case. To have the opportunity to observe the evidence *in situ*, to watch and listen as crime scene experts pore over the clues and discuss their significance, is not only crucial for setting the direction of an investigation, but also provides what is needed to effectively interrogate a suspect. Part of my process in obtaining a confession is to get a suspect to describe a crime in such detail that I can see everything that transpired in my own mind. Then I compare that to what I saw at the scene and what I've learned from the evidence. If the two scenarios match, I can trust I am getting a true confession. If they don't match, I press and confront the suspect until I can determine whether the person is making a false confession, holding back on certain facts, or minimizing to avoid full culpability.

We assembled the following morning at a makeshift command center that had been set up at a fire station in Mi-Wuk Village, a tiny burg near the car dumpsite. A large whiteboard listing assignments for the day was posted, and I noticed that my name wasn't even up there. Another agent scribbled my name in as the designated case agent, but I was not allowed to go out to the scene. Instead, I was told to stay at the command post and answer the tip line. Needless to say, I was not happy about this. Not only was it humiliating personally, but it also left me hamstrung from a tactical point of view. How could I direct the case if I didn't know all the facts? How could I interview and eliminate suspects if I wasn't privy to the evidence that would implicate or exculpate them? Information is essential, but it is also a form of power, and in a big case like this—one that had the potential to make or break careers—a lot of people were vying for control.

My role had been diminished, but I was not about to sit back and do busywork if I felt there was something more important to be done. An agent from the Fresno FBI office, Megan Nichols, came up to the command post and said she had a lead on two suspects from Modesto but couldn't get anyone to go out with her to follow up. I offered to go and we headed down to the Modesto PD, where we met with detectives Jon Buehler and Kevin Bertalotto and the parole agent who handled both suspects and knew their histories inside and out. A retired Modesto police officer had told Megan that he had gotten a call from an old informant who said half-brothers Eugene "Rufus" Dykes and Michael "Mick" Larwick may have had something to do with the disappearance of Carole and the girls. Both had long criminal records. Dykes had been in out and out of prison since he was eighteen years old for statutory rape, false imprisonment, forgery, and drug and weapons charges. In fact, he had been free from his latest bit for just three weeks at the time the women disappeared. Larwick's rap sheet included convictions for kidnapping, rape, and attempted manslaughter.

Both were currently in custody, and it wasn't so much their records that raised our suspicions, because pretty much everyone we'd looked at had a history of violence and sexual offenses. It was their recent behavior—the lengths to which they had resisted arrest—that set off alarms. Dykes was arrested March 5 on a parole violation but held off sheriff's deputies and parole agents at gunpoint for two and a half hours before surrendering. On March 16, Larwick shot and wounded a Modesto police officer who had attempted to pull him over for an expired registration. Larwick fled the scene, broke into a house, and barricaded himself inside, which led to a fourteen-hour standoff.

There were other facts of interest about the brothers as well. They were associated with a loose network of methamphetamine users and petty criminals, male and female, who supported themselves mainly through mail theft, check forgery, and other financial identity crimes. Could one of their gang have been the person who posed as Carole Sund and tried to access her account? Also, Larwick grew up in Long Barn, where the rental car was found. I had good contacts at the Department of Corrections and was able to get Dykes and Larwick's central files, which contain all the information collected on an offender while in prison and on parole, from friend and visitor information to psychological analysis. Megan and I spent all day working on Dykes and Larwick and felt that they and their associates deserved further scrutiny.

We didn't get back to the command post until after midnight. By that time the Evidence Response Team had examined the car and processed the scene. The fire that consumed the vehicle, the result of gas being poured into its interior and then set ablaze, burned so hot that it scorched tree branches twenty-five feet above the car. Tests would later determine the heat generated by the fire reached 2,000 degrees. The only reason it didn't set off a forest fire was because it was winter and everything was covered with ice and snow. As the car was consumed in flames, its shiny red paint poured off it like water and the tires popped and melted. Two bodies were found in the trunk. It would take some time to identify them through DNA testing, but it was clear from the skulls that one was an adult and the other was a youth. We assumed the bodies in the trunk belonged to Carole and one of the girls, but which one? And could the other teenager still be alive? That one of the victims was still missing heightened the stakes even further and sent all of us involved in the investigation into frenzied activity. Planes, four-wheelers, and dogs were brought in to search the heavily wooded area, but no third body, or live girl, was found.

The spot where the car was recovered was a place often used as a dumping site for old appliances and other refuse that people didn't want to pay to dispose of properly. This was an incredibly sad fact to me: that these victims, like Michael Lyons and so many other missing persons

In the Name of the Children

I had searched for, were dumped like garbage—and in this case even incinerated—when they were no longer of use to their killer. The choice of this location was also a potentially important clue. It made it seem likely the killer was a local, not a visitor, someone who knew the back roads and their hidden secrets well.

On the ground around the car some other items were recovered: a shoe, a length of rope, and most importantly, Carole's purse. At least one bank card was still inside, a curious finding if the person who tried to get a debit card issued in her name was the same one who left this card behind. (More than a dozen credit cards were still inside the wallet insert found on the street in Modesto, so again, it seemed less and less likely that robbery was the motive.) The receipt from dinner at the Cedar Lodge was there, too, along with a camera.

Because the purse had not burned, we were able to develop the film in the camera and the time-stamped photos gave us a near-perfect timeline of the victims' final hours—an incredible break that helped us narrow down the possibilities of when and where they were killed. They spent the President's Day holiday, February 15, enjoying the park. One photo shows the two teens ice skating at the Curry Village rink; in another, Juli has her arm slung around Silvina as they pose in front of Yosemite Falls. (The shoe we found matched one Juli was wearing in one of the pictures.) That evening, while eating dinner at the Cedar Lodge restaurant, Carole snapped a photo of the two girls digging into a piece of cake. The final photos captured the three back in their hotel room: a pajama-clad Juli practicing a handstand on the carpeted floor, Carole and Silvina already under the covers of their beds. If they went back into the park on Tuesday morning, as Carole had told her husband they planned to do before heading home, they would likely have taken more pictures in the park. But the photos ended in their room at Cedar Lodge.

This fact was highly relevant. Chris Hopkins and I and many of the other investigators working the case now believed the women were kidnapped from and perhaps even killed at the Cedar Lodge, and we tried to get our bosses to refocus the investigation there. But some of the higher-ups stubbornly held the view that the crime occurred either where the car was found or somewhere along one of the roads where the victims may have been carjacked. Later on I learned of a conversation between Chris and a supervisor. Despite the conflagration that engulfed the car, some of the victims' internal organs remained intact. We were able to determine that both victims in the trunk, who were eventually identified as Carole and Silvina, were killed before the car was set afire because there was no smoke in their lungs. We were also able to analyze the contents of Carole's stomach and found the ingredients of the vegetarian burrito she had had for dinner that night. The supervisor was arguing that didn't mean Carole was killed the same night. She might have taken some of the food with her, he argued, and ate some more of the burrito the next day. But we knew that Carole had forgotten her to-go bag at the restaurant. The supervisor then went on to describe how if he ate corn, for instance, he'd be "shitting it out" two days later. I recall listening with astonishment as Chris, who in my opinion had one of the best scientific minds in the Bureau, tried to explain to this man the fundamentals of digestion: how food only remains in the stomach for six to eight hours before beginning its slow journey through the intestines.

That very night when Megan and I got back to the command post, Maddock began fixating on Dykes and Larwick and shoehorning them into a narrative with Billy Joe Strange. His theory was that Dykes and Strange had been housed in the same prison at one point and that while inside they had concocted a plan to abduct and rob visitors to the park. At that point I thought Dykes and Larwick were definitely worth looking into, but the theory he was suggesting seemed really far-fetched. The prison Maddock was referring to housed about 5,000 inmates, and we had no idea at that time if it was even possible for the two of them to have had any contact with each other inside. And to tie them all together into a grand *Ocean's Eleven*–style caper, to believe that people who may never have even met had schemed to commit a particular crime years into the future and then gotten together and carried it out seemed ridiculous. I couldn't imagine that anyone would go to that much trouble for a mere robbery. And why target these particular tourists? There was nothing about Carole and the girls that would suggest to an outside observer that they'd be good for a big score. I felt this crime had to be sexually motivated, but Maddock and his coterie still did not want to believe it was a sex crime even after the case was solved. When the SAC asked what I thought of his theory I used an even less diplomatic term than "ridiculous." I think the words I used were "full of shit." That was probably the death knell for me serving as case agent, but I couldn't believe what I was hearing.

Someone reported a note was found at a restaurant with the words "help me" scribbled on it. Maddock believed that the still missing girl may have written that, and he had us knocking on doors in the area to see if she was being held around there. Then he redirected us to investigate Rufus Dykes and his associates. Dykes had already been returned to prison for violating his parole and I was sent with Modesto Detective Kevin Bertalotto to the Deuel Vocational Institution (DVI), a state prison in San Joaquin County, to interview one of his friends, Johnny Nolan Jr., who had also been taken in for a parole violation. After that interview the command center said they wanted Dykes polygraphed and sent in an examiner from the state Department of Justice, Doug Mansfield, whom I had worked with before and thought was a good choice for the task. Dykes indicated deception during the test, so Doug moved immediately into interrogating him. He started making statements that indicated he might know something about the case and began naming members of his crew and what role they would have played. That sounded incriminating, but his language was strangely subjunctive, as if he were speaking in a hypothetical context. For example, he seemed to be describing what each of his friends *would* have done based on what he knew of their specialties. He also said things that did not sound like a confession at all to me and contradicted what he had just seemingly admitted, like something to the effect of how upset he would be if his crew did this without him. He spoke in a similarly odd way in a jailhouse interview he later gave to a reporter, stating: "If I was involved, it wasn't through my knowledge."

Was Dykes making admissions or just speculating based on what he thought people he knew might be capable of doing? Was he mad at his friends and trying to settle some scores? Or was he just messing with us? Whatever it was, we needed to check out the information Doug got from him and see if any of the leads panned out. Kevin and I were up all night and in the morning we headed to the Stanislaus County Sheriff's office to plan the operation to find and question all the people Dykes had mentioned. There were about fifty people in the briefing room from many different law enforcement agencies, including people I knew from working other missing person and child homicide cases. I felt like there was a special bond in that room and was impressed and humbled by how many people had devoted themselves to the mission of finding, or finding justice for, Carole, Juli, and Silvina.

The SAC started the briefing by issuing a threat to everyone. Maddock said there had been a news leak regarding a chicken ranch near Sonora and he warned that when he found out who the leaker was he would see to it that the person was fired. I was still puzzling over what a chicken ranch could possibly have to do with the Sund-Pelosso case when I heard him say that he was going to introduce the case agent to address the day's assignments. Before I could stand up to start addressing the troops, Maddock introduced Nick Rossi, a young agent who had been our public information officer, and he took over the briefing. That was how I learned I had been officially removed as case agent.

At first I felt that I had failed, that I had let down the Bureau, my coworkers, and especially the victims' families. Then I felt angry. I like Nick and think of him as a friend. I know he cared deeply about the victims and did the best he could to solve the case. But I felt the move was really about Maddock maintaining control. He believed his theories and he wanted to call the shots and I was not going along with the program. Some people who knew me from way back in the Bureau joked that at least I was consistent, referring to my removal as case agent in UNABOM and now TOURNAP, the name the FBI assigned to the case (short for tourist kidnappings), designating it as a major case.

Terry Scott, Kevin Bertalotto, Jon Buehler, and I were part of the task force charged with reinterviewing Dykes and then trying to verify what he was telling us. It was during an interview with Dykes at DVI on March 25 that we found out the third victim, Juli, had been found. The news was terrible. I learned that a letter had come in to the FBI's Modesto resident agency that simply said, "We had fun with this one." A map was hand drawn on the note showing the vista point exit to Don Pedro Lake, a reservoir about fifty miles from Yosemite and thirty miles from where the rental car was dumped, with an X marking the spot where the person indicated her body would be found. The FBI had just started a cadaver dog program at that time and a dog from our Los Angeles division was brought to the scene. The body was completely hidden under brush. Even with the map the human searchers could not see it as they looked down the hillside toward the point the letter writer indicated, but the dog trained to detect human remains went directly to it. Carole and Silvina's bodies had been so badly burned that the medical examiner had been unable to determine the cause of their deaths, but it was obvious how Juli had died—her neck was brutally slashed. She was naked and had remnants of duct tape around her ankle, indicating she had been bound. It appeared that her killer had posed her corpse in a sexually provocative manner, which further underscored my belief that this was a sex crime.

With three victims and crime scenes spread over multiple counties (four different crime scenes if you count where the wallet was found), the SAC was convinced that more than one person was responsible for what had happened to these women. The use of the pronoun "we" in the note further solidified his belief. The FBI and other law enforcement agencies carried out a series of raids and many of those associated with Dykes and Larwick in various criminal ventures were rounded up on parole violations and other charges unrelated to the Yosemite killings. While in custody they were interrogated, polygraphed, and asked to provide hair samples and other bodily evidence to be used in the investigation. In April a federal grand jury in Fresno began hearing testimony on what Rossi was characterizing as a carjacking or kidnapping that resulted in the murder of the three tourists and what Maddock still believed was a robbery plot cooked up by Dykes, Larwick, Billy Joe Strange, and perhaps others back in the joint.

Until May I was going out to DVI and running out leads on what Dykes had told us. The interviews turned into almost comical weekly "confession" sessions, where Dykes would seem to admit something and then say something completely contradictory. As I had been urged by FBI profiler Roy Hazelwood on the Danny Hohenstein case, I kept looking for consistency, but Dykes gave us different stories every time with different details. After each interview we would try to find some facts that would confirm the latest version, but we were never able to corroborate anything he said. That meant, for example, checking to see if someone Dykes fingered had a ring that supposedly belonged to Juli (which we found Juli still wearing when her body was found).

It was not without reason that Maddock and some of the other investigators on the case became fixated on Dykes and Larwick as prime suspects. After a while, the whole crew seemed to turn on and implicate each other. Some testified before the grand jury that Dykes or Larwick had admitted involvement directly to them. One woman in their circle testified that it was she who made the telephone inquiry about Carole Sund's credit card, while another woman said she was asked by Larwick to negotiate a check in Carole's name.

The problem for me was focusing so hard on these particular suspects to the exclusion of all other potential suspects. Because this group lived largely off identity theft, it is possible that they simply tried to take advantage of a tragedy after the fact and tap into the assets of a woman who was missing and whom they heard through the media was from a wealthy family. Or perhaps they came across Carole's wallet on the street, before the Good Samaritan who turned it in, and recorded some of the information. These people were very sophisticated identity thieves. They had counterfeit postal keys that allowed them to access mailboxes unnoticed. Sometimes they opened mail, got the pertinent information they wanted, then replaced the mail in the box so they would have more time to drain an account before the victims discovered their identity had been stolen and shut down their accounts. But if they were the ones who kidnapped Carole and the girls, why did they not use the credit and ATM cards in Carole's possession? If they had control of the tourists for some period of time, they could have gotten all the financial information they wanted from them or even taken them to an ATM and forced them to withdraw money. Everything that seemed like an answer simply raised more questions.

The only piece of physical evidence that potentially implicated the crew was some fibers that the Evidence Response Team found on one of its searches, which appeared to match a fiber found under Juli's body at Don Pedro. But that was literally a slender thread, and fibers are not as unique as a fingerprint or DNA. And why would a group of ex-cons who appeared desperate not to go back to prison send the FBI a map to a body they had taken effort to hide? It didn't make sense.

In the Name of the Children

What was especially frustrating was that much of the information we were digging up and reporting back to command ended up in the media, and we began to realize that people we were interviewing were just feeding us back what they heard on the news. It became a vicious cycle of garbage in/garbage out and we didn't know what information could be trusted. Dykes told so many different stories it was difficult keeping track of the changing details. I believe he was making stuff up out of thin air just to throw a monkey wrench into the system and torment the authorities. There is a characteristic psychologists have noted in criminals with highly Machiavellian tendencies known as "duping delight," a thrill they get from deceiving others—which is never greater than when they think they have pulled one over on law enforcement. I think Dykes believed charges would never stick because there was no evidence to back them up. Or maybe he was worried about the Three Strikes law newly passed by California voters, which could send him to prison for life if he was convicted of another felony, and thought he could save himself by pretending to cooperate and throw others in his circle under the bus. Whatever his reasons, I believed Dykes was lying and I was no longer being allowed to do anything useful on the case.

One day in May, after four months of spending most of my time in Modesto away from my wife and kids, I started receiving "911" pages from my family. I got several of the alarming messages before I got a chance to call back. Lori told me our remaining five dogs had gotten out of the yard, run a half-mile down the hill, and darted out into the road into the path of a pickup. One was killed instantly and another had his legs and pelvis shattered. I couldn't let my family go through this alone again. I headed to the pet emergency, where I found Lori and the boys in shock and grief. The vet there said the only hope for saving our Great Dane, Roger (for Roger Ramjet), was to take him to a specialist in Sacramento. We placed Roger as gently as we could in our car and drove him to the specialist, but that doctor told us there was very little hope. He left to review Roger's X-rays and I lost it. All the tension of the case, all the time I had been absent, all that I had put my family through, and all they had to endure alone because of my job, all the guilt and frustration came pouring out. I had been unable to save Carole and Juli and

Carole, Juli, and Silvina

Silvina and now I couldn't even save this animal that I loved. I lay my head down on top of Roger's and cried into his fur.

The vet, walking in on that scene, said he would try to put Roger back together. He took him into surgery and we went home to wait. Several hours later the doctor called and said Roger had made it through surgery. Recuperation would be difficult, like convalescing a lame horse. I would have to build a special bed that would hold him down so he couldn't reinjure himself by trying to walk and then turn him over every few hours so that being sedentary didn't cause other health problems. I knew I had to stay around and I had to build up the courage to tell my boss without being deemed insubordinate that I wouldn't be going back to Modesto. I would instead return to the Sacramento office to work my other missing and murdered kid cases, where I would be close enough to run home and "flip the dog," as my partner Hitman put it. As a family we devoted ourselves to Roger's recovery and maybe, in some ways, we were healing our own bonds. We all slept near his bed to give him comfort—Lori, Joe, Jordan, and I and all our other dogs spread around him in the living room.

Roger slowly healed, and as spring turned to summer, I got back into the routine of my life before TOURNAP. Other agents from our office who had been called to Modesto also began to return to Sacramento as the investigation was scaled back. I heard bits and pieces of information here and there, but I was busy with my other cases and out of the loop with what was going on with Sund-Pelosso. Authorities were telling the media off the record that they believed three people participated in the killings and several others helped cover up the crimes after the fact. The FBI was refusing to publicly name the suspects they had in custody but confirmed that some had been identified in the press. And because the grand jury process is secret, rumor and speculation abounded.

Unnamed investigative sources were quoted in one story stating that Juli was kept alive by whoever kidnapped her for some period of time—from days to weeks—and was tortured before she was killed. I did not want to even imagine such a scenario. The brother and sister of a man who was found drowned in the Tuolumne River in April went to the media, claiming their brother was murdered by some of the Dykes and Larwick gang because he knew too much about the Yosemite case. They claimed their brother said he saw Juli at a house in Modesto, where she was being held captive and raped during the period she was missing. Some in Dykes's circle who testified before the grand jury started talking to the press and attempting to sell their stories. A woman who said she was Dykes's girlfriend told a reporter that she believed Dykes may have been involved in the slayings.

Someone claimed that crime in Modesto had gone way down because of all the FBI attention in the area. I don't know whether that is true or just mordant cop humor. It was too painful to follow an investigation from the outside and not be able to do anything to help, so I tried to tune it all out. I still had grave doubts that Dykes's "admissions" constituted a genuine confession, but people higher up the chain of command were convinced and I hoped they were right, because I didn't want anyone else to face the terror Carole, Juli, and Silvina had experienced.

CHAPTER EIGHT

Joie

IN MID-JUNE OF 1999, as the FBI continued to focus on Dykes, Larwick, and their associates, Maddock dismissed the discrepancies in their statements, which had bothered me and made me doubt their credibility, as crank-induced memory impairment. It made sense: most of the suspects and witnesses in the case were heavy methamphetamine users.

"These are dopers who can't remember what they did yesterday, much less weeks ago, or where a suspect was on a particular day, at a particular time," he told the press.

Despite having conducted more than 10,000 interviews, he said the investigation was ongoing and he did not expect indictments in the near future. But he said he felt no urgency because he believed that the threat had been contained with the arrest of all the suspected conspirators on parole violations and other unrelated charges. The crown jewel of the national park system was deemed safe once again for the four million people a year who come to enjoy its scenic riches.

"I do feel we have all of the main players in jail," he said.

One person who took those words to heart was Joie Armstrong. For nearly six months, the entire Yosemite community had been gripped by terror, wondering if a killer or killers still walked among them, as the mystery of the missing tourists unfolded and the gruesome details of their fate were revealed. Joie was a strong, hardy outdoorswoman. But the rustic cabin she rented within the park was so isolated that she couldn't help but feel vulnerable.

For Joie, the park was hallowed ground to be treasured and preserved for generations to come. Her goal was to teach others, especially children, to love and appreciate the natural world so they would want to protect it. She majored in parks and resource management and worked at an Audubon center on the San Francisco Bay, the Marin Headlands

In the Name of the Children

Institute, and at an outdoor education camp for school kids in Sonora before getting what looked to be a dream job with the nonprofit Yosemite Institute teaching children about nature and wildlife in the park. She moved into the wood-framed cabin that still to this day is known simply as "the Green House in the Meadow," even though its green paint has faded almost to white from the sun. She and her roommates paid just a dollar a year to live in the house, which was leased to the Institute by the Park Service. She lived in a picturesque enclave with the charming name of Foresta, just a half-hour drive west of Yosemite Valley but seemingly a world away from the hordes of tourists. There are no more than forty houses scattered around Foresta, mostly inhabited by park staff, but none particularly close to the Green House.

She had never spent the night alone in the cabin, but in the second week of July one of her roommates was going away and the other, her fiancé, was taking kids on a wilderness trek. So she made plans to drive down to the Bay Area and stay with a friend in Sausalito. She intended to head out after work on July 21, 1999, which meant July 20 would be her first and only night alone in the Green House. A local friend invited her to sleep over, but Joie waived off her own fears. That night, the night before she was murdered, Joie told her father that she felt safe again because the FBI said the Sund-Pelosso killers were behind bars. In her diary she wrote words that will haunt me to my grave: "The monsters are gone."

In the waning daylight hours on Wednesday, July 21, Joie made several trips back and forth between the cabin and her Toyota truck parked out front, loading it for the visit to Sausalito, unaware that a man was watching her from a little bridge a short distance away. The front door to the cabin was open and music from the stereo spilled outside as she went in and out to pack and water the plants in preparation for going away. She let her guard down just enough to allow the friendly seeming stranger, who approached her with small talk outside her cabin, to get a jump on her. She fought hard, almost superhumanly, to get away from her killer, which caused him to make mistakes and leave behind evidence that pointed us his way.

After Joie failed to show up, her friend in Sausalito called police. The U.S. Park Service sent a ranger around to the Green House to check on her. The door to the cabin was open and the stereo was playing but no one was home. However, her truck was still there, packed with her belongings, so it did not seem she had ever left for the Bay Area. By 7:30 AM, a dozen rangers had amassed on the cabin and began searching the area. One thing that stood out was a pair of sunglasses on the porch that looked like they might have been stepped on and partially crushed.

Around 1:30 PM the searchers found a woman's body partially submerged in a creek a hundred yards or so from the house. But they couldn't be sure it was Joie because the victim had been decapitated. It took several more hours and a trained dog to locate the severed head, which had sunk to the bottom of a pool about forty feet away from the rest of the corpse. Joie was clothed but her pants were undone and her bra had been pushed up over one breast. Vegetation leading toward that area had been trampled. It was clear there had been a chase, and she had run for her life.

It was a horrible, sickening discovery that seemed a violation of nature itself. In the preceding year there had not been a single murder in any of the fifty-plus national parks across the county. People occasionally drown at Yosemite while running the rapids on the Merced River or fall to their deaths while hiking its peaks and scaling its sheer granite faces. But the last time anyone was intentionally killed in the park was a dozen years earlier when a man on his honeymoon pushed his bride from a cliff and lied that she had slipped in hopes of collecting on her life insurance policy. Juli's throat had been cut so severely she had nearly been decapitated and now this woman's head had been completely severed. There was also a similarity in the way both Juli and Joie's corpses seemed to be positioned when they were discovered, with their legs in a suggestive sexual position. Yet Maddock continued to insist publicly that there was no indication the Sund-Pelosso and Armstrong cases were linked in any way. He still believed those who killed the tourists were behind bars and could not possibly have been involved in Joie's killing.

On the day Joie's body was discovered, I was attending a multi-day seminar held annually by the California Department of Justice's Missing and Unidentified Person's Unit. I was with Chris Hopkins, the head of our office's Evidence Response Team. Chris had been a supervisor in the famed FBI lab at Quantico and had helped develop some of the cutting-edge forensic technology pioneered there. But FBI Director Louis Freeh felt there were too many agents in headquarters and one of the many reforms he instituted during his tenure was to distribute some of those agents to field offices around the county. We were incredibly lucky to get someone with Chris's expertise in our office, but, of course, local management assigned him to the surveillance team. I lobbied hard to get him transferred to our violent crime squad, and he played an important role in the evidence gathering on the Yosemite murders.

During the first day of the seminar Chris got paged to respond to the scene of a homicide that had occurred in Yosemite Park. My services were not requested, so I stayed where I was. I don't watch the news at home—I get enough murder and mayhem on the job. I had been back in Sacramento for two months, so far outside the original Yosemite investigation that I had no idea what was going on with the case. And because I had been at the conference for several days, I didn't really know anything about the new case other than that the victim was a young woman who worked in the park as a naturalist.

On Friday, July 23, when the seminar ended, I stopped back at the office. While I was there I heard that the brother of Steven Stayner, a child who was kidnapped in the 1970s, was believed to be a possible witness to the latest Yosemite murder. That seemed like a surprising twist but only because of the notoriety of his brother's story. More than anything it just struck me as incredibly sad that tragedy had once again touched the Stayner family, but ironic coincidences and tragedies within tragedies were not uncommon in the type of cases I investigated.

Steven Stayner was just seven years old when he fell victim to a predator's ruse while walking home from school one day in 1972 in Merced, California, another Central Valley town about seventy miles southwest of Yosemite. Kenneth Parnell, a convicted sex offender, had inducted a mentally challenged accomplice, Ervin Murphy, to approach boys walking home from school, claiming to be a minister looking for donations to his church. (Interestingly, both Parnell and his accomplice worked together at the Yosemite Lodge, one of two hotels located inside Yosemite Park, when they kidnapped Steven and even held him for a brief time at the hotel.) When Murphy asked Steven if his mother would be willing to donate something, Steven said he thought she would—his family was Mormon and charity was part of its faith. Parnell then pulled up in a car and the two said they would drive him home to collect the donation. Instead, Parnell took him to a remote cabin and then over the next seven years to other cities around the state, all the while pretending the boy was his son but using him as his own personal sex slave. The single most heartbreaking fact of the case, to me, was that Parnell convinced Steven that his parents had voluntarily given up custody to him because they could not afford to raise the five children they had. Parnell pretended to speak to Steven's parents on the phone and claimed he had gone to court to legally adopt him.

When Steven reached puberty and aged out of his kidnapper's pedophilic preference range, Parnell abducted a second boy, five-year-old Timmy White. Steven had endured his fate as best he could, but he did not want another child to have to go through what he had experienced. While Parnell was at work, he took the younger boy and hitchhiked to the city of Ukiah, where Timmy had been taken. He had hoped to simply return the boy to his parents but, unable to find their house, he dropped the boy at the Ukiah police station. Steven wasn't even planning to seek help for himself. He began to walk away, but police stopped him and eventually he told his story.

For reasons I can neither fathom nor stomach, Parnell was not charged with any of his countless sexual assaults of Steven but only for kidnapping both boys and thus served just five years of a seven-year sentence—less time than Steven had spent imprisoned by his captor. Some of the sexual assaults went back beyond the statute of limitations, but certainly not all of them. So the decision seemed to be more about a desire to spare Steven the "stigma" of being identified as a male rape victim. That way of thinking makes no sense to me. Steven was always going to be identified by what happened to him; the case was too famous. I think not being able to talk about what happened to him, and not being able to see his perpetrator held responsible for all that he did to him, was far more injurious. It infuriates me that even today, at a time of great advocacy for sexual assault survivors, that talking about male victims is still considered by many a taboo subject.

I did not work on Steven's case, which concluded long before I came to California. But everyone investigating crimes against children knew about Steven Stayner because he was the shining example of hope to which all parents of missing children at that time clung: a stranger-abducted child, assumed to be dead, who returned to his family. But his story had no fairytale ending. As he famously put it in an interview with *Newsweek* magazine: "I returned almost a grown man and yet my parents saw me at first as their seven-year-old." After all he had been subjected to, it was difficult to fit back into the church-based lifestyle his family embraced. He didn't want to talk about what he had been through, and apparently neither did his parents. He didn't pursue psychological help and wasn't encouraged to do so by his parents, who were either in denial or seemed to think family and faith could heal all wounds. He didn't want to recapitulate what happened over and over again, even though the public and media would not let him escape it. Like so many sexual abuse victims, he blamed himself for what others forced on him and questioned whether he should have come home at all.

He didn't fit in around other kids his age, some of whom teased him about his abuse history under the mistaken impression that being molested by a man meant he was gay and had welcomed the sexual contact. So he dropped out of school and struggled to find work that paid more than minimum wage. According to one relative he considered suicide. He was angry, impulsive, and self-destructive, with one person close to him saying the experience left him always trying to prove his manhood. He bought a motorcycle and drove it without a license because he racked up so many tickets. Just when it seemed he might find happiness at last—he had married and had two young children of his own, had rejoined the church, and had become an advocate for abducted children—he crashed that motorcycle into a car that pulled out of a driveway into his path while he was driving home from work one day and died at the age of twenty-four, just nine years after escaping his captivity.

When the phone woke me up on Saturday morning, July 24, 1999, summoning me to work, I could never in a million years have imagined what would unfold that day. Lori and I had hoped to enjoy a romantic weekend with just the two of us alone, as our two boys were away back east visiting her family. I owed her that and so much more. Any time the phone rang I might have to drop everything and leave home at a moment's notice, leaving her to pull the weight of our family and hold everything together. The last thing I remember as I left the house that morning was Lori with a look of disappointment and frustration on her face, which made my heart heavy. I promised her I'd get home as soon as I could and try to salvage our weekend.

I didn't know where I was heading or what I was supposed to do as I got in my car. The person who called me, the night security clerk at our office, simply said my two partners at that time, Ken Hittmeier and John Boles, were looking for me but she didn't know why. Hitman knew me better than probably anyone in the Bureau and always ran interference for me when I rubbed people—mostly managers—the wrong way. While Hitman and I worked many years for the FBI before coming to the Sacramento office and partnering up to work on violent crimes, John Boles placed straight into our squad as a new agent. He had a more macho cop persona than Hitman or me, but he was one of the brightest agents I ever worked with, and boy did he speak his mind. The three of us made an interesting team, the sum at times greater than its individual parts.

I reached Hitman and John on the car radio and they told me we were to make contact with a witness who happened to be at a nudist resort called Laguna del Sol in Sacramento County. That was a first, and I tried to think how I was going to explain to Lori that I bailed on her romantic plans to go to a nudist colony. The witness was Cary Stayner, and all any of us had been told was that he may have seen something in regard to the latest killing in Yosemite Park. I thought he may have been a boyfriend or ex-boyfriend of the victim and was running out of fear.

Actually, Stayner came up on law enforcement radar quickly in the Joie Armstrong case, but only as a result of two very lucky breaks. During a canvass of Foresta residents, a neighbor who was a Yosemite firefighter recalled seeing a sport utility vehicle with a distinctive paint job—a baby blue International Scout with white stripes—parked near Joie's house the night she was killed. A park ranger also reported giving a ride that same night to a man whose car, also a blue and white Scout, had broken down on the highway between the Foresta turnoff and El Portal. He drove the man to the Cedar Lodge, where he said he lived.

A BOLO (a be-on-the-lookout alert) was issued for the Scout, and some deputies from the Mariposa County Sheriff's Department found a vehicle matching that description parked on the side of Highway 140 just outside the park. Nearby is a popular skinny-dipping spot known by locals as the 25 Mile Per Hour Beach because it is located at a sharp curve in the highway marked by a 25 mile per hour speed limit sign. The deputies and two park rangers they called in to assist encountered Stayner there, sunbathing nude and smoking a joint. They waited until he headed back to his truck, hoping to get his consent to search the vehicle. Stayner identified himself as the owner of the car and said he worked and lived at the Cedar Lodge. He denied being in Foresta the day before and agreed to let them search his Scout. But when he refused to let the officers look inside the backpack he had with him, they feared Joie's head might be inside. When they told him they were going to seize it anyway and get a search warrant to look inside he relented and turned it over. But because he had acted so squirrelly about the bag, the team at the scene decided to err on the safe side and wait for a warrant before examining its contents.

That evening a park ranger and an FBI agent from our Fresno resident agency picked up Stayner and interrogated him for several hours. He continued to deny being in Foresta and having anything to do with Joie's murder. The investigators took that opportunity to compare photographs taken of the tires on his Scout to tire tracks found outside Joie's cabin. Stayner's tire treads were quite unique because he had a different brand and age of tire on each wheel, which looked quite similar to the impressions in the dirt captured outside Joie's house. Because visitors get lost from time to time in the parks, the Park Service employs professional trackers who are expert at detecting and following trails. Without being given any information about the case at hand (similar to how scent dog handlers work a scene so as not to influence the result), a tracker named Mark Fincher picked up two sets of footprints coming out of Joie's cabin, one slightly in front of the other. The two people walked past Joie's car, then forward to where tire tracks left by another vehicle were evident. Suddenly the two pairs of footsteps morphed into one single, deeper set. In Fincher's words, it looked like someone had come down and swooped her up to heaven. In fact, her kidnapper had picked her up, making his footprints heavier and deeper as he picked her up and placed her into his car.

The backpack was ultimately searched but nothing that seemed incriminating was found inside, which only made Stayner's reluctance to turn it over more curious. They did find one item of interest: a novel about a particularly grisly serial killer who cuts women open while they are still alive. But a lot of perfectly normal, law-abiding people read books like those. There was also an X-Acto knife in the backpack, but that tiny blade was clearly not what was used to cut off Joie's head. The most innocent-looking item inside would turn out to be important: an opened package of sunflower seeds. A piece of the plastic torn from that bag was found in Joie's house, but no one had yet matched that up. The tracking evidence was the best thing they had at that moment, but they didn't feel it was enough to hold Stayner and late that night they let him go.

Stayner went back to the Cedar Lodge and sold off what he could of his meager possessions to other employees, telling them he needed money to fix his truck. He also mentioned that he might move away. When investigators showed up the next morning to talk with him further, he was gone. On mid-afternoon Friday he checked into Laguna del Sol and pitched his tent down by the resort's man-made lake. He paid for two nights when he checked in on Friday, but he had already packed up his tent and appeared ready to leave when we arrived Saturday morning to pick him up.

Hitman, John, and I were not informed about any of that. Nor were we told that the FBI had put a BOLO out for Stayner after finding he had cleared out of the Cedar Lodge. A few media outlets had gotten wind of the alert and broadcast that we were looking for Stayner, which led a guest at Laguna del Sol who recognized him to call and tip us to his whereabouts.

I thought we had been dispatched on more or less a gofer assignment, just to ferry a witness to the office. We were so unaware of the import of the task at hand that Hitman, John, and I casually bantered over the radio whether the resort would let us in with clothes on or if we would have to disrobe and strap our irons to our bare skin. I arrived first and while I waited for the others someone from the resort approached me and told me in a conspiratorial tone that the guy I was looking for was in the restaurant eating breakfast "and he is wearing clothes." I wasn't sure if this was mentioned because it was unusual in a nudist colony or if the man was thinking Stayner could be concealing a weapon on him. I only learned later that when the people who ran the place found out that one of their guests had called the FBI they went out of their way to help us by blocking the exit from the resort with some vehicles to prevent Stayner from getting away before we arrived. When the other members of the team showed up we entered the restaurant through two separate doorways and when Stayner saw us he stood up and put his hands on his head. John placed him in cuffs, as is procedure when we don't know if a situation is secure, but we told him we were not arresting him.

"I don't have a clue why we are here other than to ask if you would be willing to come back to our office to be interviewed," I said to Stayner. If he agreed, I told him, I would drive him there and bring him back to Laguna del Sol when we were done. We were also supposed to ask for permission to search his truck. He agreed to both requests and I led him to my car. We then had to wait as John went to get FBI clearance for us to proceed. As we waited, a surreal scene developed as a crowd of naked looky-loos of all shapes and sizes gathered around the car to see what was going on. This seemed to unnerve Stayner, so to take his mind off that I decided to read him his rights. Even though he was not under arrest, we were taught in the FBI that it is always better to err on the side of caution. The FBI provided us with a card-sized version of what is known as the Miranda warning and I pulled it out of my pocket and read it to him. We finally got permission to go, and with John following me in his car I drove off. I quickly realized I didn't know how to get to Highway 99, the fastest route heading north to the office, and Stayner actually guided me.

After a short distance we encountered construction on the highway that caused one of the lanes to be shut down. That turned what should have been a forty-five-minute drive into an hour and a half trek. To kill time as we drove we chatted about light things, like what it's like at a nudist colony. Stayner said he loved the outdoors and had been going to Yosemite all his life and cherished its beauty and serenity. I told him my wife was a tree hugger as well, a biologist for the U.S. Fish and Wildlife Service, and was always trying to get us to go camping. But I could never understand why anyone would want to sleep on the hard cold ground when the alternative was a nice warm room with a bed and a TV.

We talked about movies, one of my favorite pastimes. *Billy Jack* was one of the classic martial arts action films from the 1970s. Played by actor Tom Laughlin, the title character is a "half-breed" American Indian and former Green Beret who comes home to find his town overrun by violence and corruption and takes it upon himself to defend its vulnerable residents, which include a woman who is raped and children who are abused and bullied. I guess you'd call it part of the revenge fantasy or vigilante hero genre, like Charles Bronson's *Death Wish* movies, but Billy Jack was cool and philosophical and had a code, and to pretty much everyone who was a young man in that era he was an icon of masculinity. It was particularly thrilling for me, as someone who wanted to go into law enforcement but did not relish gunplay, to watch a guy overcome armed assailants with just his wits and his lightning-fast hands and feet. In one memorable faceoff, Billy Jack warns—no, proclaims to—his antagonist: "I'm gonna take my foot and hit you on the side of your face and there is not a damn thing you can do about it." To me, Stayner was the spitting image of Billy Jack. I couldn't get over the physical resemblance and kept bringing it up, but he said he'd never seen the movie.

I told him I mostly worked cases involving missing children and was always looking for ways I could help the victims' families. Because I knew he was Steven Stayner's brother, I asked him if there was anything law enforcement could have done to make things better for his family when Steven was kidnapped. He was quiet for a moment and I could see he was fighting back emotion. He talked about how unjust he felt the sentence that Parnell received was. He said his brother was held captive for seven years and his kidnapper was only sentenced to seven years. I told him I agreed that the sentence was unfair. Then he went on to talk about how when Steven came home he wasn't the same. He had spent seven years being forced to have sex, smoking, and drinking, doing all these non-Mormon things, and when he returned he was out of control, acting in a reckless manner, and Stayner believed that his recklessness was a contributing factor in the accident that cost him his life. Still, Stayner was outraged that the driver of the car that collided with Steven's motorcycle ran from the scene and fled to Mexico. The man agreed to return a week or so later and surrender but was only convicted of a misdemeanor because it was deemed that Steven was partially at fault.

It was as if Steven's kidnapper had destroyed the Stayner family three times over. There was the unexplained disappearance that ripped a giant hole in the middle of that family, and the seven agonizing years the Stayners spent not knowing whether Steven was dead or alive. Then his return as a virtual stranger to his family caused another period of great upheaval. And his death so young made the hole permanent and recapitulated the trauma all over again. I told Stayner what I believe sincerely: that he and his family were also victims of the crimes that happened to Steven. I said to Stayner that it sounded like he had not gotten over what happened to his brother. I told him how my wife and I had nearly lost a son and how it was so painful that I hid out from my family during the crisis but that avoiding my feelings only prolonged the pain. I talked about some of the child cases I worked and how much they affected me, especially the one where I helped carry the victim's body. I talked about the concept of closure, which to me doesn't mean that all the pain is done and gone but that what was once an open wound becomes more like a scar: you always know it is there but you are able to get on with your life. I told him that because of the cases I worked I had contact with people who might be able to help him feel better and come to terms with what had happened to his brother. I asked him if he had gotten counseling and he said he had tried it but felt it did not help.

Just as we pulled into the gate for my office, Stayner recited, word for word, that line from *Billy Jack* and grinned at me. So he *had* seen the movie and was just holding back. It seemed like I had passed some kind of test in his mind. It was his way of opening up, of accepting me, of saying we were friends.

I still didn't think he could possibly be anything more than a witness to the naturalist's murder. Nothing about his demeanor during that ride gave any hint of culpability. I told him I would most likely be handing him off to someone else to interview him but that I would wait around and drive him back as promised. John had parked right behind me. We walked him inside to a small interview room that was outside the locked part of the FBI building. I demonstrated to him that the doors were unlocked and that he was free to leave if he chose. Then we left to go look for someone who could give us some direction about what to do with this guy. No one was watching Stayner. He could have gotten up and walked out and no one would have stopped him.

Because it was a Saturday, hardly anyone was in the office. But I found Maddock was there, so I told him we had brought Stayner in and asked what he wanted done. He described Stayner to me as a witness in the naturalist's homicide who was running because he was afraid. Maddock said Stayner needed to be interviewed and was thinking of doing it himself but he also had a press conference scheduled that afternoon in Yosemite. The park was nearly 140 miles away from Sacramento, about a three-hour drive, six hours roundtrip. He asked me if he thought he would have time to do both. I said that I could do a preliminary interview with the witness just to gather biographical information and such and he could go to his press conference, and Maddock agreed.

I assumed he would send someone else down, more versed in the case than me, to do a more in-depth interview. After all, because I had not been part of the investigation I knew no facts about the most recent murder. Looking back today, the fact that the SAC was thinking of doing the interview himself looks like the Bureau did consider Stayner a suspect. But Maddock was so undecided about what he wanted to do that day, it didn't seem like he considered this witness very important.

I realized my workday was going to go longer than I had anticipated and called Lori to tell her that I was still hoping for an afternoon departure. John, Hitman, and I hadn't eaten anything because we had been called out so early, and we had interrupted Stayner's breakfast. So I asked the radio room to order us a pizza. I told John that he and I were going to start the interview (Hitman was acting supervisor that day, so he would monitor us but not take a direct part in the interrogation).

In the Name of the Children

Because we knew so little about the case, John suggested we call in Harry Sweeney, one of our best polygraphers. This would get us off the hook for the interview. We could simply observe Harry and be there if he needed us. Stayner agreed to take a polygraph, so we went ahead and called Harry in. John and I decided that we would do a biographical interview until the polygrapher arrived. Stayner agreed and signed an Advice of Rights form. In the course of getting this general background information, Stayner mentioned that he had an uncle, Jerry Stayner, who was murdered in 1990 and that he had been living with him at the time he was killed. I asked him what the status of the case was and he said it remained unsolved. I told him that I worked cold cases and if he wanted me to I could call Merced County, where the murder occurred, and work with them to try to solve the case.

The radio room notified us that the pizza and the polygrapher had arrived at the same time. John asked Stayner which he wanted first. Stayner could have asked for the pizza and stalled for time or he could have said he changed his mind about everything and gotten up and walked out the door. But what he said next sent a shiver down my spine.

"Let's skip the polygraph," Stayner said. "I'd like to speak to Jeff alone."

I went out to advise Hitman that Stayner asked to speak with me privately. This wasn't the first time someone had asked to speak to me alone right before a polygraph was to be administered, and Hitman kind of rolled his eyes at me like, "Here we go again." I had become known in the FBI as someone who was particularly good at obtaining confessions, and Hitman and I felt that what Cary Stayner was saying sounded like the beginning of a confession. But we were told Stayner was just a witness, so I was thinking the thing he wanted to confess might concern something different from why we were here, maybe about his uncle's murder. Hitman told me to go find out what that was, so I went back into the interview room.

Stayner was slumped over with his head down, sobbing, when I reentered the room. I asked him what he wanted to talk to me about and he said, "Jeff, I'm a bad person and I've done some really bad things." He said he struggled all the time with terrible, obsessive thoughts—thoughts about molesting and even killing prepubescent girls.

"Hold on," I said. I told him what I believed, that doing bad things doesn't necessarily mean someone is a bad person; nor does having bad thoughts. "So let's talk about what's going on with you," I offered, "and we'll figure this out together."

Stayner said that he had been molested by a relative when he was eleven years old—the same year his brother was kidnapped—and that he had never been able to get on with his life in a healthy way. He said that he was unable to achieve an erection and had never been able to have a normal sexual relationship with a woman. He talked about being in a constant state of anxiety and engaging in compulsive behaviors to relieve that anxiety, like one that caused him to tear his hair out and leave bald patches on his scalp that he usually kept hidden under a ball cap.

I tried to console him, believing he was asking for help concerning his own abuse or about his brother's victimization and death. But he interrupted, saying something that took me aback even more than his sudden request to speak to me alone.

"I can give you closure."

"On what?" I asked.

"This," he responded. "And more."

I was so stunned I excused myself again and went back to talk to Hitman. I'd told Stayner in the car about how I struggled with the concept of closure from what I experienced working cases like the murder of Michael Lyons and how that affected me and, in turn, my family. But what did Stayner mean by closure?

"I think he's saying he's the one for this," I told Hitman, referring to the killing of Joie Armstrong. "And he says there's more." By "more" I was assuming he meant that he also killed his Uncle Jerry, or maybe there was just something he wanted me to know about his life, some secret he had never told anyone. Hitman didn't know what to make of his words either and sent me back to ask Stayner directly.

When I asked Stayner what he meant by "more" he was cryptic.

"You know what I mean," he said. I could feel the tension rising inside me. The push-pull process of obtaining a confession is full of minefields. Ask the wrong question, make an erroneous assumption, push too hard or too fast and a suspect may shut down forever. I felt Stayner was subjecting me to another test and I needed to pass it.

"One more?" I asked, still thinking he must be referring to his uncle.

"More," he repeated, remaining sphinx-like. My mind raced, trying to recall any still open murder cases in the Yosemite area. All I could think of was the Sund-Pelosso killings, but my superiors had insisted that they had already arrested those responsible.

"Are you talking about the three tourists?" I asked with trepidation, and he slowly nodded. But before he would say any more he wanted something from me, something that rocked me back on my heels. This was not an attempt to plea bargain. He did not ask for any kind of deal or to even have the death penalty taken off the table but requested something extraordinary, something out of left field, and something I could not possibly deliver. We were on that fragile, delicate precipice together—the threshold of a confession—and one false move could send it crashing down. I had no idea how to get around the obstacle Cary Stayner was now placing in front of me. I went back to consult with Hitman again, for moral support and to strategize where to go from here. Hitman assured me that I could get through this, that everything I experienced in my life and career had prepared me for that moment.

The way I go about trying to obtain a confession is not based on anything I was taught at the FBI Academy or any particular school of thought and is almost the polar opposite of the controversial Reid Technique, the interrogation style taught in most police academies and used by law enforcement agencies, the military, and private security firms throughout the world. The Reid Technique has come increasingly under fire in recent years for inducing false confessions, and looking at some of its tenets I can see why that might be. In fact, the very first conviction in which the technique was trumpeted ended up being overturned decades later, and many instances of false confessions have been exposed in cases in which the technique was employed, including cases in which DNA testing by the Innocence Project later exonerated the defendants. The use of the Reid Technique with minors is especially controversial due to their greater susceptibility to coercion, and many European countries have prohibited its use on youths for fear of wrongful convictions.

Developed more than fifty years ago by John Reid, a Chicago cop who became a polygraph expert, the Reid Technique was meant to be a reform over the no-holds-barred practices used to extract confessions before that. Until the Supreme Court in the 1930s and 1940s began restricting what police could do to induce confessions, all sorts of what today we euphemistically call "harsh interrogation methods" were employed: from beatings to unremitting interrogation for days on end without letting the suspect get any sleep, to outright threats to kill the suspect if he didn't confess. Reid's idea was to bring more scientific methods, like those employed in polygraphy, into the interrogation process. In his approach, the interviewers become something like human lie detectors. For example, the interrogation may start with the detectives asking fairly innocuous questions to which they already know the answer, as one would do in getting a baseline polygraph reading, then move on to more aggressive questioning, all the while watching for physical signs of stress or evasion in the suspect's responses.

However, as any good polygrapher will tell you, physical manifestations of stress do not necessarily mean a person is guilty. And some behaviors the Reid Technique labels as signs of lying—looking down, folding one's arms, repetitively touching one's face, or tugging at clothing—could simply be personal tics or ingrained behavioral patterns that have nothing to do with anxiety, much less guilt. In fact, studies have shown that trained interrogators are no better than average citizens at detecting whether someone is lying from looking at nonverbal behavior. It is bad enough to rely too heavily on a failed polygraph as evidence of guilt. But for the Reid interrogators to rely on human lie detection—mere physical observation of what they believe to be signs of deception—is especially dangerous.

The Reid approach is so pervasive that even non-Reid interrogation manuals follow its basic principles. The trademarked Reid training lays out a series of nine escalating steps that are geared to overwhelm a suspect and wear him down, cutting off all attempts by the suspect to deny guilt. In fact, the suspect is allowed to do very little talking. Critics of the technique say that in a typical Reid interview, the interrogators do 90 percent of the talking and the suspect just 10 percent.

By the time the interrogator gets the suspect in "the box," having weeded out the obviously innocent, the person is assumed to be guilty. Rather than asking the interviewee to tell his story or explain what happened from the outset, the suspect is told that evidence already in hand clearly indicates guilt. This may be a complete lie. Interrogators following the Reid method may falsely tell a suspect that he failed a polygraph, or may lie that they have fingerprints or DNA or a slew of eyewitnesses that prove the suspect is responsible for the crime. The interviewer then moves on to a phase called theme development, during which the detective offers a series of hypothetical excuses or justifications that will reduce moral culpability in the suspect's mind in hopes of inducing a confession. The interrogator might suggest, depending upon the crime under investigation, that the killing of a child was an accident, or that a shooting was done in self-defense, or that a robbery was committed because the suspect just needed money to pay his bills. Proponents of the Reid Technique say that an innocent person will reject these scenarios, and that a guilty person will reject all but those that reflect his own feelings of justification for the crime.

As the phases of the interview continue, the Reid interrogator exerts ever more control. The questioning becomes rapid-fire and the suspect is cut off whenever he attempts to state a denial or speak at any length. The detective may continue to use lies to contradict any denials the suspect makes, such as falsely claiming to have witnesses to the crime, or implying a friend or confederate has given the person up when that has not happened. Questions are posed in a way that there are only two answers, one seemingly positive and one negative, but both constituting an admission of guilt. An example of this would be: "Have you molested other children before or is this the first time?" The detective may also use his own verbal and nonverbal language to pressure the suspect, such as expressing concern and understanding or moving physically closer to the interviewee to insinuate an emotional closeness. Tears from the suspect at this phase are viewed as an indicator of guilt.

In the final stages of obtaining a confession using the Reid Technique, elaborate themes offered earlier as justification or to reduce culpability are shortened or challenged altogether as the interrogator slowly tightens the noose, leaving the suspect less and less wiggle room in which to deny the crime. In this phase the detective is establishing complete dominance over the suspect, and dominance is measured by the cessation of denials. Under Reid's guidelines, the detective is supposed to stop the interrogation if he comes to believe any of the suspect's denials are true. However, it is easy to see how the innocent can be broken as they get further and further worn down, unable to get a word in edgewise, blocked at every turn. When the suspect finally confesses, the detective converts it into a written confession. Reid trainers encourage introducing a small mistake into the written confession that the suspect will then correct and initial, adding an even greater sense of authenticity to the document.

It probably seems unimaginable to the average person that anyone would ever confess to a crime he or she didn't commit, but it happens, and steps have to be taken to guard against it. There are disturbed individuals who come forward in nearly every high-profile case claiming responsibility due to delusional thinking or because they are seeking some kind of status and attention. There are other people, especially those who already have a criminal record, who assume they will be convicted anyway and confess to something they didn't do in hopes of getting a lighter punishment. And there are those who are broken down during the interrogation process and falsely confess out of fear, manipulation, or outright coercion.

Perhaps the most famous instance of false confessions occurred in almost epidemic fashion in what became known as the Central Park Jogger case. In 1989 a woman jogging in New York City's Central Park was raped, stabbed, and beaten so badly she was left in a coma for twelve days. She suffered brain damage and was not expected to survive, but she slowly recovered. The attack on her was so vicious that it made New York City a national symbol of urban violence run amok, and gave birth to the term "wilding" when the attack was blamed on a "pack" of juveniles police said entered the park at night with the express purpose of robbing, raping, and assaulting unsuspecting victims. Five teenage boys admitted to some degree of involvement in the attack on the jogger and implicated each other, although most of them quickly recanted their admissions, claiming they had been coerced into falsely confessing after police lied to them about evidence they claimed to possess and intimidated them. In 2001, a man already imprisoned for life for serial rape and murder claimed he was responsible for the attack on the jogger and acted alone. Semen from only one person had been found on the victim, and this man's DNA was a match to this profile. He also gave details of the crime that were corroborated by other evidence. At the behest of Manhattan District Attorney Robert Morgenthau, the convictions of all five of the boys who had already been sent to prison were vacated.

I don't profess to know what happened in the Central Park Jogger case and what may have gone wrong. But I do not believe in and would never employ some of the techniques advocated by Reid, like lying to suspects or engaging in role-playing scenarios that I view as counterproductive to eliciting truth and instead increase the likelihood of inducing false "admissions." I approach an interview—I hate to even use the word *interrogation*—not as a series of neatly articulated steps all leading in one direction but as a mutual exchange between suspect and detective.

Before forming any presumption in my mind or asking any kind of confrontational questions, I spend a lot of time trying to get to know the people I interview and to identify bedrock principles and values upon which we can agree. I can't sit in judgment of them or hold myself at some safe emotional distance. I have to be able to empathize with the suspects I interview on some level, to understand what they did from their perspective. I have to open my heart to them and expose my own vulnerability to search for their humanity—some nugget of good, something salvageable even in the most hardened criminals or seemingly lost souls. I look at what causes them to experience emotion and draw upon the source of that to help them see that, despite all the damage they have done, they can still help those they have hurt by telling the truth. Only by investing emotionally in them can I expect them to trust in me and put their fate in my hands.

In a pure psychopath like the man who killed eight-year-old Michael Lyons, there is no emotion to tap into, no kernel of humanity to leverage. But with most people there is something you can hook into in order to build rapport and positively engage with the suspect. We all want to believe our life has meaning, and what I do in interviews with suspects is help them see their value. By helping us solve the crime or leading us to the body of a missing victim their lives can still have value. I try to instill a sense that by telling the truth, providing answers and closure, they will be helping not just their victims but also themselves. This is not an empty promise, a con job just to get a confession. I truly believe that people in the grip of a compulsion to rape or murder children will actually feel more in control of their lives than they did when they were at the mercy of urges they were free to act out.

One of the steps of the Reid Technique is called "Expressing Empathy," but Reid uses empathy in a feigned and cynical manner, having interrogators suggest that they would have done the same thing under the circumstances in order to allow the suspect to confess because he felt his crime was justified. In my opinion, for someone in law enforcement to state such a position would be inappropriate for most crimes, and would certainly be inappropriate when dealing with crimes against children.

To box a suspect into a narrower and narrower frame and repeatedly cut him off, as the Reid Technique calls for, increases the chances of obtaining a false confession. You may get the answers you want, but will they be genuine? When I take a confession, I elicit as much detail as I can, both to look for consistency and to produce facts and evidence I can use to verify its authenticity. I walk the suspect through the story three different times, each from a different point of view, which deepens the narrative and provides ample opportunity to fill in holes or ferret out lies.

Initially I ask suspects for their observations and perspectives on the crime: what they saw, what they felt, what they remember. That version of the story I basically let suspects narrate, while interjecting questions to keep them on track and make them go deeper and provide more detail. One of the ways I gauge truth is by the level of detail. If people just give me a bare-bones story, I would be skeptical of its validity. But if they describe everything in the kind of detail that can be verified, I will be more likely to believe them.

In the second phase, I ask them to tell me what they think the victim was seeing and hearing. Not only do I need to know that to understand fully what happened, but it also makes offenders realize what they did to their victims, to acknowledge the pain and horror the victims experienced. Then, in the third phase, I want them to tell me what I would see if I were observing from outside the immediate event, so that I can see the crime through my own eyes and be able to investigate it and verify all the details thoroughly.

In these latter two phases I am much more active in driving the interview, asking very specific questions, probing deeper into their actions and motivations, looking for any holes or discrepancies, challenging anything that seems false or evasive or an attempt to diminish responsibility. I'm also questioning them at length about any evidence we will want to look for and all the facts we need to tie down to prove the case. I'm literally thinking in terms of the elements of the crime. This would include getting specifics about any weapon used and the location of the body or other evidence that had been concealed, as well as a detailed chronology of how the crime unfolded so that we can look for hard evidence such as blood, DNA, or surveillance footage to bolster our case.

After all that, I thank offenders for their cooperation, impress on them that they've done a really good thing, and then ask them if they will consider writing a letter of apology to their victims, the latter being a practice I picked up from Greg Stewart in the Frankie Proctor case. I've never gotten a letter of apology that didn't include something important or insightful that I missed during the interview. Taking responsibility in this way is another admission of guilt. If the confession should be attacked or excluded as evidence for any reason, the letter of apology is a statement of responsibility that can stand on its own. I hope it provides some comfort to the victim or the victim's loved ones. I also hope it helps perpetrators come to grips with what they've done and realize the positive step they have taken to set things right.

It was just Stayner and me alone in that interview room and he had dropped a bombshell, claiming responsibility not just for the killing of Joie Armstrong but also for the murders of Carole and Juli Sund and Silvina Pelosso. But now he was imposing conditions for his cooperation. I asked what he wanted. He spoke obliquely, like he didn't want his request to sound as bad as it was.

"You work all kinds of cases," he began, hemming and hawing as if he wanted me to fill in the blanks, like he did when he wanted me to guess what cases he was referring to when he said he could give me closure. Eventually he got around to the point. "I'd like to see pictures of little girls."

"Child pornography?" I asked, incredulous.

He wouldn't call it what it was, just said again, "You know, pictures and videos of little girls." He said he thought we might have such evidence stored in the building.

I could feel anger rising up inside me. I had felt a bond of trust and empathy growing between Stayner and me. He had allowed me to glimpse some of both the pain and the ugliness roiling inside him and had made the decision to reveal to me the terrible secrets he had been carrying so I could stop him from killing again. By putting conditions on his confession now, I worried that Stayner's motivation was not about "giving closure" and telling the truth because it was the right thing to do. Instead, it looked like he was seeing what he could get out of us—and not just something like a plea bargain, which would be understandable, but something so base and unspeakable even he couldn't say the words.

I needed to tamp down my own emotions and concentrate on the task at hand. Perhaps Stayner was still testing me, seeing if I would recoil in judgment of him. Or perhaps it was a battle for control, as serial killing and sexual assault are very much about control and dominance. Or perhaps it was even sadder, a last chance to satisfy a desperate craving. Whatever the reason, Stayner was asking me to do something illegal and unethical—to commit a crime to solve a crime—and I wasn't about to do that. But there we were, on that precipice, and I didn't want to risk him slipping from our grasp. I didn't know if we had any evidence against him and I worried that this could be our only chance to get a very dangerous man off the streets. I told him I had no authority to grant his request and I would pass it on to a higher authority.

I went out to talk to Hitman and he was taken aback as much as I was by Stayner's demand. He said he would pass it up the chain of command, but neither of us could imagine any scenario under which we could show Stayner such material. We would have to appeal to the "good Cary" I had already glimpsed, who was now in a final desperate battle with his dark side. Hitman suggested we move the interview to the polygraph room, which had recording equipment and a two-way mirror through which he and others could monitor the interrogation. Harry Sweeney had already set up in there for the polygraph before Stayner called it off, and we had Harry remove all his equipment, then brought in Stayner. I decided we would eat lunch first to buy some time to get our heads together. When John brought in the pizza we had ordered I asked Stayner if it was OK for John to join us and he agreed.

I invited John to stay not only because he is a great agent but also because he was a good friend and I feel more comfortable in a high-stakes situation like that with someone I trust. I wasn't in there alone anymore. John was in the room with me. Hitman and Harry were on the other side of the glass and at breaks I would go to them for guidance. I felt particularly good about having Harry looking over my shoulder because he is an expert at detecting when someone is not being truthful. Interrogations are so nerve-wracking and emotionally draining that it is hard to maintain focus at all times. So even though I was taking the lead, it was important to have others around to challenge my own assumptions, pick up on mistakes I might make, bring their own insights, and point out things I might overlook. We had a big day in front of us, but we would get through it together.

As John and I ate lunch with Stayner he began to get morose, aware he was potentially setting himself up for execution.

"This is gonna be my last pizza," he said. I tried to buck him up, told him he was a long way from that day, should it ever come. "Never got to see *Star Wars*," he continued, as random thoughts of things he enjoyed in freedom began popping into his mind.

I tried to assure him that not only would he be giving a gift by telling the truth but also that he would be getting something in return: relief.

"You're going to feel good," I said. "Not good," I corrected myself, "but you're going to feel peaceful—probably a feeling you haven't had in a long time."

"It means I can die with a clear conscience now, whenever that day comes," Stayner said. "I know they're going to give me the death penalty. Even if I confess, they are going to give me death."

Joie

I promised Stayner I would be there for him as long as it took, as far as it went. I asked him to stop and think about how what he was doing now was as close as he could come to giving life back.

"It's weird because I love life so much," he said, without a hint of irony. One minute, he said, he'd be enjoying time with friends, marveling at nature, and thinking high-minded thoughts, "and the next minute it's like I could kill every person on the face of the earth."

"It just mentally tortures you," he went on to say, "constantly back and forth like a tennis match."

"But this is over now," I told him. "You have taken control today. You are controlling you, probably for the first time since you were eleven."

I asked him if his family knew about the tremendous internal issues with which he was struggling. He said he had never told anyone until now, not even his closest friends.

"Well, don't you think it's time we dealt with this and get rid of these demons?" I asked him. In the end, I said, "Whether I live longer than you or you live longer than me, we'll both know we did what we thought was right and we took control, and that is the bottom line."

His anguish was palpable. He had first started imagining scenarios of harming women and girls when he was just six or seven years old. The thoughts were alarmingly sadistic even at a young age—he imagined having a neighbor girl trapped in an underground bunker when he was just eight—and became only more so as he grew older. He was thirty-seven now, and for over three decades a war had waged inside him.

The thoughts and fantasies that consumed him preceded his brother Steven's kidnapping, when Stayner was eleven, and his own sexual victimization, which happened about six months thereafter. Those experiences certainly were damaging and poured fuel on a fire that had already begun to smolder as Stayner grew up in an environment rife with dysfunction and twisted sexuality. According to a psychiatrist who would later evaluate Stayner for his defense team, the Stayner family tree was riven with mental illness and sexual abuse going back five generations. According to the psychiatrist's report, Stayner's father, Delbert Stayner, was ordered into therapy for molesting his own daughters. In addition to her father's unwanted advances, one of Stayner's sisters said that Cary started peeping on her and inappropriately touching her when she was ten. A cousin said that Stayner spied on her and his sisters and a neighbor girl, hiding under their beds and secretly videotaping them in the bathroom and bedroom. One relative described child sexual abuse as "like a family sickness" because it had been going on for so many generations.

The fact that Stayner's brother was kidnapped by a pedophile and abused for seven years adds an almost unfathomable dimension to the tragedy that enveloped this family. As the older brother, Stayner felt a natural if undeserved sense of responsibility for not protecting Steven from harm. He also felt more directly responsible. Stayner told another psychiatrist, Park Dietz, who was hired by the prosecution to evaluate whether he was sane at the time he committed the Yosemite murders, that as a child he worried that the obsessive thoughts he had about holding the neighbor girl against her will somehow caused Steven to be kidnapped.

Stayner's parents would testify at trial that they both withdrew emotionally after Steven went missing. Delbert swung between all-consuming efforts to find his missing son and suicidal depression. He was so bereft when Steven was taken that he pushed Cary away, saying his "real son" was gone. Stayner's mother, Kay, said her own father had told her to view Steven's kidnapping as a good thing because now she had fewer kids to worry about feeding and clothing. She said her father insisted she never cry or show emotion because it would make her appear "crazy" like her mother, and that she had raised her own kids with the lack of emotional warmth her father inculcated in her.

Despite it all, Stayner loved his family and knew that what they were about to learn about him would destroy them. He started putting other terms on the confession. He wanted his family to get the $250,000 reward the Carrington family had offered, and he wanted to be housed in a federal prison being built near his hometown of Merced. John and I told him that those latter two requests were completely out of our hands. The distribution of the reward was not up to the FBI but the Carrington family (and I could imagine no scenario in which they would agree to pay it out to the killer's own family). Nor could we ensure which prison Stayner would be sent to if convicted because, although the Armstrong case had federal jurisdiction because the murder was committed in a national park, the Sund-Pelosso case was a state matter. We knew we couldn't deliver on any of his demands and tried to get him to prioritize what was really important to him. But he kept reiterating that the porn was his number one request and, in fact, a deal breaker. He even got particular, saying he didn't want to see just a few stills but a big stack of pictures and especially videos.

I excused myself to talk with Hitman about what had just occurred. I also needed a little time to cool off. I called Lori and told her that I had no idea when or if I was going to get home that night. I told her that I was either on the verge of getting the biggest confession of my career or about to screw it all up.

I tried to put aside my feelings of frustration and disappointment as to the condition Stayner set for confessing and figure out how we were going to get around this impossible request. I reminded myself that he was the one who initiated this process, who offered us closure. I could not judge him. Instead, I needed to encourage and support the side of him that wanted to do the right thing.

I understood that realizing he was facing death or at best life in prison, another thing he was cognizant of losing was any chance of acting out the fantasies that drove him. I knew enough about sex offenders from all the interviews I had performed and attended that there is a fantasy they are chasing at the heart of their behavior. Their fantasies are highly particularized, as individual as a fingerprint. Pornography gives vision to their fantasies, feeds and fuels them. Masturbating to pornography reinforces the fantasies, and the compulsion to act them out was a classic example of operant conditioning. I usually don't even need to ask a sex offender what his fantasy is; it is obvious from his pornography stash. I've seen sex offenders living in complete squalor and chaos but the directory to the child porn collection on their computers is meticulously organized by age and "theme," a virtual psychological fingerprint.

Cary Stayner was not the first person I had met who was willing to sell his life for child pornography. Anybody who purchases child porn or exchanges images online with others is risking their freedom to see it. In perhaps the most emotionally devastating case I ever worked, an eighteen-year-old boy who knew he was about to be arrested for possessing a cache of Internet child porn made the horrific decision that if he was going to prison anyway he was going to do something to "make it worthwhile." Before being picked up he went out and acted on his fantasy and abducted, raped, and killed a twelve-year-old girl named Courtney Sconce.

Stayner said he had never seen child pornography, had been too afraid to seek it out. It was hard to know at the time whether he was telling the truth. I don't believe he owned a computer, and even if he had, Internet child porn was not as accessible as it is today. He was at the end of the line and wanted to see something that could fuel his fantasies for the rest of his life.

"It's just something that . . . that's closure for me in that respect," he pleaded. "It's perverted, it's sick, it's disgusting. I know all those things, but it's just . . . it's gotta be one of the conditions, otherwise I . . . I can't go to prison for the rest of my life and, sorry to say, be happy."

I now know Stayner had at least one experience with child pornography and it had a profound effect on him. The man who sexually abused Cary used pictures of naked girls in a magazine to groom Cary and some of his other male cousins. In his interview with Dr. Dietz, Cary talked about being "enthralled" by a particular picture of naked girls who were around ten or eleven years old. He mentioned the same picture in a phone call he made to someone from jail that was tape recorded, saying he had been "fixated" on the image ever since. It reminds me of how heroin addicts talk about how they are always chasing in vain that first high, that it is never as good as that first time. Maybe that is why serial killers keep killing. Nothing ever lives up to the fantasy they have honed to perfection in their minds over the years. Stayner told us specifically that his crimes did not live up to the fantasy he was attempting to replicate.

Stayner's latest conditions seemed less selfishly motivated than his first. The request for the reward seemed genuinely driven by his feelings for his family.

"My parents aren't . . . they're not well-off people," he said sheepishly. His dad by that time had lost his cannery job and his parents had given up their home and were living in a trailer outside Merced. He also mentioned having a nephew confined to a wheelchair who needed help. The third demand, to be housed close to where his family lived, was probably mostly to make visits less burdensome on his parents.

Joie

What hung in the air, I believe, was the sense of shame Stayner felt for what he was about to inflict on them. They had been through so much with Steven's kidnapping and subsequent death, and now they would, either actually or effectively, depending on whether Stayner was given the death penalty, be losing their other son. I tried to reach that Cary, the one who was capable of love and the deep feelings he had expressed during our car ride and just before offering closure. It hurt my heart to hear him now use the term closure in a self-interested way, as satisfying his fixation. Still, I believed he was not completely devoid of humanity. He had brutally, savagely killed four women, but he appeared to have some sliver of conscience.

I told him, and I firmly believe this, that he was not a psychopath. He asked what the definition of a psychopath was and I told him that it was someone without any remorse, concern, or conscience. "A psychopath is a person that can kill a three-year-old girl at two o'clock in the afternoon and report for work at four," I said.

"That's basically what I did," Stayner responded.

"Yes, but look at what you're doing now," I reminded him. A psychopath is someone who will never react to anything emotionally, whose conditions will only be about himself, who has absolutely no concern about anyone in his life. A psychopath doesn't think of his brother and break down or seek to feel better by telling the truth, because psychopaths don't feel anything at all. And the fact that he was offering to help us meant that there was good in him.

"You're doing the hardest, bravest thing in your life and I'm honored you trusted me to do it with," I told him.

John and I still didn't know for sure whether Stayner had anything to do with either case or whether he was just scamming us, like I thought Rufus Dykes was, and his obstinacy concerning his demands was worrying. I suspected at that point he probably did kill Joie, but I was less sure about the murders of Carole, Juli, and Silvina because of all the assurances the FBI had made. At one point, in frustration, I told him that we already had pretenders to the throne and asked why I should believe him. John put it even more directly. How could we trust that Stayner wasn't just some guy who wanted to see if he could get the FBI to show him kiddie porn?

Still holding back from completely showing his hand, Stayner offered to give us some facts to convince us that he was responsible for the Sund-Pelosso killings. I asked if there was more than one person involved in their murders and he said no. I was treading carefully because I didn't want to feed him any information he didn't actually possess but instead get him to tell us something only the killer would know. I told him I would give him one word and he should be able to explain to me its significance. The word I said was "bank," referring to the attempts to access Mrs. Sund's account.

"Bank?" Stayner repeated, with genuine incredulity. It was clear he knew nothing about the bank activity.

"Now I'm concerned," I said, worried that maybe he really was just playing us. "There are people that come in all the time who want to confess to things they didn't do," I said with some irritation.

"I didn't use any of the cards, I threw 'em out the window," Stayner responded, defensively. "There was no bank ever involved."

"All right," I said. "Give us one thing that no one knows, which you know." "Shaved pubic hair," Stayner answered immediately.

I sighed and tried to steady myself. I knew what that might mean to a pedophile, to a guy who wanted his victims to look prepubescent. I felt a little queasy to think of how that might fit into the Sund-Pelosso murders, but I had no knowledge about that fact so I asked him to tell us something we would more readily know. Stayner was hesitant to offer any more, so I went further out on a limb.

"Sometimes people make admissions and they don't say who they are, they do it anonymously," I said. "Have you ever done anything anonymously?"

Stayner answered again immediately. "Wrote a letter," he said, to the FBI at the DoubleTree Hotel in Modesto.

The letter and map to Juli's body had never been publicized. His answer and the authority with which he said it made it seem unlikely that this was merely a lucky guess. It also raised a host of questions in my mind. Why did he write that letter when he was seemingly in the clear? Why did he want Juli's body to be found? But I couldn't ask him those questions because he was still holding out for his demands. We had to get beyond this impasse.

An informal photo of Cary Stayner taken at the FBI's Sacramento office before he confessed to all four murders.

Stayner's sandal tread matched foot impressions found outside Joie Armstrong's house. He was wearing these sandals when my partners and I brought him in for questioning (visible in the photo snapped in our office).

The "25 MPH Beach" curve, a nude swimming area where sheriff's deputies and park rangers encountered Cary Stayner and asked to search his vehicle and backpack. His reluctance to turn over the backpack made them fear Joie's decapitated head might be inside and they decided to wait for a warrant before opening it.

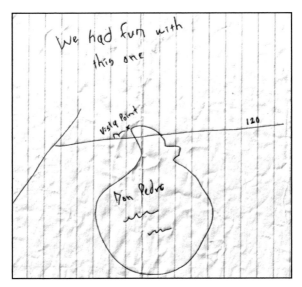

A hand-drawn map Cary Stayner sent anonymously to the FBI, indicating where Juli Sund's body could be found: downhill from a vista point above Lake Don Pedro. Stayner had gone to great efforts to distance himself from his crimes—destroying and/or staging evidence to misdirect our investigation. The fact that he sent such a letter and wanted this particular victim to be found provided rich insight into his psychology.

Aerial view over Don Pedro Lake where Juli Sund's body was found. After driving around for hours with Juli, wishing he could "keep" her but realizing that was not possible, Stayner slit her throat and hid her body under brush.

Cary Stayner and me inside Joie's cabin, where he agreed to reenact the crime on videotape the day after confessing all four Yosemite murders to me.

Stayner with Tuolumne County Sheriff's Deputy Tim Reed (left) and me during the re-creation of Juli Sund's murder at Don Pedro Lake. Keeping his word, he led us directly to evidence, including where he stashed the murder weapons, that definitively proved his guilt.

Surveillance video we retrieved at a highway pullout captured Cary Stayner driving Juli Sund to her death at Don Pedro Lake in the missing tourists' rental car. Carole and Silvina, already deceased, were in the trunk at the time that picture was taken.

02-16-01 FRI 000
06:20:54 72

A re-creation done by the FBI at the same hour of night, using a car of the same make and model as the rental car, matches eerily with the image picked up by the surveillance camera.

Nearly twenty years after the crime, a bouquet of artificial flowers remains affixed to a post at the trailhead leading to the spot where Juli Sund was murdered.

A marker erected near Joie Armstrong's cabin has become a shrine to her memory, with people leaving stones, shells, and other gifts of nature in her honor.

Sketch by courtroom artist Vicki Behringer of when I took the stand at Stayner's preliminary hearing in the Armstrong case. As the taped confession was played and Cary heard himself describe the terrible things he had done, he sobbed, buried his face in his hands, and attempted to blot out his own words by plugging his ears with his fingers.

U.S. Department of Justice
Federal Bureau of Investigation
Sacramento Division

Oct 2, 1996

Jeff,

If one of my children ever went missing I'd want you to be the person looking for them. I think that says it all.

I'm proud that you're my friend.

Don.

A letter from Don Pierce, the FBI supervisor who put me on the road to working missing children cases.

Joie

I told Stayner that I was afraid he was using us and wouldn't come through with his side of the deal even if we did meet his terms. I asked if his concern was for himself, his family, or the victims.

"Most . . . mostly my family," he stammered. Of course, I wished his greatest motivation was to do right by the victims. But I appreciated his honesty. That's what matters most in a confession. I don't want a suspect to tell me something because they think it's what I want to hear. I want only the truth.

I told him there was something he hadn't asked for that I promised to do for him. I reminded him how in the car when we talked about his brother's kidnapping I told him that I felt that those who took Steven victimized not just the boy they stole but also the whole Stayner family. And now his family was about to be victimized again.

"By me this time," Stayner said. He hung his head and began to cry.

"One of your conditions is looking out for your family," I said. "So maybe that's where we ought to focus." I told him that as soon as we were done I would go down personally to talk to his parents and break the news to them before they heard about it in the media and try and help comfort them and prepare them for what was to come. What would it be like for them, I asked Stayner, if I had to tell them that before doing the right thing their son demanded to see child pornography?

Stayner made one last plea, the saddest one of all to me, as it showed so nakedly the compulsive drive at the heart of pedophilia—a need greater than life itself. What harm was there in showing him a little child pornography, he said, using those words for the first time, compared to the murders of four people?

I know exactly how much harm there is. The children in those pictures are real child victims; I've known some of those kids. Just viewing what I've had to look at to investigate Internet pornography cases has harmed me. There was no way I was going to sit there and watch child porn with Cary Stayner even if it meant losing the confession.

Instead, I asked him if he would be willing, as a gesture of good faith, to begin telling us about Joie's killing while we waited to hear from the U.S. Attorney about his request. At last he agreed.

In the Name of the Children

At this point I need to confess my own shame. I started off by asking Cary, "Are you the one who murdered"—and then I broke off the sentence. "I don't even know her name," I uttered in horror. We had been calling Joie's murder "the Yosemite Case" all day and I realized at that moment that I still did not know the victim's name because I had not worked the investigation at all. I worried that someday her mother would hear this taped confession played in court and feel I had disrespected her daughter's memory.

I located Joie's name and a photo of her. In the picture her hair was in pigtails and I learned that was the way she wore it on the day she died. She rarely wore makeup and with her fresh-scrubbed looks she appeared much younger than her twenty-six years. In fact, someone who knew her from her previous job said she fit right in with the kids she accompanied on weeklong nature camps. I wondered if that was what had attracted Cary to her, but he claimed not to remember the pigtails, the rare detail of any of his crimes that he was unable to recall with exactitude. He denied knowing her or ever having seen her before the day he killed her. If this is true, she had the horrendously bad luck—like the three tourists at Cedar Lodge did, like Michael Lyons and Julie Connell did—of fitting the victim profile a killer craved.

Serial killers and sexual predators are on the hunt all the time, ever vigilant, scanning the horizon for victims that fit their very particularized fantasy type. For Ted Bundy it was young women with long brown hair parted down the middle. For Jeffrey Dahmer it was young men and boys he could rape in a necrophilic manner, by either drugging them into unconsciousness or actually killing them before having sex with them. Stayner's sexual fixation was with girls from about age ten to fifteen. His killing fantasy, which he would explain to me later in the interview, was even more specific—and tragically the Sund-Pelosso group fit that fantasy to a T.

From the top of the canyon, before you even begin to descend down the windy road from the highway into Foresta, you can see two buildings all by themselves on the edge of what people call Big Meadow: a barn, and nearby it, the Green House. It is such a picturesque setting that the two structures are captured in a lot of advertising photographs of the park. Stayner had been coming to Yosemite all his life. He got his love for the place as a kid going there with his family. I let Stayner first tell the story his way, and his narrative begins rather bizarrely with his own purported monster sighting. He claimed he saw Bigfoot in that barn in Foresta one day in 1982. I have to admit, when he started off talking about a fictional creature I groaned inside, wondering if he was just some crazy wasting our time. Stayner said he heard that barn had recently been rebuilt and after spending the afternoon of July 21, 1999, sunbathing nude at a favorite spot not far from there he decided to swing by the barn and check it out.

Foresta Road ends at a little bridge just past Joie's house that had been washed out and can no longer handle the weight of vehicles. He said he stopped at that bridge and was throwing rocks into the creek when he saw Joie moving in and out of the Green House, loading duffel bags into the back of her little truck.

"And I just noticed her," he said. "There she is, you know, fairly attractive girl."

It seemed to Stayner that she was alone, but to verify that he walked up the street past the house toward the barn to get a better look, then walked back and engaged her in conversation to make sure. He described this as "doing research." In law enforcement we call it stalking. She was on the porch watering her plants and he told her how long he'd been coming to Yosemite and that he had seen her house many times but didn't know if people lived there. He complimented its appearances, saying how nicely it had been fixed up, all the while inching up the path closer to the porch.

It chilled my blood how quickly he was able to hone in and ascertain the crucial fact he wanted to know, without setting off any alarms for Joie. He told her he had seen Bigfoot in that area and asked if she had ever seen the creature or heard anything about it. She said no but maybe her roommates had, probably making a joke or just trying to be polite. Stayner asked if any of them were around for her to go ask and she said no one else was home.

The moment she turned her back on him he pulled out a gun that had been shoved into the back of his waistband and hidden under his shirt. She turned around and saw the gun "and freaked out," but Stayner pushed her into the house and duct taped her hands behind her back and gagged her with the tape as well. He told her he wasn't going to hurt her, that he just wanted money and needed her to cooperate. But I believe that when Stayner pulled out the duct tape she knew that it wasn't about money. She began fighting him and it took a while to subdue her enough to bind her; she even managed to rip through the bindings twice. He then gripped her by the arm and walked her outside to his truck, which was parked down by the bridge. As they passed her truck he took the keys she had left in the trunk lock and shut the open hatch. When they got to his Scout he lifted her up, put her in the backseat, and tried to make her lie down, covering her with a sleeping bag.

Stayner told us he planned to take her to the backside of a hill away from any of the other houses in Foresta in order to sexually assault her. He flipped a U-turn, but as he drove she kept fighting, kicking and screaming through her gag and trying to sit up. Stayner was starting to panic. She was disrupting his fantasy and challenging his control. He pulled a knife out of his back pocket to threaten her into submission, but she continued to fight him with the ferocity of a tiger. He had only driven 200 to 300 yards when suddenly, to his astonishment, Joie managed to vault herself headfirst out the open passenger-side window of the Scout. I still can't imagine how she was able to do this. It seems superhuman to me and I can only attribute it to her tremendous will to live.

Joie hit the ground, then scrambled to her feet and started running. I suspect she made her break then, knowing they were near other houses in that area and she hoped she could get help. Stayner mused about how close they were at that moment to other cabins and how if someone had been looking out a window or sitting on their deck things might have gone very differently. Stayner slammed his truck into park, jumped out, and gave chase. When he caught up to her they were still in an area in plain view of some of the residences, so he tried to drag her to a more secluded area but she kept up her fight.

At this point, as far as Stayner's fantasy went, all was lost. I'm not saying he wasn't going to kill Joie all along. It was always going to end in her death and he admitted that to me. But maybe Stayner was a little different than other serial killers, in my opinion, in that he wanted control but he also wanted submission and cooperation from his victims. He desperately wanted to believe, and deluded himself to an extraordinary degree in the case of Juli, that he could have a mutual, loving relationship with someone he was holding against her will. Stayner came across to me as desperate for intimacy. I think he felt a kind of intimacy with me and that was why he agreed to confess to me. While many serial killers are sadists who enjoy torturing and terrorizing their victims and get off on inflicting pain, Stayner seemed more like a classic pedophile, who desperately wanted to believe that his victims want to be with him. He wanted them to pleasure him, and he actually believed he gave them sexual pleasure while forcing himself on them.

With the ultimate fantasy he wished for no longer possible, he moved on to the mortal alternative to regain control. He took out his knife and slit her throat. According to Stayner, she didn't die from the first cut and he continued to drag her into more obscured terrain, where he "finished the job." He then dragged her even further into the brush, down to a creek, and then ran up to park his truck, which was still sitting in the middle of the road with its engine running. As remarkable as it is to me that a few lucky breaks after Joie's killing quickly set law enforcement on Stayner's trail, it breaks my heart that no one happened by or heard or saw anything during this chaotic scene that might have scared Stayner off and saved Joie's life.

He said he went back down to the creek, and then he fell silent and didn't speak further for some time. I had to prompt him to continue with his narrative.

"And I cut her head off," he finally said. He removed the duct tape from Joie's wrists and head, then climbed into the water and tried to conceal Joie's body under some reeds and other vegetation. I asked what he did with her head, because I felt the beheading was highly significant. He said he washed the blood off her face and hair in the creek water, speaking as if in reverie. I asked what he did with it after that.

"Just kind of looked at it a couple times, didn't do anything with it, basically just kind of amazed at what I'd just done," he said.

I thought the head was more significant than that but decided to leave it there for now and walk him through the crime again from the beginning as I shifted to the more directive phase of the interview. A lot of what I asked Stayner in this stage about his thinking and preparation were things I had learned from previous cases I had worked and from specialized FBI trainings over the years, from the meetings with paroled sex offenders, and from the Sacramento Sheriff's Department's Child Abuse Bureau, where Steve Hill and Mona Feuillard worked and that was really on the cutting edge in investigating crimes against children. Apparently, some in the growing crowd of agents and supervisors that began filling the observation room as the day progressed, and word got around about what was unfolding, thought I must be a rapist or a serial killer myself to know some of the things I seemed to know about how a guy like Stayner would operate—like the fact that he would have put together a "kidnap-and-kill kit" and carried it with him everywhere he went in order to be ready to go when the opportunity presented itself.

I told Stayner I wanted to understand his fantasy, knowing it would be at the core of everything he did. I asked him when he first started feeling anxiety that day. At first he seemed not to understand the question, and then he grasped what I was getting at: that tension that starts building when predator spots prey and decides to attack. He admitted that as soon as he saw her, when he was down by the bridge, he knew what he was going to do.

"So there was never a time where you were looking for Bigfoot or you were just out there cruising around," I said. "You were out there because you had a need. Is that correct?" Stayner nodded in agreement. "And when you saw her you felt she would fit your need?" I continued, and he nodded again.

I asked him if he had a "kit" with him that day and he said he did, which he went back to his car and retrieved after doing his "research" around Joie's house. It was in his backpack and on the day he attacked Joie it included a gun, a knife, a roll of duct tape, and a camera.

"So, Cary, part of understanding yourself is to understand that this was in your backpack, you had these items, not because it hit you in the moment but because you had a constant—" Before I could even finish my sentence Stayner broke in, agreeing with and elaborating on my own thought.

"I was looking forward to it," he said.

"In terms of a drive, a devotion in your life, a commitment," I started to say and then switched to the words he had used earlier, describing himself as obsessive-compulsive. "To what degree would you say that you're obsessive-compulsive about, not this girl, but about finding someone like this in general?"

"Very," he said emphatically.

"Is it something that you feel occupied most of your thought process?"

"Every waking moment."

"And is it something that you fantasized about?"

"Quite a while," he said.

"Are there other people you have researched?" I asked.

"Yes," he said evenly. He spoke in a way I thought might be referring to Carole and the girls while still wanting to hold back on talking about that case. So I asked if any of the people he "researched" were still alive. Yes, he said. I felt even queasier learning that there had been other intended victims, but I was relieved to hear they had escaped Joie's fate. I wanted to ask more about that, but I felt I needed to be careful not to push things further than Stayner was willing to go at that moment. Taking a confession is kind of like a dance. You can't rush the tempo; you have to listen and let things flow, sometimes leading, sometimes following. My first priority was finding out everything I could about the case at hand, so I made a mental note to come back to that line of inquiry later.

I took Stayner through the attack on Joie again. I asked him what his specific intent was and he said, "To take her out of the house and to sexually molest her, I guess. I never . . ." It sounded like he was about to deny that he intended to kill her after getting whatever sexual gratification he could get from her, but I felt the need to stop and correct him about something else first. I was taking the risk of antagonizing him, but this point was important to me.

Joie was an adult, I told him, so "it's not a molest, it's an assault." I think the fact that he used the term molest confirmed that he saw Joie, at least in his mind, as a child, the girl in his fantasies.

"What was your fantasy about what you would do with her?" I asked.

"Just total control," he responded.

"If you could have whatever you wanted at that point, what would you have wanted?" I asked.

"For her to be submissive," he said, to go along easily with whatever he asked.

He had told me when he first asked to speak to me alone that he had suffered from impotency most of his life. Penetration was virtually out of the question and maintaining an erection for oral sex was even difficult, but that is what he kept hoping would give him the satisfaction that eluded him. Sexual dysfunction is actually not uncommon among serial sex killers, perhaps in part because many of them were abused themselves as children. For some, the violence and aggression is so arousing that it overcomes what they would not be able to achieve in normal consensual relations. According to Stayner, it did not work that way for him. He claimed no physical or sexual relief after his crimes, but I think the hope that he would fueled his attacks—the idea that he would one day achieve the release he fantasized about.

He claimed to get no sexual or emotional thrill from killing either, that it was just something that had to be done when everything else was over because he "had nowhere to keep them." But I don't know what I really believe about that. His answers were sometimes inconsistent. At one point he said, "To tell you the truth, I think this sex thing was just an excuse. It was the killing that was . . ." and he drifted off without finishing that thought. At another point he threw up his hands.

"These are questions I haven't even asked myself," he said. He finally described killing, the final denouement, as relieving the pent-up anxiety inside him similar to the way his compulsive hair pulling helped him relieve stress. What he claimed he felt most when all was said and done was exhaustion because of the struggle Joie had put up and how things had gotten so out of control. He said he expected to be caught because he hadn't had time to cover his tracks—literally. He knew he had left tire tracks and footprints behind at Joie's house. He realized later that he had also lost his sunglasses that day during the struggle—the broken pair we found on Joie's porch.

I got back around to the beheading. It was such an extreme act, and the fact that he held on to Joie's head for some amount of time thereafter begged a lot of questions. He said he didn't hunt or fish because he couldn't stand gutting dead animals. He claimed that even roadkill repulsed him and he would have to look away if he saw a dead animal on the roadside. Yet he said that cutting off this vibrant woman's head "didn't bother [him] a bit." He even considered cutting her up into little pieces.

Joie

I had wondered if his deep slashing of Juli's throat had been an attempt at a beheading and with Joie he had perfected his technique. I asked why he had cut Joie's head off, what he was trying to accomplish.

"Oh, God, there is no meaning at all as far as I know, just . . . compulsive thoughts that progress," he said. The thoughts, he explained, never stay at the same level but keep escalating in intensity. I asked him what he was thinking at the precise moment he decapitated Joie and he said he just wanted to do "the most revolting thing [he] could possibly do."

The great FBI profilers, like John Douglas, Roy Hazelwood, and Robert Ressler, based much of their science on interviews they conducted with serial killers. They noted that over time, the window between killings often narrows while the level of violence increases. It's almost like an addiction: what once sufficed is no longer enough to satisfy them. They may move from targeting single victims to killing multiple victims in one fell swoop, like Bundy at the end, or, like Dahmer, they may progress from just killing to dismemberment and cannibalism. Stayner's bloodlust was clearly increasing, reaching a frenzied state, even though he described the actual act of killing in clinical, dispassionate terms—"cold-blooded" and "matter-of-fact," to use his words.

I asked Stayner why he washed Joie's face afterward. He said he just wanted to see her face. I think he coveted the head. Because he couldn't "keep" a whole live woman, maybe he thought he could keep part of one. I asked him if he thought of keeping the head and he said yes, which he thought was weird because he was not much of a "trophy hunter."

"There's a difference between a souvenir and a trophy," I told him. "A souvenir is something you take to remind you of the moment. A trophy is something you take because you accomplished something." Which did he think taking the head would have been?

"It would have been a trophy most likely," he admitted.

Ultimately, I believe he beheaded Joie for a couple of reasons: as an expression of power and control but also, in a very twisted sense, of intimacy. I think the desire to keep the head was a desire for intimacy. I also think that washing her hair and cleaning her face was almost like an attempt to revive Joie, to make her appear lifelike so he could pretend that she wanted to be with him.

When he decided to leave the head at the scene he first put it into the creek face up but then decided to turn it over face down. I wondered if that meant he had some feeling of affection or tenderness toward his victim. "So you cared about her?" I asked.

"I couldn't have cared . . . too much by killing her," he responded. In fact, he claimed the reason he decided to turn the head over was not to scare anyone who might discover it.

I asked him if he ever felt at any time during the attack on Joie that he could have stopped himself.

"Once you get the ball rolling, you can't stop," he said.

From time to time during the interview he seemed to retreat back to the contention that he hadn't necessarily planned to kill Joie when things started, or at least that he hadn't thought it through in his mind. I think this was a form of denial on his part, and I did not want him to get away with the notion that Joie's actions were in any way responsible for her death. He wanted her to cooperate because that was his perfect fantasy. Her resistance was heroic. It caused him to be caught. And it may very well have saved her life if she had been able to get closer to one of the houses nearby when she catapulted herself from his car. So I wanted to clear up this point one more time with him before we ended that portion of the interview.

"Once you had control of her, did she ever have a hope of living?" I asked. Stayner didn't respond verbally, but he shook his head no.

It was time to ask him if he would be willing to write a letter of apology. I asked him if he felt bad about what he had done and if he would undo the crimes he had committed if he could.

"Of course, all of them," he said. I asked him to write a letter of apology to Joie, telling him I thought it would be therapeutic. I strongly wanted that letter for Joie's family, but I also wanted it for Stayner's sake. I had, in effect, taken everything away from him: his freedom and perhaps his life, but also his secrets, his denials and justifications, all the artifice that allowed him to live with what he had done. To me, a letter of apology is a reckoning with truth, and I hoped it would be the first step to putting the pieces of his life back together in an honest and healthy way. He said he couldn't do it right now and I didn't know if that meant he was refusing or just needed more time. If he didn't write the letter, I told him, it would make me think he didn't feel bad about what he had done.

"Cary, we've been here for a long time together," I said. "You've shed tears, I've seen your reaction. You're not the type of person that took Steven."

"I became that person, though," Stayner replied, sounding desolate.

"You did," I had to acknowledge. "But you're doing something that they didn't; you're coming back from the edge." Writing a letter of apology would be coming to terms with what he had done, I said. Writing it would be the hardest thing he had ever done, but the best thing he could do for the victim.

"I'll try," he said.

At that point I was exhausted and we hadn't even gotten to the Sund-Pelosso killings. I went out to talk to Hitman about what we should do next. The U.S. Attorney had confirmed what I knew all along: we would not be able to meet Stayner's demand. I went back to Stayner and put it in the bluntest terms. I told him that we would not show him any child pornography, that to do so would be coercive even though he was the one who was attempting to extort us. Now that I knew he sent the "We had fun with this one" letter, I told him we most likely already had evidence we could use against him for the tourists' murders, such as hairs and DNA from the letter.

"My DNA's not on the letter," he said confidently.

"How do you know that?" I asked.

"I know."

"Did you write the letter?" I asked.

He refused to answer, shrugging his shoulders in a "that's for me to know and you to find out" way. He was still bargaining and I was getting fed up with it, but even worse I began to wonder if he had lied when he told us he was solely responsible for the Sund-Pelosso murders.

"Let's put it this way," he finally said. "My handwriting is not on the letter."

"What you're telling me is that there were other people involved," I said, thinking maybe Maddock was right after all.

No one else was involved, Stayner insisted.

I was tired, exasperated, and fed up with his games. I showed him a picture of Carole, Juli, and Silvina.

"Do these people look familiar?" I asked him. "Do they bring back memories? Hard memories?" He nodded in assent to my questions but remained silent. "They're still not resting in peace and their families are certainly not resting in peace." He held the cards on that case and he knew it, and rather than vie for control I felt it was important to support and encourage his sense of agency. He alone had the power to end this nightmare for everyone and he needed to take control, not of others anymore but of himself, for the first time in maybe forever.

"The hard part is over," I said, "and it's your choice for your family, for these families, for us, but most importantly, Cary, for yourself. Do you understand that? I want you to understand that because if you decide not to make this choice, I need to go home and look at my family and know that I did everything I could to try and help your family." I could tell Stayner was struggling within himself. He covered his face with his hands, shifted in his chair, and his breathing was audible. I kept talking and he remained silent for what felt like forever, probably just a minute or two, but it was the longest he had been silent all day and his silence was agonizing. Finally, he tilted his head up, leaned back in his chair, and said, "Let's do it."

Just like we did with Joie's murder, I told him first to walk us through what happened with Carole, Juli, and Silvina in his own words and after that we would go back through it all in a more detailed manner. He narrated the entire crime in what amounted to just three paragraphs in the transcript of his confession. It was so concise and clinical it seemed as if he were reading from a police report, and it made me incredibly sad that anyone could sum up taking three lives in so few words. He ended with the letter he sent to the Modesto resident agency. I was now free to ask him what it said and he told me he wrote, "We had fun with this one" and drew a map to where we could find Juli's body. On the tape that captured the confession you can hear me audibly sigh at that moment as I took in the magnitude of that admission. Only the killer would know that.

He went on to describe the extraordinary lengths he went to in order to avoid any chance of having this letter linked to him. He went to

Modesto and bought a pen, notepad, and the envelope he used to write the letter, then threw out what he didn't use so it wouldn't be found in his possession. He altered his handwriting on the note, which was what he meant when he said we wouldn't find his handwriting on the letter. He then paid a kid he approached at a Jack in the Box restaurant in Modesto $5 for a saliva sample, telling him he was facing a paternity test and wanted to avoid responsibility for the child. He said he used that saliva to fasten the envelope and affix the stamp.

He did one other thing with that letter that showed such sophisticated knowledge of forensic techniques I was shocked he even knew about it, much less thought to do it. On the page in the notepad atop the one he used to write the "We had fun with this one" letter, he wrote some names and words, pressing hard so they would leave an impression on the page underneath. This is called indented writing and the FBI had detected its presence on the note. I knew what those indented words were from when I was the case agent, and when Stayner recited them to me—some Hispanic names, some Mexican food items, and some other notes he made up—I felt like I was hit by a thunderbolt. I no longer had any doubt that he was responsible for the Sund-Pelosso murders. Hitman, who was watching through the glass, was also aware of the indented writing. He was worried that some of the higher-ups who were arriving, who were still wedded to the Dykes and Larwick theory, might try to shut down the interview, and he vowed at that moment to prevent anyone other than John and me from entering that room.

I asked Stayner how he knew so much about evidence collection and what we look for and he said he had been carefully watching TV forensic shows on Ted Bundy and other serial killers for some time and taking mental notes on what led to them being caught. He purposely used indented writing to throw us off his trail and send us down a rabbit hole.

"Ted Kaczynski gave me the idea for the envelope," he said. Stayner knew the FBI had proof positive that Kaczynski was the Unabomber when they got a DNA match between saliva on a letter sent to his brother and saliva on the stamp used to mail a copy of his manifesto to the media.

In the Name of the Children

Stayner had begun his narration of the crime with a startling statement. Without my even asking, he got right to the point that had been weighing on me since he first alluded to it, that I had been waiting to follow up on, and it brought the fantasy that he had been trying to act out into full focus.

"It was the day after Valentine's," he began, describing the day he attacked the tourists at Cedar Lodge. "I was gone most of the day off the property. I was at a girlfriend's house and, uh, I guess this girlfriend and her two daughters were my original intended victims."

I was so shocked that I asked him to repeat what he had just said, believing I must have misunderstood, but I had not. Valentine's Day fell on the Sunday of the Presidents' Day weekend in February of 1999 and Stayner said he kept trying to call his girlfriend, whose name I will withhold, that day because he was feeling lonely, but he was not able to reach her. The next day, February 15, he went over to perform some repairs for her on the property where she was living. He had what he described as an on-again, off-again relationship with this woman, whom by his own description he didn't really like. What he did like was the fact she had two daughters, ages eight and eleven.

It was almost like that picture in the magazine his abuser had shown him had come to life. I asked him what his fantasy was and he answered with unnerving specificity: "Kill the mother and rape the daughters."

As we moved into the second phase of the interrogation, with John and I driving the questioning, I went immediately back to this original plan, as it seemed the key to his fantasy and what had unfolded that night at the Cedar Lodge. "And your intention was to kill the mother with or without having sex with her?" I asked, referring to his girlfriend.

"Without," he said.

"And then to have sex with her two daughters?"

"Force them to have sex with each other, do all kinds of things."

"And what were you planning to do with the daughters after you were done with them?"

"Kill 'em," Stayner said without any hesitation or inflection, as if he were saying something as unremarkable as "watch TV" or "eat dinner."

He admitted to me that he was just using his girlfriend to get to her daughters, that he fantasized about the girls when having sex with their mother. I was immediately concerned for the girls' well-being and asked Stayner straight out if he had molested them, but he denied it.

I wanted to find out when he moved from just fantasizing about killing to deciding he would actually act out that desire. He said it was about three or four months before the Sund-Pelosso murders. In fact, he said, he made the decision as soon as he found out this woman had two prepubescent daughters, realizing the family fit his exact fantasy profile. The first time he tried to put his plan into action was one night when the girlfriend mentioned to him that her electricity was out and she was using tiki torches for light. She had another boyfriend, who was away that night, and Stayner planned to show up unannounced. He thought he could use the torches to burn the house down when he was done with his crime and cover his tracks. But he couldn't find the house she was living in at that time.

"They were very lucky," Stayner said. He realized he wasn't fully prepared at that time anyway. He didn't have a weapon with him. After that was when he put his kit together and began carrying it with him at all times, to be ready when the opportunity arose.

He said he hadn't intended necessarily to kill his girlfriend on Valentine's Day if he had managed to reach her, "but it was always in [his] mind." The next day, after finishing the repairs for her, the woman made dinner for him and her daughters. That night he was prepared and ready to go. At one point in the confession he claimed he decided against carrying out his plan because he liked the girls and took pity on them because they were so young. But eventually he admitted the truth. A man who lived as a caretaker on the property came by and he lost his nerve.

"Had he not been around, would you have done what you wanted to do?" I asked. Stayner nodded emphatically.

Stayner's girlfriend, when later interviewed by the FBI, said she and Stayner had only been intimate on two occasions. She confirmed that he had problems maintaining an erection and was never able to reach climax. She said he seemed frustrated and ashamed by this. The last time they attempted sexual relations, right before the attack on the tourists at the lodge, he experienced the same problem and asked her to perform oral sex on him, but that didn't work either. She described him as getting so frustrated she felt something deeper than mere impotence was wrong with him.

With his original plans thwarted, Stayner returned to the Cedar Lodge. He was so worked up he decided to soak in the motel hot tub to relax, but he found the water green and dirty from lack of maintenance. So he cleaned it, but by the time he finished it was past closing hour for the use of the pool area. So instead he said he decided to take a walk around the motel grounds. He claimed he had not yet seen the Sund-Pelosso party. However, he had noticed four other young girls staying at the lodge and decided to do some research. Five months had passed since that night, but he recalled during the confession the exact number of those girls' room and what kind of car they had, just as he would recall those same facts about Carole and the girls. He saw just two cars in the entire parking area: the one the other group had arrived in and the red Pontiac Grand Prix. He walked by the room of the four girls first but couldn't see in because that particular room had only a small opaque bathroom window facing the parking lot. He ultimately decided against trying anything with them because the night before he had seen a man in their company.

He then walked on to the 500 building where the Grand Prix was parked. He said the curtain to room 509 was open about a foot and he could see Juli and Silvina in bed watching TV and Carole propped up in another bed reading a book. He had missed out on his original target that night, but here was another mother and what looked to be her two daughters. From his perspective it was almost too good to be true. He spoke like the hunter he was, like all serial killers are, describing the three as "easy prey."

"I didn't see a man in the room, so they were vulnerable," he said. "They're in a building all by themselves. There was nobody in the rooms around them. If they were to scream, no one would hear them."

Stayner admitted later that he had been surveilling guests at the lodge for an entire year as potential targets. I wondered if he knew more about the Sund-Pelosso group than he was letting on—if he really did just stumble upon an open curtain or if he had been scoping them out and knew for sure that there was no man with them and that there were no other guests in their entire building. He lived at the lodge, ate in the restaurant, used the facilities. He certainly had plenty of opportunity to do "research" during their stay.

He also had access to the master key that opened every room. He had gone to the office to get the key when he decided to clean the pool and now he thought he might need it to get into room 509. But he didn't want anyone to know he had the key if his crime were discovered, so he went back to the office and pretended to drop it in the drawer. He then went to his room and collected his kit—which included duct tape, rope, a gun, and a large serrated knife from one of those butcher-block sets he had purchased for his kitchen—and headed back over to the 500 building.

Rather than using the key, he employed an elaborate ruse to gain access to room 509. This part of his account has really haunted me. He knocked on their door claiming he was there to find the source of a leak in that wing, but to "desensitize them" from any sense of alarm he knocked on several doors near their room first, announced that he was maintenance, opened those doors, and went inside long enough to sound as if he were checking what he said he was there to check. But Carole was leery of letting a stranger into their room, and she refused for a long time to open the door. She spoke to him through the window and three times she refused him entry even though he kept increasing the consequences of the leak problem. He told her that if water was seeping into the sheetrock, they would have to move that night into another room. He said if he checked and there was no damage, they could stay put. Still she resisted. Only when he said he would go get the manager to move them to another room did she finally open the door.

In my view, Carole was a hero. She had amazingly strong maternal and protective instincts and Stayner was able to overcome those instincts only because he was a practiced chameleon who had been thinking about and preparing himself for this moment for a long, long time. He managed to fool everyone who knew him—friends, family, coworkers, and law enforcement. Stayner was so dead set on carrying out his plan that night that if Carole hadn't opened the door I think he would have burst in anyway with his key. He told Carole he needed to look in the fan duct and actually went into the bathroom, climbed up on the toilet, and pulled down the fan to make everything seem legitimate. He then put the fan back in place and emerged from the bathroom with his gun drawn. My SAC and a lot of the other investigators on the case had been convinced it would take multiple assailants to commandeer and control that many victims at once. But the minute Stayner emerged from the bathroom he had both the element of surprise on his side and a lethal weapon to quickly overcome Carole and the girls. It must have felt like the motel room had suddenly shrunk to the size of a closet with a six-foot-two armed man standing in the middle of it.

He told the three what he told Joie, that he was a desperate man who needed money to get out of the country, and asked for their money and car keys. Carole immediately went for her purse, but he ordered her back to her bed, bound and gagged her with the duct tape he brought, and then did the same to the others. He carried the girls into the bathroom and set one on the floor and one in the bathtub. He then went back to Carole, tied her hands to her feet with rope so she would have no chance to fight him off, kneeled on her back, and strangled her to death with another length of the rope.

He said he felt nothing while murdering Carole: no anger or rage, no sexual charge, no emotion at all. In fact, he described himself as killing her "nonchalantly." His lack of reaction made me wonder if this really was his first killing, but he insisted it was. He mainly complained about how physically difficult it was to strangle someone, claiming he hurt the nerves in his hands from pulling so hard on the rope. He carried Carole's body out in a sheet and placed it in the trunk of the rental car. He was not worried about being seen carrying a body through the parking lot due to the late hour and the fact that no other guests were anywhere nearby. Still, he unscrewed the light bulb in the trunk so as not to cast a light on what he was doing.

He talked about positioning Carole's body carefully in the trunk and I asked if that was out of respect. No, he explained, he was making room for more bodies.

That comment stopped time for me. I didn't want to hear any more, but I had to go on listening, asking questions, and trying to make sense of it all. Stayner said he went back to the room and brought Juli and Silvina back into the bedroom. He assumed that night that the girls were sisters and told them he had taken their mother to the room next door. I don't know whether they believed that or knew Carole was dead. Stayner said he wasn't sure if he closed the bathroom door all the way when he was killing Carole, and he said he could hear Silvina sobbing in the bathroom while he did it. I can't even imagine being in a position of such complete powerlessness. I feel Juli and Silvina were heroic, too, because they each tried in their own way to control an uncontrollable situation and to survive an experience in which survival, unfortunately, was never an option.

He cut their clothes off of them with the knife he brought. That was what left behind the little pieces of fabric that had perplexed us when the empty room was searched. He wanted to have sex with each of them but when he stripped them he realized Silvina was menstruating because she was wearing a sanitary napkin. He tried to force the girls to have sex with each other, but Silvina refused. She just kept crying and Stayner considered her tears annoying and the fact that she was having her period a "turnoff." So he took her back into the bathroom and strangled her, too, with the rope. It was like once she was of no use to him she meant absolutely nothing and killing her was no more significant than swatting a fly.

Despite what I'm feeling inside during an interrogation I try to keep my emotions to myself and my outward affect on an even keel. There was a point in the Stayner interview, however, when I got so angry at what he was saying that I was powerless to silence it. I hate to even include this here because it is such an awful fact, but it came out in court during the trial and is therefore in the public domain. I also think it illustrates the utter depravity and ruthless self-interest by which these types of killers rationalize their crimes. At this point in the confession, when I was trying to get Stayner to see the crime from his victims' perspective and acknowledge their pain, I could not let this go unchallenged because it seemed like he was trying to dehumanize his victims to avoid facing the cruelty of what he had done. He had already used an expression I found deeply offensive in describing his killing of Carole, saying the "reptilian part of your brain doesn't die as quickly as the rest of your brain does."

In the Name of the Children

After strangling Silvina and leaving her for dead in the bathtub, Stayner returned to Juli but said he heard Silvina making noises and returned to find her still breathing. He tried to pass off her breathing as merely a "reflex" and not as a sign that she was still alive. The words he used were "pretty much dead." Yet he coldly went on to cover her nose with duct tape until her breathing stopped. In my view, he killed her all over again and I wanted him to realize the monstrousness of that act.

"Cary, you're either dead or you're not dead," I told him. "'Pretty much dead' means you are not dead. She was still alive at that point, wasn't she?"

"Clinically, probably," was all he would concede.

"But she was alive," John chimed in, not willing to let this go either.

"Don't you think you might be saying that because you don't want to feel what she went through?" I asked Stayner. He hung his head but wouldn't answer the question. The whole exchange was so unnerving to me that I wasn't sure if I could continue. It is at times like this when the strength of those with whom I worked gave me the strength to go on. Having John in that room with me, knowing he was there and seeing and hearing and feeling the same things I was, enabled me to continue. I have never been able to get that imagery of Silvina's death out of my mind. It weighs on me and has adversely impacted my own mental health.

I still don't think Stayner is a full-blown psychopath, completely devoid of empathy, but he probably has psychopathic traits included in his volatile psychological stew. He felt anguish and emotion about Juli and also broke down when talking about his brother and his parents. He's no Jodi Arias or Scott Peterson, who never admitted any guilt, never said they were sorry, never shed an unselfish tear. I think he truly mourned the loss of Juli, but it was more about what he lost, not her. I think his tears before he confessed to the murder of Joie were more about shame and relief that the hunt was over, because the stress and anguish had been getting to him. The most psychopathic parts of him came out in how cold-bloodedly he dispatched Carole and Silvina and how their suffering really had no meaning for him.

Stayner sexually assaulted Juli for hours. He had the usual problems with dysfunction and forced her to accommodate him to get whatever pleasure he was able to experience. He also believed, like only a pedophile can, that he was giving her some degree of pleasure. He said he felt in control for the first time in his life. He took off her gag so she could comply with his demands and I asked him if she ever spoke to him.

"Once," he said.

"What'd she say?" I asked.

"She asked if I was gonna kill her," Stayner said, but he didn't answer her. At one point she asked to go to the bathroom and he realized Silvina's body was still in there. So he used the master key to take Juli to the bathroom in the room next door, and moved Silvina's body into the trunk of the Grand Prix. While in that bathroom he made Juli shave her pubic hair, to make her more into his prepubescent fantasy girl. He secured her so she couldn't run away and disconnected the phone so she couldn't call for help. I am so in awe of the strength of character Juli displayed over that endless horrible night. She may have known that she was on her own at this point and was just trying to survive. Or she may have thought that only her cooperation would save her mother and Silvina. Either way, she was sacrificing herself in a way no child should ever be asked to do and her actions were generous and noble.

It was around 5 AM and Stayner knew he needed to get out of there. With Juli still in the other room, Stayner began to clean up room 509 and cover his tracks. He gathered up the women's luggage and other belongings to make it look like they had checked out and loaded everything into the backseat of the rental car. He wet towels in the bathroom and left them on the floor to make it seem like Carole and the girls had showered Tuesday morning before checking out. He even took the *Jerry Maguire* video the girls were watching when he gained access to the room out of the VCR and left it on the dresser. Everything he told us matched up with evidence from the scene.

He said he knew about trace evidence and thought that he might have shed some hair on the bedspreads and planned to come back later and clean up the room a little more. Afraid that employees might be asked to provide exemplars, he shaved off all his body hair after the crime so there would be nothing to compare with any shed hairs. I was astonished he was able to stage things so successfully that no one in law enforcement, including the FBI, believed the crime originated at the Cedar Lodge.

Stayner wasn't willing to give up Juli yet. Because she had cooperated with him he felt a bond with her. In fact, he felt that he loved her and said he wanted to "keep her" but didn't see how that was possible. He told her he was taking her somewhere else but that he wouldn't hurt her. She was still naked and he wrapped a pink blanket from one of the beds around her shoulders and led her out to the red car. He put her in the passenger seat and fastened the seat belt around her. He said she was not gagged at that time and only bound loosely by her hands and he claims he left her alone in the car briefly while he stopped to drop off the master key. That she was still there when he returned was proof to him that she cared about him and wanted to be with him. I suspect she was bound more securely in a way she couldn't run. Serial killers operate on an almost primal level, with their own freedom and survival as their number one priority. No matter how much he was deluding himself that Juli cared for him, I don't think he would have risked her getting out of the car and him being caught right there at the lodge, where everyone knew him. I believe her legs were probably bound by duct tape, making it impossible for her to run even if she had been able to get out of the car. Stayner denied he ever duct-taped her legs, but in one of the photos taken at the scene on the day her body was recovered you can see a strip of duct tape around one of her ankles.

He headed west on Highway 140 to Mariposa, then caught Route 49 north. He said he didn't know where to go or what he was going to do, so he just kept driving. As they drove he said he asked Juli questions about herself, and he found out later through the news that everything she told him was a lie. Again, I was amazed at how Juli kept her wits about her, refusing to give up any more of her soul than she had to give. When he asked her name she said it was Sarah.

It was starting to get light and Stayner knew he couldn't safely drive around with this girl much longer. When I asked him where he was when he made the conscious decision to kill her, he began to cry.

"I think I knew it all the time," he said. His voice became very soft and he sounded genuinely devastated. However twisted and deluded his view of love, I think he finally felt with Juli the intimacy he was seeking and now he was about to lose it, and in recounting it he was grieving the loss. He pulled into the parking lot for the vista point above Don Pedro Lake. A hiking trail veers off from the parking lot and cuts across the ridge, and he carried Juli down the trail in his arms, in his words, "like a groom carrying a bride over the threshold." He claimed he carried her because it was cold and she didn't have shoes, so she didn't want to walk. But I believe her legs were probably still bound. That he described the moments right before her death like a mystical marriage shook me to my core.

Stayner was crying hard now as he recounted Juli's murder. I asked him if he cried at the time he killed her and he said he didn't think so.

"Why are you crying now?" I asked.

"Just remembering it," he said, his voice shaking.

I asked him to continue. He stopped at a point along the trail, spread the blanket out that she had been wearing, assaulted her one last time, and said he wished he could keep her but he couldn't. He told her that she had had a good chance of getting away from him when he first emerged from the bathroom back at Cedar Lodge because the gun was not loaded. Then he took the knife out, told her he loved her, and slit her throat. He said she fell but I think he rolled her body away from the trail down the hillside until it became caught in the brush. In a final indignity he splayed her legs in a sexual pose as he had with Joie's corpse. He removed the duct tape from her hands and hid it under a log. He cut some branches and brush with which to cover her body, and then heaved the knife as far as he could down the hill. He stood over her for a moment, taking in the view of the sun rising over the lake. Then he headed back to the car to dispose of the other two bodies.

The fact that Stayner believed love could grow out of a sexual assault is appalling and unbearably sad to me. I don't know if he was telling the truth when he said the gun he used to set off the whole plot was not loaded, but telling that to Juli in her final seconds of life seems gratuitously cruel. Or maybe that was for Stayner some way of maintaining the fantasy that Juli wanted to be with him. I felt wrung out and I was sure John did, too. But we had to go on because there was more we needed to know. We had to find whatever evidence might still be out there that would back up his confession and rule out the involvement of anyone else. His words, as detailed as they were, would not be enough to convict. So we went on.

He went back to the car, opened the trunk, and, immediately back in survival mode, cut the nightclothes Carole was wearing off her body so that it would not appear she was kidnapped from the Cedar Lodge. He also cut the duct tape off Carole and Silvina to discard, because an adhesive like that might have captured his fingerprints. He forgot the pink blanket on the hillside, but he went back and collected it later in a plastic bag and threw it off the side of the highway. He finished up at the vista point just in the nick of time. Another car pulled into the parking lot right as he was leaving. He headed north toward Sonora, still unsure of what to do. He stopped at a gas station in Sonora to get something to drink, pulling around the back to avoid surveillance cameras. When he got back on the road he found himself at one point surrounded by Highway Patrol cars. He panicked for a moment but they eventually peeled off one by one. They were not there for him; it was merely a coincidence.

He drove as far north as the New Melones Lake, a reservoir on the Stanislaus River. He planned to drive the car with the bodies still in the trunk off the boat ramp into the lake but he saw some fishermen there, spoiling that idea. He dumped a pillowcase he had taken from room 509 in a Dumpster there, which contained the trio's clothes, the sheets from the motel, and the duct tape. He then drove back to Sonora and caught state route 108, where the population is sparse, looking for an alternative place to dump the car. He checked a few places but couldn't find a road that was decent enough to get the car through in the winter conditions. Then he found the logging road near Long Barn that ended in a little clearing. He drove in as far as he could go and wiped down the car with gloves he had in his kit. He scattered some of the trio's belongings on the hill around the car—Carole's purse, some of the rope he brought, Juli's shoes—all the things we found at the scene. Lastly, he took out a pocketknife he had with him and carved into the hood of the rental car "We have Sarah"—using "we" again, just as he had in the letter he wrote to the FBI. (We hadn't even noticed this inscription, due to the condition of the burned-out car, but metallurgists in the lab were able to detect it after the confession.) He wanted to misdirect us. He wanted us to believe that multiple assailants were involved in the crime. He wanted us to think Juli was still alive somewhere, being held captive. And it worked. Many in law enforcement fell for it, as did the media, and, so it seemed, had some members of the Dykes and Larwick crew.

After ditching the car, Stayner walked to Sierra Village to catch the bus home but remembered he had not wiped down the area inside the trunk lid where he took out the light bulb. Going back to do that made him miss the bus, so he took $200 from Carole's wallet and hired a cab. He had the driver drop him off at Yosemite Lodge in the park, careful so that even this stranger wouldn't know where he lived and maybe connect him to a car dumped in that area.

Before the cab ride he stopped for breakfast, and this was another moment when I couldn't help but betray a little disgust in line of questioning.

"You were hungry?"

"Yeah."

"What were you thinking? Were you grieving for the person you lost?"

"I wouldn't say that."

"What would you say?"

"I guess I was just concerned for myself, actually," Stayner said. He was on call that night in case there was a maintenance emergency at the Cedar Lodge and he had to be back before 5 PM. He was too exhausted when he got home to go back to clean up further in rooms 509 and 510, but he did the following night. He noticed some blood on one of the pillows and in the bathtub where Silvina left menstrual blood. He was aware of Luminol testing to detect blood, so he scrubbed out the tub with bleach and changed the sheets, but he forgot to replace one of the pillowcases and the pink blanket he took to wrap around Juli. As he recounted each bit of intentional misdirection, as well as each missed opportunity when he might have been caught, I felt angry and depressed by how the TOURNAP investigation had gone so far off the rails.

Despite all the efforts Stayner had made to hide his involvement and deflect blame onto others, he was still in fear of being caught. He decided to go back and torch the car, so he drove over with a can of gasoline late Thursday night, February 18, when he thought the smoke would not be noticed. He poured the gas inside, over the backseat, and threw in a match. He took off running up the hill and heard a loud explosion behind him as the car became engulfed. He got three-quarters of the way back to his truck when he realized he had left behind his gas can. He ran back to retrieve it, and then the fire set the Grand Prix's horn off and it began blaring. He ran back again to his car and had to hide behind a tree to avoid being seen by a passing snowplow driver. He retrieved one other item from the dumpsite while he was there: the credit card insert from Carole's wallet. He drove directly to Modesto, where he threw it out the window as he passed through an intersection.

John asked Stayner why he ditched the credit cards in Modesto. So we'd think whoever committed the crime was from Modesto, Stayner said. John pointed out that he created confused motives. The credit cards in Modesto made it look like the tourists had been the victims of a robbery. But the "We have Sarah" inscription (as well as the "We had fun with this one" letter) pointed to kidnapping. Stayner shrugged. He was still learning this game and winging it as he went along. He was so nervous in the first weeks following the murders that he said he lost fifteen pounds. He was interviewed once by the FBI in those early days and kept expecting us to get back around to him because "the FBI always gets its man, so I thought for sure you'd get me." He was monitoring the news very closely and was relieved his ploys to cast suspicion elsewhere seemed to be working. He said he'd never seen Dykes or Larwick in his life, but it seemed like Larwick "did [him] a big favor by shooting a cop."

"Then all of a sudden one of their buddies comes up dead," he said, referring to the guy who was fished from the river, whose siblings said he had seen Juli being held captive in Modesto. "And I was just going, man, it's like I had a guardian angel that was working on my side."

I asked Stayner why, after hiding Juli's body and employing so much subterfuge, he wrote the letter to the FBI and led us to her body. I thought maybe he did it because he still had feelings about her. Or maybe it was his way of exercising control over her fate even beyond death.

"Like you say, closure," Stayner said.

"Closure for you? Closure for her? Closure for her family?" I asked. He didn't answer directly, so I asked him if he wrote the letter because he was trying to throw us off or because he wanted her to be found.

"A little bit of both, let's put it that way," he responded. That seemed like an honest answer and, again, that is what I want and all I can really hope for in a confession.

John and I spent most of the rest of the interview getting specifics from him about all the places where he stashed evidence. I had not been permitted to go out to the various crimes scenes but John had, so he took the lead on this questioning and also picked up on things I had missed. When we felt we had identified everything that might still be found, we asked Stayner if he would be willing to go out with us to those locations and help us look for those items. I also wanted to take him to the Foresta and Don Pedro crime scenes and have him walk us through what happened while we videotaped him. He agreed to both requests. Despite my shifting emotions to various things he said during the interrogation, I was deeply appreciative of the fact that he had kept his word. He had answered all our questions, told us everything we wanted to know, and even agreed to help us retrieve physical evidence. He had stood up and told the truth and brought this to an end, and I will always be grateful to him for that.

"You helped a lot of people today," I told him, "and the closure's worth a lot." Stayner became emotional again as I said this. Unable to act anymore on the thoughts and impulses that plagued him, that war he had described within him, his nightmares should now start dissipating, I told him.

At the very end of the interrogation Stayner asked me a question that took the breath out of me: If he hadn't killed Joie, would we have ever realized he was responsible for the Sund-Pelosso murders?

"I have a firm belief that time is the ultimate truth giver and I think eventually everything works its way out," I said, telling him I was speaking from the perspective of someone who has worked cold cases. "There's stuff we're learning now about crimes that happened fifteen, twenty years ago. And in your case, based on the way you describe yourself and looking at what you've done, you would have kept on killing until you were caught. So I think the appropriate question is, would you have stopped killing? If you had stopped, yeah, there's a chance we never would have found you. But I don't think there's a chance you would have stopped killing. Do you?"

Without hesitation, Stayner shook his head no. In fact, he nearly killed again shortly before we picked him up.

Some people assume that when a killer confesses it is because he wants to be caught. I don't believe Stayner wanted to be caught. If he did, he would have confessed everything to the FBI agent and U.S. Park Service rangers who interrogated him the night after Joie's body was found. Instead, he denied everything and attempted to flee. He was in the grip of a compulsion that he had dreamed of and fantasized about for years and he finally got to act it out. But he was not satisfied. His thirst or lust or whatever you want to call it was not quenched; it never would be. Killing the three Yosemite sightseers was not enough. He wanted to do it again, and he found Joie. And as the law closed in on him, he almost killed again.

After Stayner packed up his stuff and left the Cedar Lodge, he drove to the house of his girlfriend and her daughters, who were his original intended victims. He arrived at her house at 12:45 AM. It was unusual, she later told the FBI, for him to show up without an invitation and at such a late hour. He told her his car had broken down and it was at a friend's house, but I suspect that was simply a ruse because he had no problem driving it to Laguna del Sol later that day.

She invited him to stay the night, but her other boyfriend was there, and when Stayner realized that he abruptly left. During his confession, Stayner told us he had stopped by her house as he was fleeing town. I dreaded asking the next question because it frightened me that even more women and girls could have died before he was caught—that he may have been driven to kill again even with authorities hot on his heels, or worse, perhaps because he feared he was about to be caught and would never have the opportunity again.

"You were hoping to do this even as recently as two days ago?" I asked. Stayner nodded.

"So you were kind of out of control . . ." I started to ask, but he answered before I finished.

"I was way out of control."

It was only when he got emotional with me and tapped into the better aspects of himself that he began to think he needed to be stopped. Maybe part of that was also realizing that no killing would ever have satisfied him, that what he was chasing would never offer him the ful-fillment he craved.

The entire confession lasted six hours, and by the time we finished it was too dark to go out and look for evidence, so we decided we would do so the following day. I was still committed to fulfilling my promise—to break the news to Stayner's parents that evening—but he said they went to bed early and told me to call them and say I needed to talk to them and would come by and see them in the morning.

"I want you to know I'm not going to tell them all the gory details," I assured Stayner. "What I'm going to tell them is that you've done some bad things but in the end you've done the right thing."

We told Stayner he was going to be arrested and would be taken to jail for the night, then after going to see his parents in the morning I would meet up with him and the team and we would take him out to the various crime scenes. Before that I asked him to write letters of apology to the victims as we had discussed. I gave him a pen and paper I had torn from my notebook. John and I left him alone in the interview room for a long time and he appeared to be very pensive as he hunched over the table, writing.

When I came back into the room I was a little shocked, but probably should not have been, to discover that he had chosen to write only to Juli. Stayner was completely egocentric and Juli was the only one who gave him any ego satisfaction. The other victims were purely instru-mental, necessary to complete the fantasy, but really didn't exist for him in any meaningful way. That being said, it was a remarkable document.

He wrote:

Dear Juli,

There are not enough words in the universe or days left in my life to express to you how sorry I am for what I have done to you, your mother, and your friend. My weakness to control my evil desires has led us both to this crossroad. You, on one hand, have crossed over to a place of which I can now only dream of going, and I am going someplace far worse. My thoughts of you are of a very sweet young woman who had a wonderful life ahead of her, but as it turns out I destroyed any hope of that. No more days with your family and friends. No more breaths of fresh air. No more sun shining on your face. No more dreams of a life to be. All of it thrown away like yesterday's trash.

My memories of your last few seconds will haunt me till the day I die, and rightfully so. The things I told you before I ended your life are things I have never been able to tell anyone else. Perhaps it was fear of rejection, or perhaps it was just plain fear of love, an emotion I have never experienced from anyone but my parents. But I can't blame my emotion, or lack of, for what I did. I know right from wrong and I don't think that I am insane, but there is a craziness that lurks in my mind. Thoughts I have tried to subdue as long as I can remember. I'm just sorry that you were there when the years of fantasizing my darkest dreams became a reality in the flesh.

When the interview was finally over, I was emotionally spent. My mind was reeling at how Stayner had managed to avoid suspicion for so long despite the magnitude of the TOURNAP investigation. I thought back to how when I was still case agent and was at the Cedar Lodge interviewing employees, I'd asked around about everyone who worked there and kept hearing about an employee named Cary who was away, either on vacation or due to temporary seasonal layoff. When I was removed from the case I never got to continue with those employee interviews and polygraphs. Apparently another investigator did talk to him in those early days but nothing about him set off any alarms. Unlike Billy Joe Strange, Stayner had no record to make us look more seriously at him, just a marijuana bust for which charges had been dropped. His handsome, clean-cut, athletic appearance stood in stark contrast to the scraggly biker types, tattooed ex-cons, wizened methamphetamine "tweakers" of the Dykes and Larwick gang, and other potential suspects arrested during the investigation's massive dragnet. Stayner was a quiet loner who no one knew well but was polite and responsible—so responsible he hadn't missed a day of work in a year and a half. In fact, he seemed so trustworthy that when investigators came back in May to collect blankets from the Cedar Lodge to compare with evidence that had been discovered, the manager asked Stayner to use his master key to help them—a killer so unassuming he was inducted to help gather evidence of his own crimes.

All I wanted to do after completing the confession was get home to Lori and talk through everything with her and figure out how I could possibly prepare Stayner's parents for the news I had to deliver the next morning. The first person I saw when I emerged from the interview was Assistant Special Agent in Charge Todd Hildebrand, and I told him we needed to keep the confession absolutely secret until I could go see Cary's parents and we could recover the evidence Stayner said was still out there. Hildebrand immediately went to advise Maddock, and while I was talking to Hitman in the hallway my two bosses intercepted me. Hildebrand told me I would not be permitted to go see the Stayner family and reveal any information to them because it might leak out to the press, and the SAC wanted to be the one to release the news to the media. As exhausted as I was I still had a lot of adrenaline pumping through my veins and my blood started to boil. I looked at Hitman but the words I spoke were directed to the other two. I said I had given Stayner my word and that after all he had done for us I was going to fulfill that promise either as an FBI agent or an ex-FBI agent and offered to turn over my gun and my FBI credentials to Hitman. I wasn't bluffing; I would have actually resigned rather than go back on my word. It was about doing the right thing for the case and for the Stayner family.

Eventually I was told I would be granted twelve hours and then Maddock would make the announcement. That didn't seem like enough time to get through all we needed to get done the next day. I called the Stayners, introduced myself, and asked for their permission to visit in the morning. Cary had also called them to tell them I was coming but didn't tell them why. They agreed to see me and as I drove home dispatch notified me that they had called the FBI back to verify my identity.

It was 2 AM Sunday morning before I got home and I had to get up by 5 AM to begin the hundred-mile drive over to the Stayners. When I had called Lori in the middle of the confession she assumed Stayner was just responsible for the latest murder and she was shocked to hear he confessed to all four of the Yosemite killings. We got in bed together but stayed up the rest of the night and brainstormed as I agonized over how to tell Stayner's parents that they were about to lose another son.

In the Name of the Children

With Lori's help I decided to tell them that ultimately what was good in Stayner was better than what was bad, because he confessed without getting anything in return.

When I arrived, Delbert led me into the living room where Kay was already waiting. They told me they had seen on the news that the FBI wanted to talk to Stayner about the Armstrong case. Before I could even get to the point of what he had confessed to they started saying, "He didn't do it," that he could never have done something so wrong. When I told them Stayner explained to me how he killed Joie and also the other women who disappeared from Cedar Lodge and gave me details only the killer would know, it was like a ton of bricks hit them. They each began to cry the way only a parent who has lost a child cries—a wail of utter devastation—as I had seen so many other families over the years cry. It was a very painful thing to witness and I tried my best to offer some form of comfort. I told them that Stayner chose to confess and got nothing for it, which meant he did it for the right reason and that he stopped himself because the light of good in him was brighter than the darkness that was also there. I told them that it took courage to do what he did and that he had given his victims a gift by telling the truth and deciding to end this. I said he was now in a place where he could no longer hurt others or himself.

I knew a little about how despondent Delbert in particular had been when Steven was kidnapped and I was worried about the parents' well-being. I told them I could not leave them in such an emotional state and would stay as long as they wanted me to and answer any questions they had until I felt they were able to carry on. I suggested they call other family members to come be with them or anyone that could help them get through this. Stayner's sisters showed up and I had to break the news to them as well. We all sat together and tried to find meaning and comfort in what could not be understood. It was a couple of hours before I felt things had stabilized enough for me to leave. While I was still there the media began to call and I didn't know if the Bureau had released the information or if reporters were just figuring things out on their own. I was anxious to get out to the crime scenes and retrieve the evidence before the media or other onlookers started showing up and possibly compromising things.

Joie

As we had planned the night before, Hitman and John checked Stayner out of the Sacramento County Jail and drove him to Yosemite. I met them in Foresta along with our office photographer, Steve Grube, who brought a video camera to memorialize everything. It was actually thanks to Steve that we caught up with Stayner as quickly as we did, because it was his photographs of the tire tracks outside Joie's cabin that were matched to the treads on Stayner's Scout. A few other detectives from other agencies were there, as well as the Evidence Response Team.

En route to Foresta, Stayner made a few more startling admissions to my partners. He still insisted that the Sund-Pelosso murders were the first killings he had ever committed, but there were two other situations where he nearly acted out his fantasy that he had not mentioned the day before.

A full year before Joie's murder, in the summer of 1998, Stayner planned to attack two preteen Finnish girls who were staying at Cedar Lodge. Again, he remembered the exact number of the room in which they stayed and tried to enter it at 2 AM with the master key, but for some reason the key did not work. A woman who was with the girls woke up at the sound of the lock being jiggled. She looked out the window and banged on the glass. Stayner quickly retreated to his room. The woman was so alarmed she called lodge security, who, in turn, called Stayner to check out the disturbance. He managed to talk his way out of that situation. That was the first time he put any kind of rape and murder kit together and it was much cruder than what he employed later, containing only some duct tape and a pipe wrapped in a towel.

Just two weeks before his apprehension he almost acted again. He saw a group of women on the Merced River near the 25 Mile Per Hour Beach. He thought he would be caught if he tried to attack them because it was so out in the open and visible but he didn't care because the compulsion was too strong. He was armed with a gun on that occasion but just as he approached the women, a male companion of theirs appeared on the scene. If he had already begun his assault, Stayner said he would have shot the man to eliminate any resistance. The fact that he admitted his gun was loaded in this instance made me wonder even more if he was lying when he claimed to Juli just before killing her that the gun was empty.

In the Name of the Children

He revealed something else to my partners that if true was also highly disturbing. He said that when the rangers questioned him shortly after discovering Joie's body on Thursday, July 22, at the 25 Mile Per Hour Beach and he balked at turning over his backpack it was because he had his kit inside it. He allowed them to look through his vehicle and claimed that while they searched the Scout he removed a gun, a knife, and gloves from his backpack and hid them under nearby rocks and logs.

When I got to Foresta early Sunday afternoon, Stayner looked scared but seemed to relax when he saw me. He was dressed in the same Yosemite T-shirt, jean shorts, and ball cap he was wearing when we picked him up the day before at Laguna del Sol. His hands were cuffed in front of him but he was able to walk with us. I asked Stayner to re-create the abduction and murder for me and he complied while Steve videotaped it all, which would serve as another unimpeachable documentation of his confession. We started at the little washed-out bridge down the street from the Green House where Stayner first spied Joie, and where the tracker also captured footprints that matched those Stayner left at Joie's cabin. He showed us where he walked to case out whether Joie was alone and then how he inched his way up the stone path to her front door while he distracted her with tales of his Bigfoot sighting. It hurt to be in her footsteps as Stayner told the tale once again. I could see the flowers in the pots and planter boxes she had been watering when he accosted her. The place was rustic but very homey and well maintained. You could tell just looking at the cabin that the people who lived there really loved the place and nurtured the earth around it.

We went inside Joie's house and he started to cry as he recounted how he told her he just wanted money when that was not at all what he wanted. It seemed like some shame had set in around the lie. Maybe now that he had confronted the truth it was harder to live with the lies and the manipulation. He showed us where he thought he lost his sunglasses during the struggle with her at the house, where he walked with her out to his car and lifted her inside—matching up with all the evidence we already had. He then showed us where she escaped out the car window, where he overcame her, and where he killed and decapitated her. He pointed out the dragging trail, picked up a stick and scraped

214

through the leaves looking for blood. It was amazing to me how much he was helping to prove the case against him. He cried again as he described her murder, the tears dripping from his face because he was unable to wipe them away with his hands cuffed.

I was surprised by how close to Joie's home everything occurred. I felt some minor relief in the fact that, unlike Juli, she was not in terror for long. The area where he dragged her to kill her was fairly obscured by foliage. But one house was visible through an opening in the trees: her own.

As he fled Foresta on the day of the murder, Stayner stopped and hid duct tape he removed from Joie's body under a log. He said when he removed the tape from her wrists her watch pulled off as well and remained stuck to the tape. He also threw away the knife he used by hurling it down a hillside. As we retraced his steps, he took us right to that log and there was the tape and the watch beneath it. Chris Hopkins, Kevin Baker, and other members of the Evidence Response Team followed behind us collecting the evidence. I wasn't sure we'd be able to locate the knife in the heavy brush, but Kevin came up with it.

I later learned that as we pulled out of Big Meadow, Joie's mother, Leslie Armstrong, was driving up to her daughter's cabin. I was horrified that we had just been in that house with Stayner reenacting the crime, even though what we were doing was helping to prosecute the case against him. It still felt like we were violating her daughter's sacred space and I am so relieved that she did not arrive while we were still there.

Having finished in Foresta, we headed over to Don Pedro Lake. Hitman, John, Stayner, and I were all riding together in Hitman's Crown Vic. We had asked for a chase car to cover us for security purposes, but so many people felt a personal stake in the resolution of these cases that over the course of the day other investigators from many different law enforcement agencies kept showing up and it turned into a convoy. I could not begrudge them wanting to be there. That whole day was emotionally difficult for all of us, Stayner included, and he was being so extraordinarily helpful that we tried to keep things as light as we could for him as we drove from one scene to the next. There was no forgetting all the evil things he had done—we walked right in the footsteps where he carried out those acts. But that day he was caught up in doing good and, I believe, relieved to have gotten all the bad off his chest. It was almost like he was one of us—another cop, one of the team—as he helped direct us to every piece of evidence that was still available to be recovered.

At one point Stayner told us to pull over on the shoulder of Highway 49. I don't know how he was able to pinpoint the exact spot but when we got out and peered over the ledge, down the cliff was the plastic bag with the pink blanket he took from the Cedar Lodge. It was down a huge drop-off and the Evidence Response guys had to rappel down to retrieve it. Stayner remembered every detail with 100 percent accuracy. Everywhere he told us to look, the evidence was right there. It took the evidence team weeks to locate the knife he hurled down the canyon after killing Juli, but when it was found, sure enough, it was in the area he had pointed out to us.

When we got to the vista point parking lot above Don Pedro Lake we could see a small cross and some flowers had been placed at the beginning of the trailhead. I don't know who placed those items there, but it was very moving to see them. Stayner asked to see the memorial before we headed down the trail, and after looking for a moment he covered his face with his cuffed hands and began to cry. (Later someone erected a fairly large cross at the very site Juli's body was found. It's a very steep, slippery hillside there and I couldn't imagine the effort it took to do that. And the last time I visited, some fifteen years after the crime, some plastic flowers were affixed to a pole at the trailhead. A marker has also been placed in the woods near Joie's cabin and people leave little charms and tokens of affection there. Seeing these gestures of honor and respect, I felt like if there were such a thing as a guardian angel it was not some ethereal being helping Stayner get away with his crimes but deeply caring human beings memorializing lives tragically cut short.)

Stayner led us down the trail to the spot where he killed Juli.

"Let's stand off, out of respect," I said, stepping back a few paces and pulling Stayner with me. By the time he finished recounting the crime again he was really distraught, crying heavily and physically shuddering. As Stayner spoke he was nearly drowned out by the sound of helicopters swirling above us. I worried they were media choppers that had tracked us down, but it turned out they were there responding to a crime in commission. An arsonist had been setting fires all along Highway 49 and the copters were dumping water on the fires. There was also a serious car accident in the area and some members of our team actually peeled off to assist the victims. It was as if pain and tragedy were all around us.

As we finished and got ready to head back to Sacramento, Hitman and I looked at each other. We had worked together so long that he knew exactly what I was thinking and I knew the same about him. We'd been at it all afternoon with only a stop for a bottle of water. I remembered Stayner's comment, just before confessing, that the pizza we shared with him would be the last thing he would ever eat in freedom. Not only had he confessed, but he had also come out with us today, filled in every detail, provided us with all the evidence prosecutors would need, and literally put the murder weapons in our hands. It seemed like one last meal outside jail and the penitentiary was the least we could do for all his cooperation.

We let Stayner choose and he decided on a casual place so he could keep his hat on indoors. At least eight of us went along to ensure security. We asked for a booth and sat him in the middle surrounded by the biggest among us so that there was no chance he could make a break for it. While we were eating it occurred to me that the twelve hours I had been promised before the FBI was going to announce Stayner's arrest had expired. In a moment of panic John and I ran outside to a newspaper box, but we were relieved to see Stayner's picture was not there, so we let him finish his dinner.

In fact, we were still out with Stayner gathering evidence when the SAC made his announcement at a press conference outside our Sacramento FBI office. Francis and Carole Carrington stood beside him, but Leslie Armstrong declined his invitation, choosing instead to go to Foresta and take care of her daughter's affairs.

Maddock said that Stayner had been arrested for Joie's murder and that information had been developed in the last twenty-four hours that also tied him to the Sund-Pelosso killings. It was a shocking revelation considering that just two days before, the day Stayner had fled town after his first FBI grilling, Maddock had continued to insist there was no link between the two cases. That was the same day Stayner had stopped unexpectedly at his girlfriend's home, planning to kill once again, but Maddock had said he had "no reason to believe there [was] a continuing threat."

Attempting to address the question on everyone's mind before it was asked, Maddock braced himself for the deluge of criticism and second-guessing he knew was to come.

"I ask myself whether we could have done anything differently that might have prevented the murder of Joie Armstrong," he told a stunned press corp. "I have struggled with that issue for the last twenty-four hours and continue to do so." But then he concluded by saying, "I am confident we have done everything that reasonably could be done [considering] the resources that have been brought to bear on these cases, the dedication of the men and women on the task force, the quality of information we've received from a wide variety of sources, and the extraordinary efforts taken to conceal and destroy evidence."

Still, he refused to rule out Dykes and Larwick and others previously arrested by the FBI as playing a role in the Sund-Pelosso case, saying that was being evaluated, but that he believed that "no other person involved in any of these murders was still on the loose."

That refusal continued, at least internally, for three years—pretty much up until Stayner's trial for the murders of Carole, Juli, and Silvina. Reputations, even careers, were on the line. Maddock and many others had invested so much in the Dykes and Larwick theory that it was hard to let go. At one point, the SAC called me into his office and asked me if I thought Stayner had acted alone. I told him I had no doubt. For one thing, I had never seen a man who suffered from erectile dysfunction sexually offend in the presence of other men. I told him that Stayner had accounted for everything that occurred with the exception of the bank lead that had not been resolved. I pointed out that the suspects who had previously been arrested had provided no information that could be confirmed, whereas all the evidence we had discovered backed Stayner's detailed confession. I also added that Stayner denied having ever even met any of the Modesto suspects.

Maddock and others in his circle continued to ask me that same question for a long time and each time I refuted it, but still they clung to their theory. They kept investigating, looking for a connection between the original suspects and Stayner. They even bugged the jail cells of Dykes, Larwick, and Stayner, listening for some acknowledgment that they knew each other, but they never found any. Other police agencies also continued to investigate the Dykes gang for a very long time, insisting they must have played some role.

What should have been my greatest triumph as an FBI agent was somehow turned against me, as if I had set out to damage people's careers and stolen the glory that should have belonged to others. Subtle messages were sent, and then more direct ones, that I was persona non grata. The first couple of things seemed like fraternity pranks but then took on a darker cast. Some staged photos were left on my desk. In one, a mannequin was seated in my chair and Maddock was giving the mannequin an award plaque, as if he were giving me an award for solving the Yosemite cases. In another photo, the mannequin was sitting in the driver's seat of a Mustang GT (which everyone knew was the type of car I was always trying to get from the pool) and the second in command in our office was handing the keys to the mannequin. I found a swastika one day underneath a pile of files on my desk. At another point, a bag of cat scat was deposited on my desk.

FBI headquarters had designated TOURNAP a major case—like UNABOM, TRADEBOM, the first attack on the World Trade Center in 1993, and OKBOM, the bombing of the federal building in Oklahoma City by homegrown terrorist Timothy McVeigh. Major case designation means that solving those cases is considered a national priority and extra funding and manpower are allocated accordingly. The agents responsible for solving major cases are lauded and sometimes even financially rewarded for their efforts. Not only was I never acknowledged for solving the four Yosemite murders, for getting the confession of Cary Stayner, and for preventing more murders that Stayner made clear he intended to carry out if he had not been arrested, but my role was also virtually erased. In his press conferences, Maddock ascribed responsibility for the confession to an unnamed "task force member"—a description that was not only belittling but also untrue, as I wasn't even on the task force at that time. When he was later asked to account to headquarters for the mistakes that had occurred—the arrest of the wrong suspects, the leaks to the press, the murder of the fourth victim whose death might have been avoided—he described Stayner's confession as almost a nonevent and again assigned "credit" to an anonymous "task force member."

There is a form in the FBI, known as an FD-515, in which the case agent is supposed to report any statistical accomplishments, such as an arrest or an indictment. Management reviews these forms to determine the quality of our work. No FD-515 was ever filed on my obtaining the confession, except by someone at the Fresno resident agency who referred to me as a supporting agent who merely helped. I was so discouraged by this that for the rest of my career I gave credit for anything I did that would constitute a statistical accomplishment to other people for investigations in which I was serving as case agent.

I kept my head down and tried to keep doing my job, but that, too, was altered in ways that hurt me tremendously. I was forbidden to have any unchaperoned contact with any of the Yosemite victims' families. That was very painful because trying to help and support victims and their families is the part of the job that matters most to me, and I wanted to do for the Sund, Carrington, Pelosso, and Armstrong families what I had tried to do for the Stayners: offer comfort and answer any questions they had. I was also taken off my beat investigating crimes against children and basically busted down to doing interviews of candidates applying to the FBI. I was still getting calls from local law enforcement agencies asking for my assistance when a kid in their jurisdiction disappeared, but I wasn't being assigned those cases. I couldn't bear not helping, so I did what I could without authorization and made sure the locals took all the credit for what we accomplished together.

The United States Attorney General and the California AG vied over who should prosecute Stayner first. The state intended to charge Stayner with special circumstances for the murders of Carole, Juli, and Silvina, which would make him eligible for the death penalty. The feds also decided to charge him with the death penalty for killing Joie. The wait for execution in the federal system is much shorter than the twenty-plus year wait for prisoners on the state's death row.

Joie

It was decided that the federal case would proceed first, but it never went to trial. Instead, in September 2000, a deal was struck in which Stayner was allowed to plead to life in prison without the possibility of parole. Leslie Armstrong told a reporter that she wavered between her Christian beliefs and days when she wanted to "personally beat him to death." Ultimately she decided to go along with the deal to avoid the agony of prolonged appeals, also realizing that seeing Stayner die would not bring her daughter back.

The state proceeded with its capital case and I was called in June 2001 to testify at the preliminary hearing at the Mariposa County Courthouse. Lori and our older son, Joe, came along to support me. We tried to make a family outing of the trip, enjoying the sights along the way even though I was going there for such a grim task. Just knowing they were there meant so much to me, as my strength at that time came from my wife and the boys. We were put up in the same inn as the other witnesses and the victims' families.

After settling in, we went for a walk, and as we arrived back at the inn we saw a woman approaching people and asking why they were there. As we got into the elevator to go back to our room the woman got in with us and asked my identity. When I told her my name a guttural sound emerged from deep inside her.

"You're the one," she said, recognizing my name as the person who took the confession. She fell to her knees and began to cry, saying no one would tell her what happened to her daughter Joie. I realized, as did Lori, that this was Leslie Armstrong. I had never met her because I had not been permitted to speak to the victims' families. And because her daughter's case did not go to trial, she still didn't know much about what had transpired. I told her I would tell her anything she wanted to know and she came with us to our room. Lori couldn't hold back her own tears and told Leslie how sorry she was and excused herself and Joe so we could talk alone.

Leslie was distraught. She told me that the SAC had asked her to stand with him at the press conference at our FBI office in which he announced Stayner's arrest but she declined, saying she needed to get to the morgue and to Joie's home to take care of things. She said he was upset that she didn't go and no one would ever talk to her about what happened to Joie. I told her she had a right to know and that I would answer whatever questions I could. I told her I had not been at the crime scene, so all I knew was what I had been told by Joie's killer. I apologized for not knowing her daughter's name at the time of the interview. I told her how I had no idea who Cary Stayner would turn out to be when I met him that day at Laguna del Sol. I shared with her how the interview had come about and how it proceeded.

I was desperate to say something to ease her pain. I told her that the only reason Stayner was in custody and being prosecuted was because of her daughter's fight for her life, which caused him to leave so much evidence behind and for us to catch up to him. I told her that in taking his confession, I was merely Joie's tool; it was Joie who caused the case to be resolved.

I also asked Leslie a question that I hoped would not offend her in any way but which I thought would give her some peace. I asked her that if Joie had had to make the choice, was she someone who would have sacrificed herself to save others, or would she choose to save herself and let others perish? Leslie said without hesitation that Joie would have chosen to save other people's lives. I told her that because of Joie, others would live and Stayner would not be able to hurt anyone else.

I then told her of the many people who had worked so hard and sacrificed so much to ensure that Joie's death would not be without meaning. I explained the courage of the other victims and said that I was just one of the many people from many different agencies who participated in the investigation who cared. I ended up by telling Leslie that when she looked at me in court she would see her daughter because I was an extension of her.

We had been talking for less than an hour when there was a knock at the door. It was Nick Rossi. He asked me what I was doing and I told him the truth. I would have liked to talk to Leslie a lot more, but he whisked her away.

I testified the next day and the whole six-hour confession was played in its entirety. It was a highly emotional day I remember almost in snapshots, like slides in a slide projector. It was the first time I had seen Stayner since those two days we spent together and he motioned in acknowledgment to me, then got very emotional and buried his face in his hands. As the confession played, he plugged his ears and wept, seemingly horrified by his own words. I remember José Pelosso, Silvina's father, becoming so enraged by what he heard on the tape that he leapt to his feet and lunged toward the man who had killed his daughter. I recall Mark Fincher, the tracker, telling me he didn't understand until he heard the confession that Joie's killer had picked her up and forcibly placed her in his car and that is why the trail of her footsteps ended so mysteriously outside her home. I remember looking at Lori as I testified and how just the sight of my wife calmed my nerves and gave me courage to get through the day. And I remember Leslie Armstrong. As I entered the courtroom I saw her stand and turn toward me. Then she noticed Lori, and when she did she patted her heart and mouthed the words "thank you" to Lori for giving Leslie that hour alone with me where she could begin to put the pieces together and fill in some of the void left by her daughter's absence.

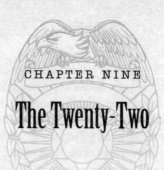

CHAPTER NINE

The Twenty-Two

WHEN I WORKED FOR THE FBI there was a mandate that every citizen who calls the Bureau should be able to speak to a live person. I believe the practice was put in place by Hoover himself, who wanted the FBI to be accessible and accountable to the people it served. It was also intended, like some of Hoover's other innovations, such as the Ten Most Wanted List, to encourage average citizens to help law enforcement—to serve, in effect, as the eyes and ears of the street. This is crucial, considering that FBI agents don't walk beats like police officers and thus don't have contact with the public other than what we initiate on the cases we are working. Today when I try to call the FBI I get an automated answering system like pretty much every other government agency has instituted. I think of all those calls I took from people who decided on the spur of the moment to call for help or report a crime and wonder how many are dissuaded by the prospect of having to leave a message or navigate a bureaucratic phone tree.

Some of the FBI's biggest cases have originated from these cold calls. We've also received invaluable leads on existing investigations and information that has helped us locate suspects at large. In every office, agents took turns answering the public line, and separating the wheat from the chaff could be a time-consuming and frustrating task, as a large number of the people who called in unsolicited were cranks and people with a loose grip on reality. Agents referred to this part of the job as "complaint duty," and that is no understatement. I learned from these callers that Martians were landing on Earth with incredible regularity and that everyone is being watched at all times, including in their bathrooms. Some callers even claimed to be the human antennas through which this massive surveillance was conducted. Others insisted imaginary people were being held in federal custody. There were "frequent flyers," who called repeatedly and every agent on complaint duty came to recognize the numbers of local psychiatric facilities from which many of these calls originated. Some people had personal grudges or grievances they insisted we handle. Others called about a legitimate criminal matter, but it did not constitute a federal violation that would give us jurisdiction to take action. These conversations could last hours, as the caller tried to convince us in scrupulous detail that there was, indeed, a federal violation. Chances were good that if you heard anyone in the office having an adversarial phone call they were on complaint duty.

The only way I could deal with the more outlandish and persistent callers was with what I came to call "martial complaint arts." It did no good to tell them the crimes they were reporting did not exist. So I gave them tips on how to communicate with extraterrestrial life and how to use tinfoil to avoid becoming an unwitting listening device. That advice seemed to work because I got several thank-you calls. When a new feature was added to our phones that allowed us to forward calls, I would sometimes transfer the call to another agent and watch how they dealt with it. Then I realized, why keep it within the office? One woman called me at least ten times one day from a mental health facility. I still had to handle all my other casework while pulling complaint duty and she was eating up precious time I needed to devote to active investigations. I couldn't take it anymore and told her I was going to have "Agent Scully" (from *The X-Files*) pick her up, then patched Lori into the call and gave her instructions, addressing my wife as Agent Scully. That was the last call I received from the woman that day.

One day in 2003, while working complaint duty, I answered a call that would affect my life forever. The call came from Del Oros, who at the time was a deputy district attorney in Sacramento and is now a judge on the Sacramento County Superior Court. Del was also a former FBI agent and knew from his work with the Bureau that transporting a person across state lines for the purpose of illegal sexual acts was a federal crime. He told me that two families—one in the Sacramento area and one in Fort Worth, Texas—were essentially trading their children back and forth for the purposes of molestation. The Sacramento DA's office had charged the local couple with nearly a hundred counts of molestation, but for reasons unknown to this day, Texas authorities would not prosecute the subjects who lived in Texas for the sexual offenses committed there. Del was hoping we could bring the Texas couple down on federal charges.

What Del described was a case with clear federal authority, exactly the kind of case the FBI is set up to pursue and the reason to have real live agents staff the help line. After several years and some changes in management I was back to being able to work directly and proactively on investigations of crimes against children. I told Del that this was precisely the kind of case I handled and offered to help. The story he laid out for me was almost unbelievable, except that at this point I had seen just about every depravity imaginable perpetrated on children. In recounting it here I will use the real names of the adult perpetrators, who were named in court and reported in the press for committing these crimes, but pseudonyms for all the victims.

Allen Harrod, like Ulysses Roberson, invented his own religion. In the case of Harrod, it was a bastardization of Mormonism and Judaism, with himself at its center: the god-like figure that controlled the lives of the women and children around him. And like Roberson, the pseudo-religious overtones were simply a trumped-up cover for sexual and physical abuse. He had many children with his first wife, Ila, and then more children with his wife's sister, Irene Hunt, whom he converted into the fold as a sister wife.

But Harrod took the polygamous cult route a step further than Roberson had. He molested nearly all his children and had a friend named Michael Labrecque, a buddy from when they served in the Air Force together, who shared his proclivity for sexually assaulting children. Labrecque and his wife, Juliette, became the only disciples of Harrod's self-styled "religion," what he called the Universal Church of Jesus Christ. The two couples gave themselves biblical names. Allen and Irene became Isaac and Rebekah. Michael and Juliette became Joseph and Mary. Harrod was the patriarch and Labrecque was given the title of bishop. Harrod wrote his own scripture, all of which revolved around a system of elaborately ritualized child sexual abuse.

They created, in effect, their own rape club. Operating by what they called divine "commandment," Labrecque began molesting each of his daughters when they turned seven, "preparing" them for "presentation" to the patriarch for further "religious training." Once in Harrod's clutches, they were required to undergo a three-stage sexual ceremony that was couched as necessary to attain spiritual enlightenment and become a woman. The Harrod girls were also forced to perform sexual acts with their father as "offerings." All the Harrod boys, except one named Martin, were shipped off to live with the Labrecques, where they were subjected to physical and sexual abuse. Some of the older Labrecque girls were so thoroughly indoctrinated that they considered themselves to be Harrod's wives, and one bore a child by him. Harrod also had sex with Labrecque's wife and there was a question as to whether some of the Labrecque kids were actually fathered by Harrod.

The children were required to address Harrod as "Lord" and keep journals of their weekly "offerings" to him, using biblical terms like "loaf" and "fish" as euphemisms for different sexual acts. Refusal or disobedience to any commands was punished by "spankings"—which were actually naked whippings with a belt—and other vicious beatings. To further keep the kids under their control and prevent anyone from discovering their secret, the kids were kept out of school. Ostensibly they were "homeschooled" by one of the older kids, but that really just meant some rudimentary English and math skills—enough to record their weekly "offerings"—and instruction on how to please the "elders." The kids were told they would be killed if they ever told anyone what was happening. Irene and Juliette were accused of participating in the abuse as well, molesting some of the boys and teaching the girls how to perform various sexual acts. Through violence, intimidation, and isolation, this arrangement remained secret for more than a decade. Investigators believed at least twenty-two children were victimized during that time.

That one or two or four individuals could hurt so many children and get away with it for so long, could force their children into what can only be described as sexual slavery, was beyond horrifying. It was one of the worst cases of sexual exploitation I had ever seen in terms of the sheer number of victims and the acts perpetrated against them, the age of the victims (as young as four), and the monstrously manipulative and psychologically corrosive system within which the abuse occurred. Child sexual abuse is damaging in any context, but when the abuser is a parent, the person who is supposed to care for and protect the child, it is even more emotionally deleterious. In this case, the abusers were not only the children's parental authority figures but also the ultimate authority—God himself, or his appointed disciples. Some have described the damage caused by prolonged child sexual abuse as "soul murder," and I can think of no case that fits that description better than this one, as the abuse came from someone who literally claimed to sit in judgment of the children's souls.

This devil's bargain that was struck by the Harrods and the Labrecques came to light only as a result of the extraordinary courage of Harrod's eldest daughter, whom I will call Samantha. Two years before Del called the FBI, in 2001, Samantha was a young adult, out from under her father's control. She was a mother herself, living with her boyfriend, but still tormented by the abuse inflicted on her by her father. Harrod began molesting her when she was in first grade and it continued until her mother, Ila, gathered up her children and fled with them when Samantha was eleven. One day, after waking from a particularly distressing nightmare, she confided her abuse to her boyfriend. He insisted on confronting her father, and Samantha discovered that a bunch of young girls she had never seen were living at her father's house. At least one of the girls was wearing an anklet and Samantha instantly knew what that meant from her own experience—that she had "passed" her sexual initiation by Harrod.

Samantha decided she was going to do whatever it took to free her siblings and whoever these other kids were from her father's control. She went to three different police agencies before anyone agreed to look into the matter. Samantha was persistent and found a sympathetic ear when she went to police in the city of Folsom, a suburb of Sacramento, where her father lived. Detective Rob Challoner opened an investigation and obtained a warrant to search the Harrod house.

When Rob and his team executed the search warrant in the fall of 2001 they were shocked by what they found. There were six children living in the house, including several girls from the family in Texas. One of Harrod's own daughters, a seven-year-old who suffered from a noticeable skin condition, had been shunned on Harrod's orders due to her physical "imperfection." The social and intellectual deprivation she suffered had reduced her to a feral-like state. She could barely speak, crawled on all fours, cowered in fear, and growled at the officers. The Folsom PD removed the children from the house as well as lots of documentation of their abuse in the form of calendars and journals detailing sex acts; those journals would prove harrowing to review for those of us working the case.

The journals showed how narrowly proscribed the kids' lives had become. In addition to listing every sex act they were required to perform, the journals included everything else they did to seek favor and please their master, from fulfilling chores to exercising enough to remain thin and thus more sexually attractive to their "Lord." In the emotional desert that was their lives, it was heartbreaking to note the meager joy they took from any acknowledgment of their worth: the treat of a soft drink or piece of jewelry for a particular sexual accomplishment, some movement up the status of the family pecking order in the futile hope of some better treatment.

The date set for the trial of Harrod and Hunt in state court was approaching and Del was anxious to get something going against the Labrecques. We could not go after the Labrecques for the molestations themselves: those are violations of state statutes that could only be brought by the authorities in Texas. But we could pursue violations of federal law, which would include trafficking the children across state lines to engage in sex or to produce pornographic images of them. I told Del I hoped we could bring federal charges against both couples and would consult with Laurel White, Assistant U.S. Attorney for the Eastern District of California, to see what needed to be done.

Those of us who worked crimes against children in that part of California always liked to take our cases to Laurel. She was driven by a genuine passion for protecting the most innocent and vulnerable, the kind of passion and commitment that is required to make the system work for child victims. With the rise of the Internet and the opportunities it opened up for child exploitation, as well as the trafficking of children for forced prostitution across state and national borders, she had developed a ready arsenal of ideas to apply federal law in prosecuting offenders for child sex crimes. She really held our feet to the fire when gathering evidence and taught us how to conduct investigations that would proactively address anticipated defense tactics and strategies.

In the Name of the Children

The prohibition against interstate travel for the purpose of illegal sexual activity dates back over a century to what was originally termed the White-Slave Traffic Act and is more familiarly known as the Mann Act, after its original sponsor, Illinois Congressman James Robert Mann. The law was originally intended to crack down on forced prostitution, which at the time was termed "white slavery." But for a long time it was also used to go after people involved in any kind of sexual activity deemed unlawful: from "consensual" prostitution to premarital and extramarital sex to interracial sex to sex with someone below the age of consent. In recent decades the law was amended to remove enforcement against consensual relationships and to focus on forced sex trafficking and sexual exploitation, with special emphasis on protecting children.

Laurel told me we would need to prove that the transit of the children to and from Sacramento was for the purpose of molesting them and instructed me to interview the children to obtain details about their interstate travel. If we could find the evidence, she said she would prosecute. Most of the kids had denied being abused at the time they were removed from the two homes, which was not surprising to me. They had lived in fear for so long—their will subverted to the needs of others, their bodies so thoroughly dominated—that it would take time for them to feel safe enough to acknowledge and articulate what had happened to them. Two years had passed since they were freed from Harrod and Labrecque's all-encompassing authority and I hoped we might now be more successful in getting them to open up.

Del put me in touch with Rob Challoner and he was on board with the plan. Del and Rob told me that some of the Labrecque girls were with their maternal aunt, Franny, and the Harrod children could be reached through Samantha. We decided I would interview Trisha Labrecque first and Franny agreed to bring Trisha to Sacramento. The federal government would pay for the travel and, anticipating the children's needs, I immediately set up with the Sacramento FBI's Victim/Witness Coordinator, Laurie Smandra, to start providing services to all the victims.

On the day of Trisha's interview, I drove out to the airport to pick up her and her aunt. Franny was bubbly and spoke in a tone that was very nurturing. She was a nurse, a profession for which I think she was perfectly suited. Perhaps Franny's voice stands out so much in my mind because it took me so long to hear Trisha utter a word. She remained silent as we drove from the airport and while we stopped for refreshments. It was clearly going to be a challenge to draw her out and I didn't know if I would be successful. I also was worried about doing or saying something that might hurt her further. So I decided to enlist all the help I could get.

When we got to the office I asked Harry Sweeney if I could use his polygraph room, because it had equipment to record the interview and the two-way glass through which others could observe. I put Trisha in the polygraph room and Franny in the viewing room next door. Then I went and found a couple of other people in the office whom I wanted to observe the interview and give me their thoughts and advice. Neither was an agent but they were two of the most insightful people I have ever worked with at the Bureau. Sharon Dorl was an FBI clerk who had a master's degree in abnormal psychology. I consulted with her on every case I worked and this would be no exception. Kathy Lux worked her way up from clerk to an analyst position. She was the person I always turned to for a workup on a suspect or a witness. She also lived and breathed the Bureau for the majority of her life and knew more than almost any agent. I asked Harry to join them. Laurel White was also there to observe and advise.

When I sat down to interview Trisha I was extremely anxious because I still had not heard one word from her. She had been so horribly violated she had no reason to trust me or any other figure of authority. It would be her choice whether to talk or remain silent and keep the secrets locked inside her. As I had in my interview with Cary Stayner, I needed to encourage and support her sense of personal agency. I had noticed her doodling and what she was drawing were pictures of a woman dressed in armor. Her aunt had told me that was how Trisha saw herself, as a warrior queen. I realized these were self-portraits and that inside she had not surrendered to her circumstances. Harrod and Labrecque may have been able to control her physically, but she would not relinquish her mind to them. Through these drawings, she was taking back her power, and I needed to help her find her voice.

In the Name of the Children

As the day progressed, I treated Trisha like the warrior queen she was and she began to speak to me. She was around seventeen at the time of our interview and she revealed that her father began sexually abusing her when she was six years old. This gave her something in common with her two older sisters, something she would eventually share with her younger sister as well—an observation that broke my heart. She described the development of the pseudo-religion, the adoption of biblical names to reflect divine designation, the rules and regulations of the perverse ideology. Her father continued to sexually assault her in different ways to "train" and "prepare" her for "presentation" to Harrod, which according to the system the two men devised was to occur at the time she experienced her first menstrual cycle. At that point she, like the other Labrecque girls, was delivered to Harrod. Within one month of her arrival, the time in which her return ticket was valid, she would be put through her three-part initiation, which involved being assaulted three different ways by Harrod.

If she "passed" the initiation, she would remain living with Harrod and continue to "serve" him. If she "failed" she would be sent back on the return ticket for further "training" from her father. Her older sisters, who had been living with Harrod far longer and were more fully indoctrinated, tried to help things along by serving as "eye candy" for Harrod to get him excited. But Trisha's defiance, the warrior queen inside her that allowed her to resist as much as it was possible to resist in her circumstances, caused her to fail her "presentation" and she was sent home. I continue to be amazed that a man who considered himself to be God was concerned with meeting the validity requirements of an airline ticket.

Trisha flew back to Fort Worth, where her father continued to "train" her for her next presentation opportunity. When Labrecque deemed his daughter adequately prepared, he sent her back to Sacramento. This time she passed and was forced to stay in Sacramento until the efforts of Samantha and Rob caused her to be rescued and removed from her chamber of horrors.

What Trisha had to say took the wind out of me and deeply affected everyone in the observation room, including Laurel White. It was one thing to hear a cold hard recitation of facts from Del, but listening to the firsthand account of this sweet, brave young girl being forced into sexual servitude by her own parents was emotionally wrenching. Tips from Sharon and Kathy helped me keep Trisha focused and enabled her to work through her anger. As she told her story, she became that warrior queen right before our eyes, adopting a tone of resistance that had not only helped her survive her own ordeal but would help all the victims of Harrod and Labrecque. I was amazed by her strength and resilience. I committed myself to making sure that, one day, her voice would be heard in a court of law, and those who wronged her would have to answer for their crimes.

I conferred with Laurel about what we needed to do next to build the federal case. We decided to try to interview Harrod's son Glen. After Rob Challoner served his search warrant on the Harrod house and found the Labrecque girls there, he realized the Harrod boys were in Fort Worth and worked with Texas authorities to have them removed from the Labrecque home. Samantha didn't even know most of her stepsiblings at the time she went to police because she had been out of the Harrod house for so long. But in the aftermath she provided shelter to as many of them as she could, at one point squeezing five of her newfound siblings into her small home to help them get a fresh start on life. (Franny had taken in several of the Labrecque kids in addition to Trisha.) I called Samantha and we made arrangements for Glen to fly by himself to Sacramento. She described him so that I would recognize him when I went to pick him up and said he walked with a strained gait. She said this was because he had gained 100 pounds since being removed from the Labrecques' custody.

While interviewing Glen, I asked the same group of people to observe us through the glass. Glen did not display any of Trisha's reticence or her anger. Instead, he seemed very open and upbeat. He smiled throughout the interview, even when describing the beatings and abuse he suffered. His affect was so startling I didn't know whether to be concerned for his mental health or worried about whether we were getting the truth. But by the end of the interview I realized that Glen was happy because, for him, every day outside the control of his father and Labrecque was a good day to him.

Glen said he believed he had trouble learning and felt somewhat challenged in expressing himself. I told him we would go slow and not to worry about me understanding him. To gauge his level of truthfulness and understanding, I directed him to look at the carpet in the interview room, which appeared gray but when you looked at it more carefully was really composed of many colors that gave the overall appearance of being gray. I explained to Glen that if I asked him what color the carpet was I would consider him to be telling the truth if he described it as being made up of many different colors. If he simply answered "gray," I would not consider that accurate. In other words, truth for me is in details, not generalities.

I then presented Glen with another analogy, the same one I explained to Cary Stayner when I was trying to get him to summon the courage to tell me the truth. I used the example of a soldier in battle and told Glen that in my opinion courage is not running into fire without fear of the consequences; real courage is doing something you know is right even when you're scared to death of doing it. Glen told me he understood the difference. He said that he did not do well in school and that as a result his father beat him a lot. There were times he feared he would be beaten so badly he would not be able to recover. When Glen was seven years old, his father told him he was going to be sent to live with the Labrecque family in order to have better teachers. Glen said he didn't want to go and did not want to be separated from his brother, Martin, whom he loved. What he didn't realize, but our investigation showed, was that Harrod wanted the Labrecques to prepare Glen sexually to assume the role of patriarch in the future.

Glen's mother, Irene Hunt, took him on an airplane to Texas. Soon after they arrived at the Labrecques' house, his mother walked him to an upstairs bedroom where Mrs. Labrecque was waiting. He was told to get undressed and get in bed with a naked Juliette. His mom took pictures of him with Juliette, posing them in sexual positions. Glen recalled details, like those colors in the rug. He remembered the sound of the camera clicking as his mom took pictures. He remembered Juliette's husband asking him, when he came back downstairs, how it was.

Glen went on to describe what daily life was like at the Labrecque house. He said Labrecque beat him on a regular basis with a leather belt, a wooden two-by-four, and other objects that were at hand around the household. He said that during the eight or so years he lived with the Labrecques, Michael wore out at least three leather straps beating him. The beatings would be worse if he did not master the school subjects he was supposed to learn. Fearing failure, he cheated on a math test and got caught. As punishment he received one hundred lashes with a belt. He said the teacher at the Labrecque house was Nina Labrecque, one of the Labrecque girls who was even younger than him and had not yet been "presented" to Harrod. I couldn't imagine how a child could teach another child a subject that she had not had the opportunity to study in school. It seemed like Glen was set up for failure and that both Harrod and Labrecque used his learning difficulties as an excuse to act out their sadism. Maybe they worried that he would grow big and strong as he approached manhood and so they needed to undermine his sense of intellectual competence and break him down physically so he would be unable to challenge their authority.

Glen described beatings so severe that he would not be able to use his leg or arm or fingers for some time thereafter. He said once he was unable to walk for a month because he could not use his leg and had to stay in bed. The Labrecques also did not feed him enough, perhaps to keep him from growing. As Trisha had mentioned to me, Glen stated that he had gained over 100 pounds since being freed from the Labrecques' custody. When Trisha brought up this fact, I was expecting Glen to be overweight, but he was not at all. I shuddered to think how starved and skeletal he must have been that gaining 100 pounds put him at a healthy, normal weight. I could not help but think of the images, captured in newsreel footage, of the skeletal figures liberated from Nazi death camps during World War II. No wonder every day since his "liberation" seemed like a good day. I began to suspect that Glen's strange way of walking was not the result of any weight gain but due to permanent injury from the beatings he suffered.

I cannot adequately express what it is like to listen to someone describe their everyday life in this way, to imagine children being raised in an environment where sadism was the norm. As Glen went on, I could feel myself falling into a bottomless well of sorrow. I became obsessed with helping Trisha and Glen and all the Harrod and Labrecque children, but what could I ever do to make right what had happened to these kids?

In the Name of the Children

There is no true justice or closure in the types of crimes I investigated. I cannot bring Michael, Danny, Alexia, Salaam, Juli, Silvina, and all the other murdered kids whose cases I worked, back to life. I could not even bring Danny's killer to court. And I could never give Trisha and Glen back their childhoods, their innocence, their untrammeled trust. All I could do is try to give victims and survivors a measure of justice. Sometimes that meant simply getting to the truth and providing answers to what happened. Sometimes it was locating the body of a missing child and "bringing him home" to his family for burial. Sometimes it meant conviction and punishment. I would do whatever I could to send Harrod and Labrecque away, but no sentence would ever be enough to make up for what these children had stolen from them.

I had to concentrate on what Glen was saying and not my own reactions, so I did my best to tamp down my feelings as we got further into the area of his own sexual victimization. As Glen started to approach puberty, Labrecque forced his daughters to perform sexual acts on the boy. Labrecque also started using handcuffs on Glen, sometimes leaving him cuffed for days and even weeks. He described to me the degradation of having to beg for help to go to the bathroom. He said that he was sometimes allowed to visit Sacramento as a reward, but on one such visit home he was forced by his father to engage in sexual acts that left him feeling ashamed and further humiliated.

Glen revealed that when his mother and father were arrested by the Folsom Police Department, Labrecque flew with him back to California to try to assist the Harrods and destroy evidence. Labrecque bailed Harrod and Hunt out of jail and made Glen help him destroy pictures and documents hidden at the Harrod home to prevent police from getting them, and they burned them in a trash barrel.

When we finished I took Glen back to the airport. Rather than simply dropping him off out front, I walked him to his flight and waited with him until he boarded. I did this in part because I was not certain of his ability to look out for himself but also because I wanted to show him respect and acknowledge his value, as I had endeavored to do with Trisha. It seemed like it was the first time he had ever been treated like he was important, and the fact that it took a stranger to do what his parents should have done made me incredibly sad.

The Twenty-Two

After he boarded, I went back to the car, called Lori, and broke down sobbing. I had told Glen in the interview that I was going to prove to him that this should not have happened to him and I was going to show him there would be justice. Since meeting Trisha and Glen I could not understand the extreme emotional reaction I was experiencing. I headed home and, as I made the last turn into my driveway, I realized that it was because for the first time in a long time I was dealing with victims who were still alive. The responsibility I felt for Trisha and Glen was overwhelming. I worried about the promise I had made to Glen. What measure of justice could we possibly be able to deliver that would be adequate compensation for the suffering of these children?

I called Laurel White after Glen's interview. I was anxious to know if she thought the interviews were providing the evidence needed to prosecute federally and to get the go-ahead from her to continue the investigation. By that point Del Oros had been transferred to another position with the Sacramento County District Attorney's office and Deputy DA Chris Ore had been assigned the state case against Allen Harrod and Irene Hunt. Laurel had been in contact with the DA's office and had identified several things she thought could yield federal prosecution. She believed that Glen's initial travel to Fort Worth, where he was immediately directed to pose in nude sexual photos with Juliette Labrecque, was a possibility, because that appeared to fit the definition of interstate sex trafficking. Laurel believed sending the Labrecque girls from Texas to California for their sexual presentation to Harrod was a violation of federal law as well as state statutes. Through Laurel's coordination with Chris Ore, Harrod was charged with additional state molestation charges for what we had learned he did to Trisha.

Once the prosecution strategy had been formulated, Laurel suggested that I interview Polly Harrod. I checked with Rob and he signed off on that plan. Polly was living with a foster family in Sacramento. I contacted her foster parents and arranged for her to come to our office. Polly, like all the Harrod kids, spoke in hushed tones—which was not surprising considering how brutally they had all been silenced. What was amazing was that they were able to trust that anyone was interested in their welfare, that they had any belief that their words and their wishes had power. I was relieved to hear Polly say that she was very happy with her foster parents. I'm so grateful for people like Samantha and Franny and Carole Sund and Polly's foster parents who open their homes to abused and abandoned children and allow them to experience what it is like to live in a loving family.

Polly said she had been required to provide sexual services to her father since she was five years old. (All the Harrod and Labrecque kids were teenagers when I interviewed them.) She told me she was scared and did not want to engage in any sex acts, but her father demanded it and her mother forced her to comply and "taught" her how to do what was required. I cannot imagine how she or any of the kids survived what she described because the whole system was set up to rob them of any sense of self, safety, and value. Through absolute control of his home and family, enforced through vicious beatings, Harrod created the image that his children lived to please him, when really they were in fear for their lives if they did not act as instructed. It was as if he were a director and the kids were actors required to give the appearance that they wanted to be assaulted and controlled. His "religion" evolved out of this same theatrical vein, a grand fiction to rationalize and ritualize his seemingly unquenchable desire to have sex with children. Polly was immersed in this environment for so long that she was only now learning what a normal life is like.

One by one, the Labrecque girls moved in as they reached the stage of "presentation," until there were finally four living with the Harrods. Her father played the girls against each other in a most insidious way. He told Polly he did not find her as desirable as the Labrecque girls and would give them her favorite clothing. They were all expected to vie for his attention and compete for whatever treats he would throw their way. The girls were expected to wear sexually provocative clothing purchased from places like Frederick's of Hollywood and to flash their breasts at Harrod (flashing being one of the "offerings" they could claim credit for in their journals).

At one point Michael Labrecque traveled to Sacramento for "religious training." While he was at their home, Polly's mother told her she had to go in and do for Labrecque what she did with her father. Polly said she was repulsed but was given no choice. This assault on Polly became a criminal count by which Chris Ore could also prosecute Labrecque in California state court. Chris also added other charges against Harrod to his state prosecution based on my interviews, which meant I would be a witness in that proceeding.

In addition to the interviews with the children, there was physical evidence that had been seized from the Folsom house that we needed to go through to reconstruct what had happened to the children. We all worked together—the FBI and the U.S. Attorney's office, the District Attorney's office and the Folsom PD—building the federal case and helping to bolster the state action. There were the journals kept by the children, which were found neatly organized in binders on a bookshelf of the living room of the Folsom house. A computer was also seized along with discs and paper records and receipts. Art Dorl, Sharon's husband, a forensic computer examiner for the Bureau, did most of the computer excavation. Art, Sharon, a new agent named Jim Harris, and I went through the plethora of diaries, calendars, and other forms of written documentation. It turned out that Harrod and Labrecque kept meticulous records of their conquests, often in code. We also found the airline tickets purchased for Trisha's "presentation" to Harrod, which was crucial to our interstate trafficking case.

Laurel presented the evidence we uncovered to a federal grand jury. I testified, relating what the children had told me when I interviewed them. I remember the jurors responding with great emotion to what they were hearing. At one point, Laurel herself was so overcome she burst into sobs and ran from the grand jury room. I had to sit there on the stand, literally biting my lip to keep myself from breaking down.

The grand jury indicted Harrod, Hunt, and the Labrecques. The violations of federal law included transportation and travel with intent to engage in illegal sexual activity with minors and transferring and obtaining custody of a minor to create child pornography. Harrod and Hunt were already in jail in Sacramento awaiting their state trial. I tracked the Labrecques down in Iowa, where they had fled after authorities removed the Harrod boys from their home in Texas. It was cathartic to put together their arrest warrants, but I decided not to go out on the arrest because I wasn't sure I could remain professional. I couldn't get the image out of my mind of how Labrecque had left Glen in handcuffs for weeks at a time, and I was afraid I might do something cruel, like cuff Labrecque too tightly. I asked Rob Challoner to go in my place. He started the ball rolling on this case, and I felt he had earned the collar. I just asked that when he put the bracelets on Labrecque he tell him that Glen was thinking about him.

Rob went out with Hitman and some other members of our crimes against children task force to make the arrest and serve a search warrant at the Iowa residence. Two minor children who were living with them, a young son and daughter, were taken into the custody of Social Services. It was later determined that they, too, had been sexually assaulted. The two oldest Labrecque girls, Barbara and Helen, were also there, the ones who had been living with Harrod and considered themselves to be his religious wives. They declined help and refused to cooperate in the investigation. It was hard for the arrest team to leave them behind when they returned to Sacramento, but they were adults now and there was nothing else we could do.

As the state and federal cases moved toward trial, I interviewed more of the kids. Each interview was a challenge. Some of the kids had a conflicted sense of loyalty. Others were too afraid or ashamed to articulate what they had experienced. I had to tread a very careful line. We needed the information from the kids to prosecute the parents, and I also felt that they needed to talk about what had happened to them to begin to recover from it. But I was afraid of pushing them to places they were not yet ready to go. I broke off interviews with two of the younger Harrod boys because I felt that continuing would cause them further emotional trauma. Lucas, one of the three Harrod boys sent to live with the Labrecques, was willing to talk about the beatings and vividly recalled Labrecque counting out the hundred lashings he administered to Glen for some purported misdeed. But he couldn't talk about the rest, which he said he told himself to forget. He said he just wanted to focus on his "new" life.

"When you tell me you told yourself to forget, you didn't really forget, did you?" I asked. Lucas, who was still only thirteen, eleven years old when he was liberated, acknowledged that was true. I told him I was ending the interview for his sake but said I hoped he would talk to his therapist or his foster parents when he was ready and not just bury the pain inside him.

"What you could tell us is important," I said. "But it does not mean more than you being OK. We're not going to hurt you or make you feel worse just to get what we need from you."

Nina Labrecque was so reluctant to speak she wouldn't even look at me or say my name when we began the interview. Then she wanted to question me about my life before she agreed to answer any questions about hers. She was a remarkable young woman, seventeen at the time of our interview, very bright and perceptive. But she had only known life with Allen Harrod at its center, and his dictates had controlled her life so thoroughly she said she didn't even know if it was wrong for adults to have sex with children.

"That's all I was taught," she said. To survive what she went through, she used her own form of psychological distancing.

"I blocked my conscience a long time ago—my right and wrong, too much confusion," she said. I told her that I didn't believe that she actually blocked her conscience but resigned herself to a situation she could not avoid.

"You don't deserve to go through life blocking out of your mind what is right and wrong," I said.

Taking in my words, Nina's denial dissolved. She said her dad began forcing her to perform oral sex on him when she was seven years old. "Isaac," as she called Harrod, would call her father once or twice a month and announce that the next day was a "Day of Rejoicing," which meant it was the day she would be required to pleasure her father and she would rue the approach of the day. At one point she asked her mom, "What does this have to do with religion?"

"But she said I just have to do what he says, that we all had to," Nina said. "I told her that it had nothing to do with religion; it was just about sex."

I asked her how this situation made her feel. Angry? No. Hurt? No.

"Lost," she said. There it was, that sense of resignation.

"And how do you feel now?"

"Lost," she repeated, which broke my heart.

"You're not lost, you've been found," I sought to assure her. I told her how proud I was of her for acknowledging what had happened to her and that this was the beginning of a new life for her, of healing and making sure nothing like this ever happened to her children if she decided to become a mother.

When she had her first period, at fifteen, her father told her it was time for her to go to Harrod for her "presentation." Under the rules of the "faith," she had to go within a year of her first menstrual period, and Labrecque had been mad at her sister Trisha for delaying the trip and then failing her presentation. Nina said she wanted to go right away. I asked her why, startled by her eagerness.

"I was trying to escape," she said. She didn't anticipate that Harrod was going to demand something even worse from her.

Two weeks after Nina got her period, Labrecque put his daughter on a plane to Sacramento. Again, it was the details she recalled that leant credence and poignancy: her mom not crying as she sent her daughter off to be deflowered; her dad buying her a bag of Cheez-Its, a final little bribe to mollify her. Irene Hunt, whom she referred to as Rebekah, was at the Sacramento airport to collect her, along with her sisters Trisha and Helen.

"They needed Trisha there to recognize my face," Nina said, an observation that stabbed me like a knife to the gut. Harrod met her at the house and spouted a bunch of spiritual mumbo jumbo that she didn't understand. Then he said he wanted to take some time getting to know her. She had been sent out with only the clothes on her back. Harrod told her he would buy her some things to wear, which did not include pajamas. She noticed no one wore pajamas, just walked around naked. She asked some of the other kids about it and noticed their embarrassment. Harrod let her sleep in the shirt and pants she arrived in for a week and then took them away from her, telling her by that time she "knew better."

Nina had the same one-month time frame to complete her presentation as Trisha had, because of the terms of the return ticket. Harrod explained the three stages to her and that intercourse was included. But he waited for two weeks, and then had trouble getting an erection and reaching climax. She mentioned the fact, like it was no stranger than any of his other unholy rules, that "he wore a condom because he wasn't allowed to get anyone pregnant unless they were eighteen." It took seven tries before he was fully able to consummate the assault. She said she forced herself not to cry because she wanted to get it over with and be able to go back home—the place she had wanted to escape, only to find this place was even worse. At least, she said, her father "didn't do that!" She didn't understand that if she had completed her initiation, she would not have been allowed to return home but forced to live permanently with Harrod.

Adopting Harrod's lingo, Nina said she never "crossed over," meaning that her presentation was not completed because the Folsom Police showed up and dragged Harrod and Hunt away. Nina empathized with her mother and wanted to help Juliette. In fact, she only wanted to speak against her father if her mother would as well. She seemed to think Harrod still had god-like powers over her. She believed he was omnipresent and was even spiritually aware of our interview. I told her that he was not God, just a man who was evil and hurt many children for his own needs. She was shocked to hear that we had identified twenty-two victims. There were brothers and sisters she didn't even know she had and "cousins" she had yet to meet.

Everything we learned in the investigation added new dimensions of horror. For purposes of prosecution we had to make sure the kids could distinguish between perpetrators. It was devastating to hear children describe in detail the difference in appearance and taste between their perpetrators' offending organs. I felt shock, dismay, disbelief, numbness, intense anger, and overwhelming sorrow. I could understand how these kids wanted to force themselves to forget and "block their conscience" because I couldn't bear to know what I knew and wished I could unknow it.

I felt a tremendous sense of responsibility toward the victims in this case and decided that, if they were willing, I wanted to always remain in their lives and try to be there for them however I could. At one point, Martin Harrod asked me if I was there for the case or if I was there for them. I told him that the two were inextricable. The case was *for* them. Sending their parents to jail was to protect them. Everything I was doing was in their names. But I would not abandon them no matter what resulted in court.

In the Name of the Children

Lori and I have been there for them to this day. We consider them part of our family and some of the kids send me cards on Father's Day. We've celebrated many milestones with them. When Glen continued to suffer health problems I took him to my own doctor. Neither his parents nor the Labrecques had ever taken him to a doctor despite, or more likely because of, all the damage they had done to him. The doctor told me that nearly every bone in his body had been broken at some point, including several vertebrae, and that he was suffering from spinal compression, which explained his altered gait. He lives with constant permanent physical pain. It's not just Lori and I who have remained in close contact with the kids. So have Laurel White and Chris Ore and his family.

Harrod and his disciples were unrepentant to the end. The legal proceedings against them took many strange twists and turns as they played every trick in the book to avoid being held accountable: from stalling tactics to bizarre legal maneuvers to attacking the children and those of us who sought to help them. But we were determined not to let them win and fought back at every turn.

At first, it seemed as if even the system was against us. The state was forced to drop seventy of the ninety-seven counts against Allen Harrod and all but five of the twenty-seven counts against Irene Hunt after the U.S. Supreme Court redefined the statute of limitations on child molestation, limiting the number of years after the fact that allegations can be brought to trial. That would have cut the sentence each defendant could receive nearly in half, but Chris Ore added on additional charges that were uncovered by our investigation. Then on the eve of trial, Harrod's attorney questioned his client's sanity and the judge had to delay proceedings in order for him to be psychologically evaluated. He was ultimately deemed competent to stand trial and the state case proceeded against Harrod and Hunt.

Several of the children testified. Even though the charges involving Samantha had to be dropped because they exceeded the statute of limitations, she got her day in court. The judge allowed her to testify about the abuse she experienced and witnessed among her siblings to show the pattern of behavior in question. Some of the Harrod boys also testified about being molested by Juliette Labrecque. The jurors reacted to the children's testimony with the same kind of emotion the grand jury had displayed when I related their stories. In one instance, a juror recoiled and audibly groaned in horror and disgust at what the children had to endure.

The defense took the same tack the couples' lawyers would in the federal case, the defense that has been employed since the infamous McMartin preschool case in the 1980s: that the children were lying, that the whole concept of ritualized abuse was fiction, a kind of mass hysteria implanted in the minds of suggestible children by police, therapists, and the media. Harrod's lawyer, Dani Williams, compared the case against her client to the Salem witch trials and cast Samantha not as someone who rescued her brothers and sisters but as the mastermind of a conspiracy who influenced her siblings to back up her lie. She also accused me of lulling the children into false testimony during my interviews, likening me to Kaa, the evil snake in Disney's version of *The Jungle Book,* who used hypnosis and other mind tricks to control children.

But the evidence backed up the victims' assertions, just as it would to the federal charges: photos of the adults having sex with the kids, the journals the children were required to keep documenting their weekly "offerings" to Harrod as well as the logs kept by Harrod and Labrecque, the Frederick's of Hollywood dresses the girls were required to wear to look alluring, the biological fact that Harrod had fathered a child by one of the Labrecque girls. In January 2004, the jury in the state case convicted Harrod and Hunt on all charges, including a special circumstance that made Harrod eligible for life in prison.

"We were the children's voice," one juror told the media afterward.

Half the panel returned to court to witness the sentencing. Two of the children did as well. Martin addressed his parents face to face. "I just want to say to my father and mother that I'm not their slave anymore," the eighteen-year-old told them, noting that while he had once been their captive he was now free and they were the ones behind bars. One of the Labrecque girls sent a letter lamenting the ongoing depression that "scars [her] soul" from "being forced to grow up too fast."

In the Name of the Children

Hunt's attorney, who had denied during the trial that any sexual abuse occurred, changed course at sentencing and put on an expert in battered woman syndrome who said Hunt admitted the molestations to her but had been powerless to stop them. She was given twenty years. Harrod was sentenced to two life terms plus sixty-two years. He lashed out at the children, the court, and all who "wronged" him, warning they would be subject to his own "sword of justice."

It was an impressive sentence; the judge who issued it told Harrod, "You have earned every day." But it was not enough time for Chris Ore. First, Harrod had only been charged with crimes against six of his victims and then the Supreme Court had substantially reduced the time frame of offenses for which he could be charged. Now the time the judge meted out did not match what Chris had calculated based upon the number of violations.

The prosecutor took the exceedingly rare step of appealing a life sentence and in 2007 Harrod's sentence was amended to more than 400 years. It may sound ridiculous to sentence someone to more years than they could possibly live. But I can guarantee you that enhanced sentence meant something to Harrod's victims and to all of us who worked on their behalf, and, I hope, sends a message to anybody in the future who seeks to abuse children or dismiss ritualized abuse as collective hysteria and "moral panic." To Chris it was a matter of principle and precedent. The added time wouldn't meaningfully affect Harrod's circumstances— barring a successful appeal he would certainly die in prison—but Chris believed that clearing up how a sentence should be calculated might be of great importance to some future case.

After her conviction in state court, Hunt agreed to plead guilty to transporting her seven-year-old son to Texas to have sex with Juliette and help prosecutors go after her husband and the Labrecques. I'll admit I wasn't feeling much sympathy when I sat down to interview Hunt. If she really was an unwitting accomplice, forced to comply with the wishes of a tyrant (as Nina saw her mother, Juliette), I wanted to know how her husband was able to get her to do the terrible things she had done. She told me that she was still a young girl when Harrod married her sister, Ila. While visiting the couple, she said Harrod raped her with what she believed to be the tacit approval of her sister. She stayed with the couple and came to be considered a second wife.

Hunt expressed fear unlike I have ever seen from a witness. She said Harrod controlled her every move. She described one occasion when Harrod and Ila were away and she took the opportunity to go visit some other relatives nearby. When Harrod learned of it he told her to go to the upstairs bedroom and wait for him there. What she said ensued was almost beyond belief but wasn't out of character with the kinds of things the children told us. Hunt said that when he came into the room he first punched her in the face, knocking her to the ground. He then grabbed a fistful of her waist-length hair and chopped it off with a pair of scissors. He dragged her around by her remaining locks to another room, where he produced a jar containing feces and urine and forced her to consume it. She said from that point on she never challenged Harrod and did exactly as he told her to do.

I thought about the women in Ulysses Roberson's cult and the violence and intimidation that kept them in line. They did not participate in hurting their children, but they did nothing to stop it, and did not report the murder of Salaam. We all know what we think we would have done, what we would like others to do, but can any of us really know how we would react in such a situation?

Hunt fully cooperated in helping us prepare for the federal case. For example, I had never understood how Glen's contention could be true that he and Michael Labrecque had destroyed evidence at the Harrod house, as the Folsom Police had thoroughly searched the place at the time Harrod and Hunt were arrested and seized what evidence was there. Hunt told us that there was a secret compartment hidden behind a wall where pornographic photos taken of the children were stashed. Labrecque knew that taking and exchanging those photos set them all up for substantial federal time. That was why he burned them.

As it came time for the federal trial to take place, Harrod did not want to face another jury like the one in state court that had sympathized with the victims, so he attempted something truly novel. He requested a trial by judge only, what is known as a bench trial. In federal court, both sides typically have to agree to waive a jury, and the U.S. Attorney adamantly opposed the request. But Harrod's attorney said he would not be contesting two of the major prongs of the case: that sex acts occurred or that the children traveled between California and Texas. Instead, he said, the defense would focus solely on intent, specifically arguing that the government could not prove he had knowledge or intent as to the purpose for transporting the children, and that the abuse testimony would be so inflammatory that a jury could not focus purely on the issue of intent. The judge set to try the case in U.S. District Court agreed and granted Harrod's motion, which meant he alone would decide the case, not a jury.

In almost every murder or sexual assault case, and pretty much any case involving child victims, defendants try to exclude from the trial certain pictures, evidence, or testimony they say will inflame the passions of jurors and prevent their clients from getting a fair trial. The test employed by judges to decide these questions, based on well-established legal precedence, is whether the evidence is "more prejudicial than probative." The tipping point is when a piece of evidence—say, a crime scene photo or personal testimony—is so gratuitously graphic or emotionally laden that it is being introduced simply to evoke anger toward the defendant or sympathy toward the victim, rather than having true evidentiary value. In this case, all the facts were terrible, but they were the facts and thus of evidentiary value. Rather than letting the case proceed before a jury and ruling on individual objections to evidence as they might arise, the judge said that the conduct, charged and uncharged, against the defendants was so "heinous and repugnant" that jurors would be incapable of ruling dispassionately on purely technical arguments regarding interstate commerce.

Harrod still wanted to rule the children's lives, to dictate the terms, to take away the one thing that made reliving their experience slightly less onerous to bear. Laurel was outraged and so was I. She had me contact the children to see if they wanted a jury present and to ask them how they would feel if there was no jury. They all told me that during the state case they were comforted by the reaction of the jurors to their testimony and they absolutely wanted a jury to hear the federal case. Laurel appealed and another couple of years dragged on before the question was decided.

This was a particularly bitter pill for me to swallow, because the defense knew that I had been planning to retire at the conclusion of the case and now, with yet another delay, I would no longer be an FBI agent when it finally came to trial and therefore unable to testify. I believe in our system and that defendants are entitled to the best defense possible, but in this case the defense went beyond any bounds of propriety. The defendants and their attorneys seemed more motivated by a personal, petty vendetta than by any concept of justice. As we left the courtroom the day Laurel announced her appeal, each defense attorney individually asked me when I was retiring, relishing that I would no longer be able to take the stand on the kids' behalf.

Five months after I retired, the Ninth Circuit Court ruled that a defendant has no constitutional right to a trial by judge only and that the government's failure to consent to a bench trial does not violate a defendant's right to a fair trial or due process. The "able and skilled" judge to whom the case had been assigned would have an abundance of tools at his disposal to ensure a fair trial, the court stated.

Then Michael Labrecque asked for permission not to attend his own trial, saying his scruffy appearance might prejudice him in the eyes of the jurors. He, like Harrod, had grown his hair and beard out to resemble Old Testament prophets. That was denied, and he tried to have the proceedings delayed while he appealed, but his motion to stay was also slapped down.

At long last, in 2008, six and a half years after Samantha went to Rob Challoner and told her story, the federal trial commenced. When I left the FBI, I assigned the case over to Special Agent Jim Harris and he assisted Laurel with the prosecution. Four of the children, by then adults, came to court to rebut the defendants' claims that the sex was unforced. The defense had claimed no jury could fairly hear their case, but the decision by the jury in the federal trial was quite nuanced. Harrod and Labrecque were found guilty on multiple charges of transporting minor children for sexual activity and Harrod was also found guilty of transferring custody of Glen to Labrecque for the purpose of making pornography. But they deadlocked on another interstate travel count against Labrecque and hung on charges against Juliette Labrecque, who portrayed herself, like Irene Hunt, as another victim of the cult. Still, due to the number of counts and the force involved, the two men received life in prison. For her cooperation, Hunt was sentenced to another fourteen years to be served concurrent with her state sentence. Juliette was acquitted and went free.

In imposing his sentence, U.S. District Judge William Shubb called Harrod and Labrecque the worst of the worst and noted that they never exhibited an ounce of remorse or sympathy for the suffering they imposed on their children. He refused even to address any idea of supervised release in the future, saying he fully intended for them to die while in custody.

"I never want them to get out," he declared. "I am convinced they would do these things again if given the opportunity."

I'd like to say everything ended in resounding victory. But with the conclusion of the legal cases, the services the kids had received from victim/witness coordinators ended and they were on their own to pick up the pieces of their lives. Trisha and Nina Labrecque went home to Franny's house, and the Harrod children went home to their aunt and uncle in El Dorado County, California. The relatives who took in the Harrod children were in a more financially precarious position, and the kids were immediately faced with having to find work and more settled places to live. They were left with virtually no education and had to take manual labor jobs to cover living expenses. Yet each has persevered. Several of the kids graduated from college or trade school, and Trisha and Nina are both accomplished graphic artists. Lori and I are enormously proud of what all the kids have been able to achieve and continue to be amazed by their character, fortitude, and resilience.

My wife and I have tried to be there for the kids in any way we can, but I cannot help but ask hard questions that they sometimes do not want to answer. They see us as caring but are understandably wary, as their ability to trust has been deeply strained. When the legal process ended, I made a point of introducing myself to their various apartment managers and provided my number so they had someone to call if there were problems with the rent or other issues. When their financial situations appeared to be beyond the ability of the children to address, Lori and I provided funds so the children would not be put out on the street. Our ability to do this was limited, but luckily, they have been able to get by.

We have attended three of the kids' weddings and many graduations and birthday parties. We consider ourselves unbelievably fortunate to

The Twenty-Two

have met the two children we didn't even know about for a long time, who were removed from the house in Iowa when the Labrecques were taken into custody. As with Steven Stayner, however, there is no fairy-tale ending to the story. There is no ability to go on to a completely normal life after what they experienced. They struggle with PTSD and still have difficulty fully grasping all that happened to them. Glen lives with unremitting physical pain, and I believe that as he ages, his ability to work will diminish. Parenting for some has been a particular challenge, robbed as they were of any semblance of a happy childhood.

But life goes on and despite their ongoing hardships, happiness does exist—because anything is better than the life that they once had to endure.

CHAPTER TEN

Lori, Joseph, and Jordan

THE THINGS THAT I HAVE WITNESSED and experienced investigating crimes against children have taken a toll on me and caused my family to suffer as well. It is not easy for me to acknowledge the damage inside me and the struggles I have endured. It is even harder to face the shame of knowing that I have harmed my family, whether directly or inadvertently. But the truth is that my wife and sons were victims, too, of the cases' effect on me. Their love and support helped pull me through and restored me to life. We have worked hard to heal each other and get to a happier, healthier place as a family. I hope by discussing this, people outside law enforcement may get a better understanding of what we experience on the job. I also hope that people within the profession who need assistance can talk about it and get help.

Like a lot of cops, like a lot of men in general, I wanted to be the strong, silent type. I wanted to be composed and in control—like a pilot who remains calm even when faced with catastrophic failure and methodically tries to remedy the crisis. But I've always been a man of great emotion. For the first ten years of my life, teased and bullied due to my deformity, I felt scared, insecure, and powerless. After surgery gave me more normal physical abilities, the anger I had been bottling up came out in violent and defiant outbursts.

By the time I became an FBI agent I was able to exercise a greater degree of control over myself. The running I had taken up helped me de-stress, organize my thoughts and feelings, and experience a sense of physical competency that I had longed to feel. Marrying Lori and starting a family gave me center and focus, happiness and acceptance. My relationship with Lori grew from friendship to best friends to love and we considered ourselves partners and equals. But looking back, I wonder if she and the kids might have been happier if we never moved to California. We loved the New Jersey farmhouse we had painstakingly worked to make our home, and she had a great job as a research biologist with Merck pharmaceuticals. We said the move was a mutual decision, to find the best place to raise our kids and enjoy the splendor of nature. But was she really putting her needs secondary to mine?

Lori would eventually find work with the U.S. Fish and Wildlife Service, which was not on par financially with the job she left behind but had a mission she believed in. I was so proud of being an FBI agent and helping kids that I somehow did not expect it to interfere with my family life. Lori always knew me better than I knew myself. But even she had no idea how bad it would get.

With Joe being so sick upon our arrival in California, we barely even noticed the beauty of our new surroundings. For the eighteen months it took him to recover I lived in a fog of fear and anxiety. I didn't recognize it at the time, because I was so consumed by my own feelings, as the uncertainty of Joe's recovery revealed a new vulnerability in my life, the vulnerability that every parent feels concerning the welfare of their child. It was even worse for Lori, who had the continuing emotional and physical burden of caring for a very sick child, causing her to put aside her career. I had the daily escape of the job and then retreating to the garage when I got home to work on some seemingly important project when I was really hiding from facing what I couldn't bear to deal with: the fear of losing Joe and watching him suffer.

I will never forget the day we began to believe that Joe was in remission. There had been a long hospitalization and countless doctor visits but slowly the follow-up appointments became less frequent. One day in 1992, I took Joe to his appointment with his pediatric nephrologist, Dr. Sudesh Makker. It had been quite a while since our last appointment and at first the receptionist and then the doctor asked where Joe was. I pointed to the normal-sized, healthy-looking boy next to me and they were shocked by the change in his appearance. Everybody in that office welled up with emotion. We sent at least thirty-five thank-you letters to everyone who helped care for Joe and give us back our son. That had been the big turning point for Lori and me, in deciding what we wanted to do with our lives and our careers. We wanted to mean as much to others as those who had meant so much to us.

In the Name of the Children

With Joe in remission, we were able to enjoy our new home. In the winter the fog has a way of coming up and settling just below our house, which gave us the feeling we were living on a cloud. We were ninety minutes from San Francisco and an hour from Lake Tahoe. We had ten acres that Lori would not let me touch except to clear for fire danger, which left plenty of room for animals—both our ever-growing menagerie of pets and the deer and other wildlife that wandered free on our property. Lori arranged trips for us to explore California. I began my quest to customize our home for us and engage in my favorite hobby of restoring classic muscle cars. My own two children were thriving, and life was great.

When the Frankie Proctor case ended in such a wonderful way, being able to return a living child to his parents, it provided an opportunity for Lori and the boys to see what my job in Sacramento was all about and why it was becoming such a passion for me. Working Danny's case, however, was an exercise in frustration. The irresolution of it was very hard to take. Despite our best efforts, despite identifying his killer and getting a confession, there was nothing we could do to bring that person to justice. Vern Kelch and I worked at that case for nearly a decade and the satisfaction we did experience was in identifying his killer and enabling his family to give him a proper burial. How we believed Danny died was hard to take, but so were the sad facts of how he was forced to live.

The brutality of Michael Lyons's murder and the horror that gripped me at his crime scene is something that still affects me. It's one thing to take a class or read a text on death investigation, but to see a child so much like your own in a setting like that changes you forever. For a long time during and after the case I had difficulty concentrating. My mind was forever replaying what I saw, heard, touched, smelled, and felt that day. I would sit and watch TV with my family and have no clue what program I had just seen. I could not sleep, could not think about much of anything other than Michael's suffering.

I isolated myself in an escapist way, hoping to avoid any and all interaction. I believed there was something wrong with me, that I was weak and letting down my family. I was ashamed that I could not shake the depression I was experiencing. Eventually, I went to see FBI Chaplain

Lori, Joseph, and Jordan

Mark O'Sullivan, who had helped me previously recognize how I avoided my family when my son was so sick. I told Lori how much the cases were living inside me, and I shared some of my difficulties, in simpler terms, with Joe and Jordan. Lori's concern and care helped me in the moment, but the symptoms I was suffering continued. Michael's crime scene was the first thing I thought of when I awoke and the last thing I saw as I went to bed. And then there were the nightmares. Sleep became scarce and my energy suffered.

At one point while talking to my supervisor Don Pierce, he commented that Michael's crime scene was a particularly bad one. I felt so much emotion I had to immediately leave his office and go someplace alone to grieve anew. I don't think he was intending to send me a message, just making a comment, but it legitimized for me what I was feeling. It took away some of the shame, but I still felt like I was looking at the world through a dark pair of glasses. I was able to share some of what I was experiencing with Steve Hill and some of the other crimes against children investigators I knew from the Department of Corrections parolee interview sessions. While they understood perhaps better than anyone else what I was going through, the problems remained and I was still plagued by nightmares, the intrusive thoughts and memories, and the sense of a darkness overcoming me. Eventually, I was able to regain some sense of normalcy, but the pain remained within me.

I was still working Danny's case with Vern when I began to think that there were a lot of people who should not have children, and it scared me to think how many kids were at the mercy of people who were not qualified to be parents. That fear increased as I encountered people like Barbara and Larry Carrasco, Ulysses Roberson, and Allen Harrod and Michael Labrecque, who inflicted unfathomable cruelty on their children. There are other cases I haven't even written about in this book that rival these in horror: a father and son teaming up to rape and murder a nine-year-old neighbor girl; a man who buried his young niece and nephew alive because they screamed and cried while he was raping their mother. As hard as it was to handle the emotions these cases stirred, I was honored to receive them. With each case, the value of the victim involved kept me from saying no. Working these cases also made me feel like I had value. I had a purpose and I was driven to help these kids and their families. I hoped that I would reach a point where I could resolve a case and move on to the next without feeling so haunted and unable to let go.

A lot of people in the office could not understand why I was so involved in cases that did not necessarily fall under federal jurisdiction. I resented those who could not understand the pain, sorrow, and responsibility that was felt by those affected by crimes against children, and I cherished those who did appreciate the value of these very special victims. At Michael Lyons's crime scene, I remember Mike Ernst, an agent I knew from New York, down on his hands and knees in that awful primordial "river bottoms" area, scouring the earth for evidence, and Steve Grube trudging through water and muck trying to piece together what had happened. Then there were those of us who carried Michael's body out in our arms, away from the media copters, to give him the dignity and respect he deserved. I feel like we share a timeless bond.

The pride I took in being an FBI agent was always there and driving me. When my sons were old enough to appreciate what an FBI agent was, it made me try even harder to impress them. All the darkness I had absorbed was still inside me but under control. Our family grew, not with more children but with more animals. To Fred and Barney, the dogs we brought out from New Jersey, we added a St. Bernard we named Toby, for Beethoven. When a family in our community found out we had a Saint, they were sure we'd take in another one needing a home, so George joined us, a dog so massive that when we saw him being delivered to us in the back of a pickup truck he made the truck look tiny. Then Lori found a Great Dane that needed adoption, and he became our beloved Roger. When I met Roger for the first time he was taller than me while standing up on his back legs. When I tried to wrestle with him he quickly put me down and "playfully" put his mouth around my neck. That was the end of wrestling with Roger.

We subsequently acquired an African grey parrot, a green-winged macaw, and a blue-and-gold macaw. It's quite something to have three talking birds. On one occasion, while Lori and I were out on a movie date, we got a "911" page from our babysitter, who exclaimed that someone had broken into our home and was telling the dogs to get away, lie down, and sit. As we were about to tell her to call 911 for real she heard another voice say "bad dog" and she realized that all the commands were coming from the birds—literally parroting words they had heard us say. Between the birds, dogs, and numerous cats, you could stand outside our front door and think there was a party going on inside when, in fact, no one was home. At night we would gather in one big group with all the animals and watch movies. That was special family time.

In February 1999 the Yosemite case began, and I was back and forth to Modesto and Mariposa for the next few months. It caused issues because everything involving home and kids fell again on Lori. As the investigation progressed, my anxiety increased because of the controversy of the case and my diminished and then prominent role in its conclusion. I initially did not realize that in getting Cary Stayner to confess I had caused anger and resentment toward me from some people in the office. As a division of the FBI, our office put a serial killer behind bars and solved the murders of two women and two teenage girls whose loss was a catastrophic tragedy. That's the way I chose to look at it, and I don't know how obtaining that confession could possibly be construed by anybody as a bad thing. Some people in the office were very supportive and tried to mitigate the ill will directed toward me. For a long time, however, my daily life and career were thrown into an uproar. My success on the case caused a lot of resentment from a lot of corners. The anonymous acts of belittlement, like the cat feces and the swastika left on my desk, were bewildering and upsetting. But the worst was not being allowed to have direct contact with the Stayner victims and help them through their difficult time. Having a relationship with victims or victims' families after a case is resolved, seeing them move forward with their lives and assisting them any way I can, is the closest I get to a sense of closure. Without that, I felt even more adrift.

Every day when I got up the anxiety would begin. It would grow as I got closer to work, and hit me full flush as I entered the office. At home, I was full of pent-up emotions. It wasn't just about what was going on in the moment, but the current situation seemed to unleash everything I had pushed down and fought to keep in check. I was desperate for a sense of control, wanted everything to be in order, in its place. I could not tolerate chaos and in a home with two young boys and a zoo's worth of animals there was always going to be a certain amount of chaos. I would throw items that I felt were out of place across the room, just to get them out of my eyesight. I was suddenly unable to feel the comfort I normally experienced from my home and family. I began lashing out at Lori, Joe, and Jordan, as if they were against me. I felt alone even though my family was doing everything they could to keep me close. It was completely irrational. Lori and my sons were what I most valued in my life, but I was so on edge, my emotions swinging so wildly, that I did not appreciate them and instead made their lives difficult.

Around this time my doctor told me that I needed double knee replacement surgery. I was only forty-eight, but he told me that my knees had degenerated to the point that all the cushioning material in the joint was gone and it was just bone rubbing against bone. I was in so much pain I was gulping down handfuls of anti-inflammatory meds so I could keep running. Finally, my friend Chris Hopkins told me that it was hard for people who cared about me to see how much pain I was in just trying to get around, so I opted for the surgeries. I had the left knee replaced first, and then the right one three months later. Both procedures seemed to go without incident. Then in July 2001, five months after the second surgery and exactly two years after the Stayner confession, my right knee began itching and hurting while I was at a homicide conference in LA. By the next day the pain was excruciating and it was hard to walk. That night I was beset by chills and sweats and had to keep getting up in the middle of the night and taking showers to try to warm up and cool down. I called the doctor and he told me to get back as soon as possible. My partner who was at the conference with me, Chris Campion, got me on a plane back to Sacramento. He saved my life by getting me home.

When I got off the plane in Sacramento I was so obviously sick I remember several people approaching me trying to help me walk. I looked so frail, Lori walked past me without recognizing it was me. When I got to the doctor's office, he immediately prepped me for surgery. I didn't really know what was happening, but I knew it was bad. I remember being asked if I wanted extraordinary measures to keep me alive. I had never considered that question before and had to puzzle through for an answer. I said that I did not want extraordinary measures. Other than for the sake of Lori, Joe, and Jordan, I had no desire to stay alive.

When I woke from anesthesia, Lori was with me. Soon a procession of priests and nuns started visiting, then a doctor I did not recognize—I'm guessing a psychiatrist—came in and asked me why I said I wanted to die. I realized that I didn't. Waking up and seeing Lori there made me want to live again.

It turned out that I had developed a staph infection in my knee, which spread throughout my system and caused sepsis: inflammation throughout the body that leads to shock. I had, in fact, been dying. The infection was so advanced that the doctors were forced to remove the prosthesis in my right knee and replace it with a temporary spacer that contained a reservoir of antibiotics. Because I had no right knee, I had to live on the couch in our downstairs great room for five months. That entire time, Lori slept on the couch with me, and Joe and Jordan moved their mattresses down next to the couch. The pain was the worst I had ever experienced and I was completely dependent on their care. When the infection was finally vanquished, the prosthesis was reinstalled. By the time it all ended I had been virtually immobile for almost seven months. I had been put back together physically, but emotionally I still felt out of control.

Eventually, I was able to go back to work. I will always be grateful to the many colleagues who donated their leave to me so I could take the time to recover from the infection. By the time I returned, the SAC and ASAC had been removed and I had the pleasure of working under a series of supportive and highly effective bosses. One of these managers, ASAC John Pikus, personally came out to the site where the body of a victim, a seventeen-year-old girl who was strangled by her boyfriend and buried in the woods, was recovered to make sure we were OK and that we and the sheriff's department we were working with had everything we needed. That was a first for me and while it might sound like a small thing, when you are in a place where vultures are circling, the flies are swarming, your arms and legs ache from digging, and you can only bear to breathe by smearing Vicks under your nose, having a manager at that level standing with the troops meant a lot to all of us. He also came with me when I was awarded Investigator of the Year in 2003 by the California Sexual Assault Investigators Association.

Because I worked with so many outside agencies on their cases, I was exposed over the course of my career to hundreds of cases in which children were brutally victimized. All the scenes and pictures and memories became this unending river of horror in my mind. Being intimately familiar with all the ways in which a child could become a victim changed me both as an investigator and as a father. I worked cases of children who were killed by their best friends over a trivial or even unwitting slight. Realizing that we cannot ensure the safety of our children made me overprotective to a fault with my own sons. I did not trust their friends, or the parents of their friends that I had not met.

I made the boys check in with me all the time. One day my son Joe did not come home after school. I went ballistic and had his school bus stopped and searched. I had forgotten he was going to a friend's house. Another time one of the boys was downloading games from the Internet, which tied up our home phone number all night long so I couldn't reach them. By the next morning I was so anguished I had the local sheriff's department do a welfare check on my house. My wife and sons woke up that morning to the startling presence of armed and uniformed deputies in our home. This preoccupation with the safety of my own loved ones became all consuming and I would say things like if anyone harmed my family I would send back my credentials and badge to the FBI but I would keep my weapons. It was not a healthy mind-set.

My time at home as a father was constrained, because my assistance was required more and more by other children in far-flung places. The staff at Jordan's daycare center was very accommodating of our situation and would let me talk to him when I called in from the road. On one occasion I was away from home for a whole week and I promised Jordan I would get back on Friday and we would have a great day together. As I was heading home that Friday on Interstate 5 I got a call that I was needed in Colusa County to search for a missing fifteen-year-old boy. I felt so bad about breaking my promise to Jordan I started crying when I called him to give him the news. I got off the phone until I could regain control of myself and then called him back, but the queasiness in my stomach was in full spin. We soon found the boy's body in a field with his head beaten in and his throat slashed. It turned out that his friends had killed him because they felt he had embarrassed them. These were supposedly good kids, on the college-bound track, and after it came out their friend was dead they pretended to be bereaved. My paranoia and sense of all-encompassing doom increased.

At one crime scene, the agent I was working with found a missing little girl because her feet were sticking out above the level of kitty litter the girl's mother had covered her with to absorb the fluids of decomposition. In another case it was the porcelain whiteness of the body we dug from a clandestine grave that registered and stayed in my mind. The smells, the observations, the comments of investigators at the scene, and the acts of compassion from those with whom I worked occupied my thoughts without end. It was not a constant replay of one event but more a cascade of all the related thoughts. An aspect of one crime scene would bring back the memory of another. Eventually, most of the memories seemed to organize themselves by geographic location. I identified places by who had died there or who had been victimized there.

Being home at the end of the day, seeing Lori, Joe, and Jordan, holding them, became something I could not do without, under no circumstances other than if I was called out on another case. Any activity that did not allow me the ability to predict what was to come could be a catalyst for bringing up these thoughts. Movies, which I loved so much and which once had been so relaxing for me, became a catalyst when a scene depicted in a movie mirrored a scene I had observed.

When college came into sight for my kids, I begged them not to choose schools far away. It was selfish of me, but having my family close to home was the only thing that gave me any peace. When Joe announced he would be attending college at least five hours away I was devastated. On the way home from getting him settled, instead of thinking how many miles we had to drive to get home I thought of how many miles were separating us from Joe. It turned out to be a learning experience for Joe and for us. Ultimately, his decision helped us all grow.

Another thing that made my work confusing was the elusiveness of feeling satisfaction about any outcome. Lori began describing me as having "suffered a successful career" because my success in solving cases and getting confessions was never really an experience that could be considered joyful. People expected me to see all offenders as monsters, but I saw people suffering in their own right. I don't mean to say that they do not need to be punished. In most of the cases I dealt with, the perpetrators should never be freed. They are simply too dangerous to live among us and would rape and kill again if given the opportunity. But many, if not most, of the offenders I dealt with had once been victims themselves.

As Lori and I tried to figure out why I was successful in getting confessions and closing cases we decided it was because I cared and had empathy. I gave something of myself and others gave back to me in return. In many instances I was able to show the offender that in spite of what they had done they still had the capacity to help, which meant they had value. I am not a social worker or someone who believes that everyone is redeemable. I just know that on some occasions I was able to get through to someone, which enabled us to recover victims, answer anguished questions, and prevent others from being harmed. For me, the pain of both the crimes and the confessions live within me.

I take no joy in disrupting the lives of the offender's family, who cannot be blamed for everything a loved one has done but have to live with the pain and the stigma and a feeling of responsibility. In one case, while we were serving a search warrant on an offender's home, his mother was in the master bedroom dying of cancer. She was at the very end of her life, receiving hospice care from an attendant, when we came busting in and upended her whole world. How do we leave feeling OK about pain we caused this woman in her final days? People said that it was not our fault, that her son committed a crime and we were just addressing it. Yet it is still hard to live with. Even harder to live with is the pain and disruption I caused my own family, for which there is no excuse or adequate apology.

I became so fixated on death that I began to crave my own demise. I had come back to my senses temporarily after my surgery, seeing Lori by my bedside and realizing I wanted to live. But as I became consumed again by all the sadness and destruction not only caused by the subjects who committed the crimes but also by the trauma we caused during our investigations, I became increasingly self-destructive. I was fighting with Lori all the time, unable to appreciate the love of my family. I hated the person that I had become but felt powerless to do anything about it. I fixated on the dead children, and came to believe that they wanted me with them, and I wanted to be with them.

One morning I was lying in bed with Lori. We were in the midst of an argument and I had this overwhelming feeling that I just wanted to end it all. Lori couldn't believe that I would really kill myself. But inadvertently questioning my resolve made me want to do it all the more. I took the gun I kept for protection by our bed and held it to my temple, preparing to squeeze the trigger. I could see Lori's face turn immediately from anger to the most indescribable look of fear. That broke through to me like a bolt of lightning and ended the incident but, unfortunately, not the underlying condition that was driving me to suicidal thoughts. It is unbearable to know that I caused her the same kind of pain that exists in me from experiencing a traumatic event. To this day, any scene in a movie or TV show when someone holds a gun to his head sets her off and she relives the memory of that morning with me. I take responsibility for this, but that does not make up for how I caused her a hurt that she will have to deal with for the rest of her life.

Still, I am ashamed to say, I put her through it again, and my sons as well. We were arguing again and in my mind I just decided that was it. Except for the home protection pistol, I always kept my guns locked in my FBI car. It was a practice I had begun so the children could never get to them and had stuck with ever since. I told Lori to call 911 and tell the dispatcher that the authorities would find me in my car at the bottom of our hill. Lori, Joe, and Jordan knew what I meant, and for the next half hour we were all engaged in a physical struggle—with me trying to get to the car and them trying to hold me back. I was committed, but so were they, and they prevailed.

When I got into these really dark places, Lori would call my closest friends, like Ken Hittmeier, Chris Campion, and Chris Hopkins, and enlist their help. The day after my last attempt at suicide, Lori called Chris Campion and he came to our house and tried to get me to go stay with him. I couldn't stand to be at home, but I couldn't bear to be away either and was unable to leave. Chris called Joe and Jordan into the living room. I guess this is what you call in addiction treatment circles an intervention. We all sat down together and Chris had each of my sons tell me what it would have meant to them if I had been able to get to my gun. What they said, how they sobbed, stays with me always. I cannot ever remember a time where I felt so much emotional pain. I realized that no matter what happened from that point on, I would never commit suicide. I realized how selfish and self-centered it would be to inflict that kind of wound on my family. Instead, I live with the knowledge of the harm I caused my wife and sons and that their memory of it will never go away.

In 2006, doctors discovered that the systemic staph infection that had raged through my body had affected my pituitary function, leading to deficiencies in several hormone levels that affected my body's ability to deal with stress. Low levels of certain hormones can cause or exacerbate symptoms such as depression (sadness, hopelessness, despair), irritability (increased anger, agitation, loss of patience), and anxiety. For five years, I had lost all ability to cope with stress. The doctors started me on hormone therapy to bring my levels back to a functional range. It took a while to start feeling better, but eventually I did.

The thoughts, dreams, and emotional issues are still present, but I am better able to live with them and tolerate the trauma. I still experience frequent nightmares and even "daymares," where flashbacks intrude into my waking mind. It would be too simplistic to say that my emotional dysregulation was all due to my pituitary failure. Maybe my controls were lacking, but my feelings were and still are my feelings. I continue to awaken many times at night and find Lori holding me, trying to calm me down.

During Cary Stayner's murder trial, I was cross-examined for many days, which was basically a prolonged character assassination—not a pleasant experience. As the person who took his confession, I was the key prosecution witness. But what may seem unbelievable to some is that I volunteered to also testify as a defense witness. The defense wanted me to talk about his emotions and make him sympathetic, but I did not think that was a good road to go down because I would have to say that his emotions were really only directed at one of his victims: Juli. The confession spoke for itself and I thought the jury could hear the moments when Stayner was more empathetic and the times when he was simply cold. I did not need to point that out. What I did offer to say was that Stayner chose to confess even though he knew he was not getting anything in return. I thought that was worth something; it certainly meant something to me. If people were going to weigh the value of his soul, I thought it was important that they know that.

He was convicted, and then there was a final penalty phase in which the state asked for death to be imposed and the jury recommended the ultimate penalty. I had no desire to go to the sentencing, which was a few weeks before Christmas in 2002. It was not a joyful occasion for me, but I was ordered to attend by the SAC. I had so many conflicting feelings about the case and wanted to maintain a low-key presence. I drove down to the courthouse in San Jose, where the trial had been moved after a change of venue request, and took the elevator alone up to the fifth floor, where the courtroom was located. As I stepped off the elevator, I bumped, rather awkwardly, into the group of jurors who had come back to attend the sentencing. I had, obviously, not had any personal contact with the jurors before that day, but they recognized me from my long testimony. Before I knew what was happening, they pulled me into their center. Some shook my hand, others hugged me, and they told me what a great job I had done on the confession and on the witness stand.

I had never spoken to jurors before and didn't know what to do. As I started making my way out of their midst, the Stayner family saw me and they grabbed me. I remember those hours I spent with them the day after the confession and how I tried to help them cope with such earthshaking news. Suddenly, next to the Stayners, I observed Mr. Carrington and his family, the Pelossos, and other members of the victims' families. They also approached me and I was surrounded by all these people from different sides of the case. It was almost an out-of-body experience. I was not sure how the victims' families would feel about me comforting the Stayners. I did not know how the Stayners felt about me being hugged by the victims' families and by the jury that had convicted their son and asked for him to be executed. And I had no clue what the jury made of it all. As we stood there waiting to get into court, I overheard the Stayners apologize to Mr. Carrington for what their son had done.

In the Name of the Children

Finally, the doors opened and we all went inside. I sat off by myself in the back. Judge Thomas C. Hastings was the same judge who presided over the murder trial of Richard Allen Davis back in 1996 for the kidnapping and murder of Polly Klaas. The judge began by summarizing the facts of the case. His words were so genuine, so measured, so meaningful, that I was in awe of him and wondered how such great men are formed. When he got to the loss of Carole and the girls, he was so overcome that he left the courtroom to compose himself. When he returned after several minutes, his face was red and his eyes were teary as he sentenced Stayner to death.

People constantly ask me whether it feels good knowing Stayner is going to die and the answer is no. What happened between us during those two days resulted in him being sentenced to death, and while I am glad and relieved he was caught and can't hurt anyone else, I cannot celebrate that he, too, may one day be killed. I worked the cases I did to honor life, to give it value. How can anyone feel good about the loss of any life?

I have been asked frequently for my position on the death penalty, and I feel I am being asked so that my name can be associated with an argument for it or against it. It is a highly controversial subject and I respect those who hold opinions on both sides of the debate. I am personally aware that the fear of the death penalty has prompted many to confess to crimes they have committed and, even more importantly from my perspective, to help us recover victims. For that reason alone, I believe in it. But I would be content for no one to be executed. In California, the death penalty is in place, but in practice as I am writing this, it is always delayed and rarely carried out. I don't wish to see Stayner executed. I would prefer he die in prison of natural causes.

In 2005 we got a new SAC, Drew Parenti. Many SACs make a point of meeting with people individually when they take over a new office, but I always thought of it as lip service. Still, Parenti called me in and I told him of my concern that the FBI was focusing so much on terrorism that it was detracting from our contribution to the cases involving children. I gave him examples and provided him the names of people to talk to about the issue. When I finished he asked me, "How are you doing?"

That question, coming from someone in his position, was so unexpected that my lack of emotional control kicked in and I told him truthfully that I did not think I was doing well. More importantly, I told him, I was afraid of what I had done to my family. He promised me that he was going to get me healthy enough to retire and asked me to promise him not to obtain any more confessions and to stay away from homicides. Without me realizing it, he started me on the path to retirement. I don't know if I would have been able to do it of my own accord. He sent me to a therapist in Southern California who does Eye Movement Desensitization and Reprocessing (EMDR) treatment for PTSD, which is a way of trying to reprogram the brain to desensitize the person to traumatic memories and end the constant replaying of these events. I only had a week with this therapist, and I couldn't get past the debriefing stage. I would start talking about one case and that led to another and another. The therapist seemed taken aback by what I was telling her and said it was the most cumulative trauma she had ever encountered in a single person.

My focus turned toward closing down my cases and my career. I was addicted to making a difference in peoples lives, but I realized from my friends in the office, and especially from Lori, that it was time to make a difference in the lives of my family. Ironically, shortly before I retired I was reassigned as case agent of the Yosemite murders, and I made it my mission to get rid of all the evidence that was not required for the appeal process. I'm referring to Stayner's car that had been impounded and other things I feared might end up one day for sale on the Internet to people who collect serial killer memorabilia. I asked permission from Mariposa County to have what was left of the red Pontiac rental car destroyed. We got Delbert to arrange to get the title from Stayner for his Scout and his other car and they, too, were destroyed.

I retired on the last working day of May 2006 so I could leave for the Memorial Day weekend and not come back. The office threw a retirement party for me. Chris Hopkins was the master of ceremonies, and he was very good about pointing out my embarrassing quirks. Many people attended from outside the Bureau, which was a huge honor. I received a lot of plaques, but the gift that touched me the most was a large wooden sculpture of a bear protecting a cub. I was proud to present my family to everyone I worked with, and then I was officially retired from the FBI.

In the Name of the Children

For the first six months of my retirement, I could barely get out of bed. I think all the stress and emotion were oozing out of me. But my family and the love of my wife and sons was the best therapy, helping me to fully recover. I'd taken the private investigator exam, passed, and set up my own business, which got going and I was able to start living and working again. It was difficult not feeling a mission, that all-consuming dedication to a purpose. The idea of working to make money should have seemed normal but was, in fact, foreign to me. I have not been able to stay away from helping victims' families, especially where children are concerned. I have been particularly honored to help a family whose daughter has been missing since 1996. They have never given up trying to find her, and I will never give up trying to help them.

In 2007 I came up with the idea that we could prevent children from becoming victimized via the Internet by developing software that would identify when a child's online activity put them at risk. Louis Freeh had recognized the dangers of emerging technology for delivering children into the hands of predators and got us involved proactively. I wanted to continue in that vein. Chris Hopkins joined in, and together with Lori and others, I tried to become an entrepreneur. Along with some smart, compassionate, talented people from California State University, Chico, we succeeded in developing the prototype that would prove our concept and that would identify risky activity by children. We tested the prototype and it worked, but we could not raise adequate funds to get the company off the ground. We were attempting to start this during the 2008 global financial crisis, and while I know most start-ups do not succeed, I hoped that would not apply to a business dedicated to preventing child victims and saving lives. However, I learned that the concern expressed by many on the issue doesn't necessarily translate into action.

In 2012, an inmate on California's death row reached out to me and I went to see him. Because I was retired and not a sworn law enforcement officer, I went to San Quentin with Matt Buechner, an agent with the California Department of Corrections Special Services Unit, and Susan Kane, a supervisory parole agent with the corrections department. The inmate, a serial killer, provided information that helped us locate six of his and his serial killing partner's victims. I met the victims' families and for their sake I have stayed involved in the case as a private investigator.

After coming to terms with how the cases impacted my emotional welfare and affected my family, I try whenever I can to help other law enforcement officers and anyone else I encounter dealing with PTSD. I have met many wonderful, caring people this way, and I let them know that they are not alone and that there is a reason for how they are feeling.

Both of my children are now out of school and, I must say, remarkable young men. Joe became a mechanical engineer and married his high school sweetheart, and they are about to make us grandparents. I was especially honored when they asked me to officiate at their wedding. Jordan is a police officer and engaged to be married. When both boys moved out, we became empty nesters. I take pride in the lives the boys have built and the new adventure Lori and I are embarking on, as we are now free to do as we please. Our main goal now is for Lori to retire, so that we can enjoy our time together and the everlasting love we feel for each other.

But the mission still calls me. The emotional heartache from the cases I have worked and continue to work still affects me, but also spurs me to go on. There are children still missing who must be found, abused and exploited kids who must be freed from their suffering, and child killers who must be brought to account. We all must continue the fight to seek justice in their names.

Acknowledgments

TO MARILEE STRONG, my coauthor, and more importantly, my friend: Authors use words as art and to convey meaning, but there are no words that can accurately describe your value and the quality of your character. As a father, I leave behind my sons and the beginning of other families. Marilee, by virtue of your books, you leave behind a contribution to society that transcends time and can be appreciated by many generations to come. Your respect for life, your empathy, and your ability to understand emotion, and especially pain, make you a portal through which we can all achieve a greater understanding of the ramifications of victimization. This project was difficult, but with you, it also became one of catharsis for me, my family, and some of the victims described herein. Thank you for your concern, care, and genuine love, and for making this book speak for all victims, both known and unknown.

I would like to thank the following individuals for their love, help, support, patience, wisdom, and partnership. If I accomplished anything as a man, and as an FBI agent, it is because of my family and the people listed here. There are many more individuals who contributed to my life and career, but there is insufficient space to list them all.

Dale Anderson: You made so much possible while providing a role model of morality, goodness, patience, and honor. Tim Tracy and Randy Ewy: You traveled the journey with me to becoming Special Agent "Accountants."

Don Pierce: You helped me find my path and showed me how to walk it with humor. You showed me how not to be angry, and also embedded in me the importance of the mission and the people. "Love you mucho."

Ken Hittmeier, Chris Campion, and Chris Hopkins: For friendship, brotherhood, and helping my family keep me alive.

Acknowledgments

Joe and Marjorie Pelcher: Although we are not blood relations, we are family.

My college family at Albright: John Diamond, Steve Nee, Jeff Ronner, and the brothers of Alpha Pi Omega.

FBI Director Louis Freeh.

From the Sacramento Division of the FBI (happy 50th anniversary): Tony Alston, Lenny and Michelle Ammond, Paul Artley, Linda Bakula, Joan and Bill Barcklay, John Boles, Shirley Bridges, Steve Broce, Rich Davidson, Sandy Disney, Sharon and Art Dorl, Todd Drost, Karen and Mike Ernst, Tom Gibberson, Sheila Glover, Bonnie and Steve Grube, Emily Hatch, Vern Johnson, Cathie and Ron Krouse, Randy and Beth Leben, Mamie Lim, Kathy and Ralph Lux, Mike McHale, Dale Miskell, Gaye and Lee Myers, Bill Nicholson, SAC Drew Parenti, ASAC John Pikus, Gary Schaff, Harry and Michelle Sweeney, Barb Williams, Ken Van Gundy, and Ron ("Wojo") Wilczynski.

From the FBI's Child Abduction and Serial Killer Unit (Behavioral Analysis Unit): Bill Hagmaier, Roy Hazelwood, and Mike Morrow.

From the FBI Laboratory Division: Dr. John (Jeb) Stuart.

From the U.S. Attorney's Office for the Eastern District of California: Prosecutors Laurel White, Michelle Rodriguez, Samuel Wong, and Jody Raskin.

U.S. Postal Inspector Bob Lieske.

From the Sacramento County Sheriff's Department: Mona Feuillard, Steve Hill, Tom Roloff, and Sheriff John McGuiness.

From the Sacramento Police Department: Greg Stewart, Joyce Thorgrimson, and Glenn and Donna Walters.

From the South Lake Tahoe Police Department: Chuck Owens.

From the Modesto Police Department: Jon Buehler and Kevin Bertalotto.

From the Tuolumne County Sheriff's Department: Tim Reed.

From the Butte County Sheriff's Department: Vern (I miss you) and Vera Kelch, and Sheriff Perry Reniff.

The Mariposa County Sheriff's Department and Sheriff Doug Binnewies.

From the Placer County Sheriff's Department: Des Carrington and Bob McDonald.

Acknowledgments

From the California Department of Corrections and Rehabilitation: Matt Buechner, Susan Kane, the Special Services Unit, and the High Risk Sex Offender Parole staff.

From the California Department of Justice: Prosecutors Mike Canzoneri, Mike Kelley, Jeanine Willie, and George Williamson.

From the Douglas County, Nevada, Sheriff's Department: Stan Lamb and Rory Planeta.

From the Reno, Nevada, Police Department: Alan Fox.

From the California State University, Chico, Human Identification Laboratory and Department of Forensic Anthropology: Dr. Turhon Murad, Eric Bartelink, and Amy Zelson Mundorff.

Denise and Stan Smart (may your suffering end).

Mark Connelly, Esq., and Lisa Connelly.

Drs. Bruce Jensen, Richard Heater, Christopher Olson, and Mauro Giordani; RN Cindy Anderson; and RN Tina Arce.

—J.R.

I would like to thank, first and foremost, Jeff Rinek, for letting me into his world, opening his heart, and sharing such deep and unflinching truths with me. It has been a pleasure and an honor to be your partner on this project and to "speak" through you in one voice, as I share your mission of trying to protect society's most vulnerable from being victimized. I am in awe of the bravery you showed not just in bringing down predators and perpetrators but even more so in your willingness to confront and share the battle within, which is an inevitable casualty of doing the kind of work you pledged to do. I owe Lori Rinek enormous gratitude for her unwavering support of this project and her willingness to share so much of her and her family's lives.

Amy Rennert made all my dreams as a writer come true. Amy, you literally gave me voice, and I can never thank you enough for that. If my time on this earth is deemed to have had any value or meaning, it is because of you.

Mark Powelson has always made me feel that I have an interesting story to tell and the passion and insight to tell it.

Acknowledgments

Publisher Glenn Yeffeth, Deputy Publisher Adrienne Lang, Editor Vy Tran, and all the staff at BenBella have been unwavering in their support of this book. Their respect and sensitivity to the subject matter and what we have tried to accomplish in this book is truly remarkable and has sustained Jeff and me throughout the process.

I was the victim of a no-cause eviction in the middle of writing this book, booted from my home of eighteen years by an avaricious landlord, and I was forced to completely uproot and resettle in the midst of the tightest real estate market in decades. The process was anguishing and upended my life for several months, and I appreciate the patience and understanding of my publishers at BenBella and the love and support of those who helped me through a very difficult time. They include Rick Clogher, Susan Rutherford, Susanna Praetzel, Susie Haufler, Lauren Chambliss, Lisa Falls, and Maria Brown. I would also like to thank Randall Aiman-Smith, Reed Marcy, Hallie Von Rock, and the entire team at Aiman-Smith & Marcy who have made it possible for so long for me to maintain a writing career.

I write to give voice to those who cannot speak for themselves. I am humbled by the bravery and the suffering of the children whose stories we have told in this book and I hope by telling their stories that their voices will be heard.

—*M.S.*

About the Authors

Retired Special Agent **JEFFREY RINEK** served thirty years with the FBI primarily investigating cases of missing and murdered children and is internationally renowned for obtaining a surprise confession from serial killer Cary Stayner to four bru-

tal slayings known as the Yosemite Park Murders. In the Sacramento office of the FBI he was responsible for assisting police and sheriff's departments throughout Northern California in active and cold-case investigations involving missing children, child kidnappings, and the abuse, exploitation, and murder of children. He also served as a certified profiler for the National Center for the Analysis of Violent Crime. In 2003, he was named Investigator of the Year by the California Sexual Assault Investigators Association and in 2006 received an Award for Excellence from the International Homicide Investigators Association. He was the Sacramento division case agent in 1993 for the UNABOM case. He has also worked for the FBI in the areas of white-collar crime, foreign counterintelligence, and organized crime; served on the Bureau's SWAT team; and was a copilot in its aviation program. He and his work have been featured on numerous TV documentary crime shows, including A&E's *American Justice*, TruTV's *Crime Stories*, and Investigation Discovery's *Real Detective* and *Deadly Sins*.

About the Authors

MARILEE STRONG is an award-winning journalist who specializes in reporting on crime and psychological and social issues. She is the author of two previous books: *A Bright Red Scream*, on the aftereffects

of childhood abuse and trauma, and *Erased*, which presented an original criminal and psychological profile of a particular kind of intimate-partner homicide. She has also written widely on topics such as child abduction, women in prison, gang violence, hate groups, and psychological treatment for sex offenders. She is a graduate of Columbia University's Graduate School of Journalism, where she was awarded a Pulitzer Fellowship, the school's highest honor. She is the recipient of more than a dozen writing and reporting honors, including a National Headliner Award and the Society of Professional Journalists Excellence Award. She has been a guest on NBC's *Dateline,* Fox television's *On the Record with Greta Van Susteren,* the BBC, and numerous other TV and radio shows around the United States, and has appeared in several film and television documentaries on the subjects of her work.

PHOTO BY MANOLO GARCIA